THE FRENCH EXCEPTION

Still so special?

D0733677

Andrew Jack was for over four years Paris correspondent for the *Financial Times* before becoming the paper's Moscow correspondent. He has won several British and French journalism awards. He is married with an Anglo-French son.

Andrew Jack

THE FRENCH EXCEPTION

Still so special?

P

PROFILE BOOKS
LONDON

First published in Great Britain in 1999 by
Profile Books Ltd
58A Hatton Garden
London ECIN 8LX
www.profilebooks.co.uk

This second edition published in 2001

Typeset in Bembo by MacGuru
info@macguru.org.uk

Printed in Great Britain by
Bookmarque Ltd, Croydon, Surrey

A CIP catalogue record for this book is available from the British Library.

ISBN 1 86197 319 5

Contents

A Victor

Conçu dans l'esprit de l'entente cordiale, né avec ce livre

The schizophrenic state

Anyone who has tried to negotiate the Place de l'Etoile in the heart of Paris has experienced the tension between the disciplined Napoleonic form of the Arc de Triomphe and the Latin chaos on the roundabout that envelops it. That awkward but enduring relationship symbolizes the many schizophrenic conflicts and paradoxes that characterize – and even determine – the face of modern France.

With economic growth outstripping most of its European peers, the export of Airbuses and influx of tourists helping to swell its trade earnings, and tens of thousands of its more adventurous citizens creating a full-scale ethnic 'Petite France' in South Kensington, an optimism based on free trade and ease of movement might seem to be the logical spirit of the age. Yet the Frenchman who probably captured most public attention around the world at the turn of the millennium was someone with entirely different values, a farmer with a rabble-rousing walrus-moustache from the remote south-west of the country, who was fighting for greater protectionism. He epitomized all that is defiantly different about France, encapsulated in the widely-used phase *l'exception française*.

José Bové was facing prosecution for vandalizing a branch of

McDonald's in the town of Millau in August 1999, selected as the ultimate symbol of the evils of globalization. But that did not stop him from taking a prominent role among the protesters who picketed the World Trade Organization meeting in Seattle in November of the same year. Nor did it prevent him from being invited to dinner by Lionel Jospin, the French prime minister, on his return to Paris, where he was feted as a national hero. Yet Bové himself does not fit the simple stereotype of a narrow-minded Frenchman or *franchouillard*. English-speaking, the son of an academic from Luxemburg, he spent much of his early childhood at the University of Berkeley in California, before drifting around different parts of France. He quickly picked up some distinctly gallic methods, combining violent protest with anarchic humour, handing out alternative 'burgers' made with local beef, roquefort and *baguette*. He perfectly encapsulated the love-hate relationship of France with the Anglo-Saxon world, and its continuing struggle with modernity.

Such tensions between old and new, liberal and egalitarian, inward- and outward-looking approaches to the world, permeate French society. Its citizens know how to live with their contradictions, which are a natural, integral part of their character – even a strength on which they thrive. What other nation, after all, could have had the panache to discover the 'French paradox', showing that a moderate but regular intake of one its finest products – red wine – is actually good for the health? The French may pride themselves on their vast high-brow literary heritage – from Molière to Maupassant, Zola to Proust – but most of their many bookshops devote large sections to a very different class of literature. The continuing adventures of Asterix remain a best-seller among children and adults alike. There is a multitude of lightweight books on serious subjects, written by intellectuals who do not bother to include either academic references or an index. There is an almost equal number of intensely serious books on lightweight subjects, pontificating on the psychology of the (Belgian but francophone) cartoon character Tintin, for example.

France may boast of its rationalist and secular traditions. Yet Europe 1, one of the most influential national news radio stations, found time until recently just before 9 am each day among its more worthy analytical items to broadcast horoscopes by Elisabeth Teissier, a self-styled *voyante* and one-time pin-up who used to provide advice to François Mitterrand. A survey cited by the magazine *La Recherche* showed that over half of the French claim that astrology is a science and a third that the stars influence personality. At almost any Parisian *soirée*, it is easy to find believers who can knowledgeably and with complete conviction describe individuals' character traits purely on the basis of their signs.

This permanent state of contradictions makes it a perilous exercise to draw out any common threads. Just as you master the fact that most French walk as they drive – on the right-hand side – and try to do the same, so you bump into people on the pavement who recklessly break the rule. Any generalization, in short, is doomed to contradiction. A country with a highly scientific approach to medicine, illustrated by a record drug consumption per head and a disproportionately high number of specialist to generalist doctors? Perhaps, but also one whose pharmacies are stocked with homeopathic remedies despite the most tenuous evidence of their effectiveness. Or whose health insurance service operates an office in the new quack 'thalassotherapy' treatment centre in Vichy to offer swift refunds to patients seeking to cure their ills by bathing in water and seaweed, washed down with some herbal tea.

France may be a society obsessed with secrecy, to the point that many Parisian families do not even put name-plates on their doors or bells, leaving unsuspecting first-time visitors to wander the corridors of apartment buildings in frustration. But it is also one where you can theoretically demand to inspect the amount of tax paid by your neighbour, and where estate agents systematically demand to see your salary slip as a condition for renting a flat. A nation where the state and the government seem to interfere in almost every aspect of daily life? Perhaps. But also one which never nationalized its water supply and waste treatment companies, with the result that it boasts two private-sector utilities groups – Vivendi and Suez-Lyonnaise des Eaux – that are the envy of the world, busy swallowing up everything from Northumbrian Water and the London suburban railways, to the water and electricity companies of Malaysia and the US alike.

Such contradictory features do not simply apply to individuals, but lie at the heart of contemporary France. Many of the country's achievements and detractions are as intimately linked as two sides of the same *franc* coin. Indeed, the common criticism by foreigners crudely put that 'France would be great without the French' is flawed for the obvious reason that the country without the French would simply not be France. Its citizens still bask in the past glory of an undeniably rich heritage, with world-class philosophers and writers, artists and film directors; high-speed trains and modern telephone systems; sophisticated food and wine; striking landscapes, beautiful historic buildings and bold modern architecture. And yet they are also confronted by another more anachronistic side, with corruption, nepotism, a heavy-handed interfering state and a corporatist trade union movement. In spring 2000, marches by teachers and tax inspectors showed just how brightly the revolutionary spirit still burns. The demonstrators succeeded in forcing swift reversals on two important policy decisions by the left-wing administration of Lionel Jospin, pushing two ministers to resign and triggering a cabinet reshuffle.

France reported growth of more than 3 per cent during 2000, placing it in a position of confidence during its six months of presidency of the European Union. Unemployment edged down for the first time in many years beneath 10 per cent, and the prospects of the prosperous 'new economy' driven by the Internet were on everyone's lips. Its designers were winning contracts and awards for their work on blockbuster Hollywood animation films. While its less skilled workers were staffing the restaurants of London, its top managers were imposing themselves abroad through takeovers of foreign companies. What better symbol of the country's participation in globalization than when that most British of businesses, Marks & Spencer, chose Luc Vandevelde, the Belgian-born chief executive of the French supermarket chain Promodès, to take the helm at the start of the same year?

Yet while the French have an external image as arrogant, headstrong and self-confident, behind the façade the country has probably never been so lacking in self-confidence and consensus about the path it is taking. Countless opinion polls have shown its citizens to be among the most pessimistic in Europe, with a very high suicide rate and record consumption levels of anti-depressant drugs. The shelves of its bookshops have all but buckled under the weight of multiple highly critical tomes by French analysts on their own society – from '*l'aveuglement français*' or French blindness to '*les trente piéteuses*' or the 30 pitiable years that followed '*les trente glorieuses*' after the second world war. Far more such books than exist in other countries. Such apparently defiant gestures as the short-lasting resumption of nuclear testing unveiled by President Jacques Chirac in 1995 were less firm gestures from a proud and united nation than the nervous reflex action from a divided population under the pressure of considerable change, and hovering on the verge of a nervous breakdown.

This book attempts to use France's most notable exceptions as a way to tease out these tensions and to analyse the nation today. It is not meant as an attack on the country and its people.

It is a selective critique of some aspects of France and the actions of some of the French, reflecting views which are shared by many of its own citizens. It aims to highlight those elements that are changing in society, and those which are resisting change. And to point out how the good and the bad aspects are often intimately connected if not inseparable. How there are strengths within its weaknesses; and weaknesses even among its best acknowledged strengths.

Food for thought

While Mao may have long gone out of fashion even among most French intellectuals, another little red book is still going strong a century after it was first produced. The *Michelin Guide* was originally offered free to motorists by the tyre company to help locate garages, hotels and restaurants around the country (and hence wear out their wheels more quickly in the process). Today it sells well over a million copies a year, and has become synonymous with one of the most universally admired aspects of France: its culinary excellence. The phrase 'three-star restaurant' has entered common parlance, and while French may be diminishing as a world-ranking language, it remains *de rigueur* in the kingdom of the cuisine.

But French food is now suffering from considerable indigestion, and its characteristics mirror many of the issues facing the rest of the society. Its very success in the past has become a significant problem today, by creating a dangerous sense of complacency. Take the year 1997, which hardly proved to be a good vintage for the restaurant sector. Pierre Gagnaire was forced to close his three-star restaurant in the industrial town of St-Etienne. Marc Veyrat, a three-star chef based in Annecy in the Alps, entered into delicate negotiations with his bankers. And several well-known restaurants collapsed in Lyon, France's self-proclaimed culinary capital. Nearby, the nation's only centre of *Hautes études* for cooking teetered on the brink of bankruptcy, even as the neighbouring Japanese-owned Tsuji school teaching its student chefs French methods prospered. And in 1998, the British designer-turned-restaurateur Terence Conran even had the gall to export to Paris his concept of upmarket French-style brasseries that he had developed in London.

With its rich land and weather to nurture high-quality and varied produce, and its many regions to furnish different ingredients and cooking styles, the French are endowed with some extraordinary raw materials to explain their gastronomic success. Their food has also been heavily moulded by the country's inhabitants and their practices. Historically, that reflects the influence of the Revolution in putting the cooks of the aristocrats out of jobs while creating a new and hungry middle class, which sparked the creation of the first modern restaurants and the spread of fine cooking into the burgeoning *bourgeoisie*. Culturally, food has been elevated to a national obsession, a topic of conversation that is at least as dominant (and rather more interesting) than the weather is for the British. Socially, the long-standing rural character of French society has helped maintain the links to the soil and to fresh, artisanal produce. Foreigners may complain that the baguette goes stale very quickly. But that is not a problem for the French, most of whom would never dream of holding on to ageing bread rather than buying and consuming it fresh from a bakery every day.

The state and its intermediaries have also been involved in moulding culinary tastes and gastronomic practices in different ways, just as they have in so many other parts of society. Since the 1930s, for instance, the Institut des Appellations d'Origine has meticulously classified, defended from competitors and ensured the quality of the output of over 90,000 vineyards, not to mention cheeses weighing 170,000 tonnes a year and other products as varied as lentils from Le Puy and butter from Charentes. The battle of the baguette became a matter of government policy in 1996 when Yves Galland, consumer affairs minister, introduced legislation to prevent anti-competitive pricing by large retail groups which risked driving small shopkeepers out of business. He warned that there would be particularly vigilant examination of attempts by the out-of-town hypermarkets to dump bread at below cost price, citing examples where baguettes had been sold at Ffr1 each. The Juppé government even attempted to limit the use of the word *boulanger* to those bakers who could show that they made their bread on the premises rather than from pre-prepared frozen dough. Political banquets – like business lunches – have long been a central feature of French life. In the same way as Kremlinologists used to study in detail who stood next to whom at the May Day parade in Red Square, the President's choice of guests for a meal at the Elysée Palace is still closely watched for signs of who is in and who is out of favour.

There is an elitist, intellectual approach to cooking – like so many other things French – which enriches the fare on offer, while not always taking into account the wishes of the client. You rarely find salt and pepper on the table of a top restaurant, for example, because the chef knows the 'correct' proportions to add. Highly complex dishes accompanied by rich sauces remain widespread, although there is growing demand for simpler, lighter, more health-conscious menus. To request any form of coffee other than an *espresso* at the end of the meal – let alone to chose the 'wrong' wine to accompany the food – is sacrilege. And while the quantity of service in the best restaurants is often generous, it is not always matched by speed or friendliness. 'If we had treated the young better, they would not have switched to US-style fast food,' says the three-star chef Alain Ducasse. 'We have been obsessed with formality and unfriendly service. We have lost out to foreign restaurants as a result.' Another Paris-based chef points a finger towards the Michelin rating system itself, which became the reference for too many of his colleagues. 'In their efforts to win stars, they thought they understood the system so well that they forgot the client,' he says.

It would be ridiculous to sound the death-knell for French restauration. *Haute cuisine* – like *haute couture* – has rarely been very remunerative in itself. But unlike the fashion trade, where the products of the catwalk create an image that sells perfumes, accessories and profitable ready-to-wear clothes, restaurants have been rather less effective in creating similar spin-offs. French cooking has understandably become a victim of its own success: why take inspiration from others when your own food is so good? The unfortunate consequence is that French restaurants abroad have remained expensive and elitist, and been a far less commercially successful 'export' than their Italian, Indian, Chinese or American equivalents. And while the average restaurant within France remains far better than its counterparts in many other countries, it is not difficult to find disappointing venues too, with pre-prepared and microwaved food, and menus without the slightest attempt at innovation.

Since 1960, the number of brasseries and cafés has declined from an estimated 200,000 to a little over 50,000. Much of the drop is the result of rapid postwar urbanization, which has left smaller villages across the country depopulated and their restaurants deprived of clients. Combined with the parallel trends of a rise in the number of working women, and the growth of the nuclear family and lifestyle, the time spent at home to prepare high-quality food around the dinner table has diminished sharply. Central Paris, with its high density and prosperous population, can still support good-quality food markets. Elsewhere, a trip to pick up frozen goods from an out-of-town hypermarket is becoming the norm: more than half of French households use giant out-of-town centres as their principal shop, and a further two-fifths per cent primarily use supermarkets. Increasing time pressure on employees and greater scrutiny of managers' expense accounts have made eating out less extravagant. And the higher rate of value-added tax that applies in cafés than in take-away outlets has not helped.

If the French continue to change their lifestyles in the same way as their counterparts in the US and other industrialized countries, the future for the country's restaurants can be positive. Nearly 70 per cent of the French go home to eat lunch during the week, for example, while in the US dining out is the norm – suggesting considerable potential for growth. Outside Paris in particular, the cult of the lunch-hour (or rather hour-and-a-half or more) remains strong. There will always be scope for *haute cuisine* at one extreme in France. And some interesting initiatives are being undertaken by the Conseil National des Arts Culinaires, for example, to try to foster greater culinary understanding by schoolchildren. But at the more basic level of street cafés, adaptation to take into account the changing habits of contemporary French society has been slow. Relatively high prices, uninspiring decor, poor service and disappointing food are far from atypical.

It is no accident that among the more commercially successful French-owned restaurants today are those which have heavily imitated US-style chains at the expense of more elaborate culinary choices, such as Bar B Q Grill. While Flo has built its reputation as a company restoring and maintaining historic and traditional brasseries, its main money-earner is the hamburger and child-oriented Hippotamus chain. It is in the absence of greater domestic innovation that McDonald's has done so well. Its success represents a combination of marketing with providing what customers want. The chain has even proved adaptable, tweaking its standard menu to adapt to French tastes, selling beer and modifying its salads and hamburger fillings to the local palate. What a telling sign of the difference between the two cultures that even if *frites* were developed in France, it is the Americans who have popularized and cashed in on them around the world – under the name 'French fries'.

Daring to be different

Frogs' legs may be among the more unusual items to feature on French restaurant menus, but that does not stop British popular newspapers from regularly indulging in a bit of nationalistic 'froggy bashing'. In October 1999, the publication best-known for such cross-Channel salvoes as 'Up Yours Delors' struck again. 'We don't want WAR, but the French are wrong', the *Sun* screamed across the front page. To ensure that the message got home, it even took the unprecedented step of producing a parallel French language edition. Its latest gripe was the refusal of the health authorities in Paris to allow the import of British beef, in the wake of the 'mad cow' crisis. Inspired by William Hague's call for a boycott of French products, the *Daily Mail* shrieked from the cliffs of Dover: 'Merde! What a Flaming Cheek.' Such anti-French media attacks were not simply restricted to the tabloids. Even a *Guardian* columnist thought fit to pronounce: 'The English love affair with France is over. Their food is out of fashion … Even Majorca is more fashionable as a holiday destination.'

Such rhetoric left little room for nuance, of course. The French might have been flying in the face of scientific arguments about the safety of beef that had been accepted by agricultural and medical experts within the European Commission. But there was no mention in the tabloids of the fact that they were not alone in their stance, since the Germans had also adopted a similar policy. There was no discussion of the fact that

France had long taken a far more aggressive approach to tackling the disease than their British counterparts, killing the entire troop of cattle if a single case was discovered – and had suffered far fewer reported human victims than the UK. And there was certainly no understanding of the radical restructuring and painful reflection which took place after the contaminated blood scandal of the 1980s in France, which traumatized a generation of political leaders and civil servants and helped lead to the creation of a health regulatory body which was independent from the state.

There is nothing new in such anti-French media attacks. The *Telegraph* and the *Times* regularly report horror stories of British citizens hassled and harassed during their holidays or once they have settled down for a peaceful retirement or a new life in France. When Jacques Chirac relaunched nuclear testing in 1995, the *Guardian* wasted little time in publishing a tongue-in-cheek article entitled 'Twenty ways to make the horrid French hopping mad'. A tempting trigger for a humorous parody of 'tabloidese' perhaps, but would the same paper ever have dared to print an equivalent piece on the Jamaicans, the Irish or even the Germans?

In fact, nuclear testing released a shock-wave of anti-Gallic sentiment for weeks around the world. Australian restaurant-owners poured bottles of valuable Bordeaux down their drains, Scandinavian demonstrators burnt *tricolore* flags outside French embassies and Japanese clients boycotted Club Méditerranée holiday resorts across the southern hemisphere. Yet the reaction seemed disproportionate compared with the much more destabilizing effect of the nuclear tests carried out by India and Pakistan in 1998, for example. The near-unanimity of condemnations from abroad also masked a fiercely critical internal domestic debate on the subject. The popular left-wing daily newspaper *Libération* was among many publications to quickly criticize Chirac's move. The president's opinion-poll ratings dropped sharply – proof, if any was needed, that the French public was ever less isolated, ever more influenced by the way in which it was regarded and the trends taking place in the outside world.

Chirac's potent gesture – so soon after his presidential election – was less the culmination of a style of centralized, defiant postwar Gaullist governance than a defining moment in its death throes. His television and newspaper interventions on the subject contained no God-given self-righteousness in the style of Bill Clinton or George Bush when they launched attacks on supposed terrorist bases in the Middle East. Nor did they mirror the highly nationalistic tones of Margaret Thatcher as she announced the Falklands war. Chirac's announcement lacked strong political rhetoric. If anything, it was characterized instead by dry technocratic arguments about the need to carry out scientific tests to complete national defence databases.

Of all the nations who attack the French, it is perhaps the British who demonstrate the strongest and most negative reaction. Even many highly intelligent and politically tolerant Britons who would never dare express similar views towards other nations show little reluctance in voicing their suspicion of and distaste for their nearest neighbours. It is often expressed in the formula 'we love France, but we hate the French'. Charles Gancel, a partner with Inter Cultural Management Associates in Paris, who advises companies on crossborder differences, says: 'There are tensions between France and Britain because they are so similar in many ways.' Both, after all, are former great powers with widespread colonial empires now on the wane. Both, too, have pretensions to be able to continue to propagate their own model of society in other countries. And both objectively remain significant and competing economic and cultural powers vying for influence around the world.

If the British expect the French to feel a similar hostility towards them, they are increasingly mistaken, however. In a

survey carried out for the 'Marche du Siècle' television programme in late 1997 among 1,000 citizens of each country, 50
per cent of the French expressed positive feelings towards the
British and just 13 per cent negative ones. The equivalent proportions for the British views of the French were 35 per cent
and 20 per cent respectively. There was even a marginally greater
number of French who could imagine themselves living in
London (18 per cent) than of British who would consider
moving to Paris (17 per cent). The figures are borne out in the
250,000 or more French who live in the UK, compared with an
estimated 65,000 Britons in France. The most trivial example of
a French businessman decamping to Ashford to reduce his operating costs is eagerly picked up by the British media. And the
suggestion that the Corsican model Laeticia Casta, whose image
was used for the busts of Marianne on display in French town-
halls around the country, had abandoned France for the UK was
reported with glee by the media.

'For the French, it's more a case of love the British, hate
Britain,' says one young Frenchman. He reflects a widespread
French resistance to the weather and food across the Channel,
while admiring British pragmatism and creativity, modesty and
self-deprecating humour. Qualities, incidentally, that the recent
arrogant 'Cool Britannia' triumphalism under the Tony Blair
government has helped to erode. In fact, the contemporary
French view of the British is probably more than anything one
of indifference. You will search in vain for vociferous anti-
British sentiment in French newspapers, for example. Partly
because it is not the Gallic style to throw around such 'humorous' insults, and there are no equivalents of the UK tabloid
press to act as the mouthpiece for such sentiments. But also
because there is relatively less interest shown by the French
towards the British than vice versa. Surrounded by other countries and supported by a different history, the nation's reference
points are elsewhere: to its neighbours in Germany, Spain and

Italy; to North Africa, the Middle and Far East; and to the US. Why is the price of a return trip on the Eurostar cross-Channel train service from Paris to London cheaper than one that starts in London? Because there are far fewer French and other mainland Europeans who want to head into the 'dead end' of the UK than there are British wanting to travel on to the 'continent'.

France has long had a far greater fascination – of both attraction and repulsion – with the US than with Britain. Both nations in their present form were founded on the basis of an intellectual, republican idea backed by a constitution. They have traditionally shared a distinctive and open approach to immigration, for example. While some tourists now mistake it for a memorial to Diana Spencer, the golden torch flame sitting above the Pont de l'Alma in Paris is in fact a model of the one clutched proudly by the Statue of Liberty in New York harbour, a gift constructed in the workshops of Gustave Eiffel and presented to the Americans by the French as a sign of international friendship and Republican solidarity.

Yet like the British, the Americans regard their transatlantic neighbour with suspicion. France may be part of the Western alliance, and provided troops during the Gulf war. But it has also long stood apart, with its refusal to join NATO, its insistence on an independent nuclear deterrent, and its ambivalent attitude in the Gulf war and in subsequent stand-offs such as with Iraq. It remains a force to be reckoned with, a country willing to stand apart in the fora which wield influence – whether the G7, or the United Nations Security Council, where it retains one of five permanent seats. In short, what irritates its partners is that France dares to be different. Yet, to the infuriation and incomprehension of its allies, it is still ultimately loyal on the most fundamental questions.

For the historian Douglas Porch, the ambitions of France's foreign policy now far exceed its information-gathering capacities – let alone its ability to act as an independent military force. Its defiant activities sometimes seem superfluous or point-less. When heads of state of 49 nations gathered in November 1997 for the seventh summit of *francophonie*, it seemed to some more like a manifestation of francofolly. The network had been grandiosely launched in 1986 at Versailles by François Mitter-rand, supposedly with the aim of uniting French-speaking nations in a fight against the 'abolition of difference'. There seemed to be more than a little desperation in the location of the latest gathering in Vietnam, a country where less than 2 per cent of the population speaks French. Let alone in Jacques Chirac's attempts to broaden its focus to discuss democracy, press freedom and human rights: subjects on which some of the affil-iated *francophone* nations had themselves yet to make much progress. These themes continued to dominate at the follow-up summit at Moncton in Canada in 1999, so much so that the organizers of the next gathering in Beirut in 2001 publicly resolved to try to move away from the idea of a defensive 'fortress France' trying to protect itself from the Anglo-Saxon onslaught.

There is a certain paranoia linked to France's diminishing role in the world. Its diplomats seemed only to be showing their insecurity when they so often insisted on their role in de-fusing the 1998 stand-off between the UN weapons inspectors and Saddam Hussein, or in shaping the emergency financial package brokered by the International Monetary Fund to help strug-gling emerging economies later the same year. So too when they point to conspiracy theories engineered by others against them. Writing on the decision to begin withdrawing French troops from much of Africa in 1997, Dominique David of the French Institute for International Relations argued: 'Even if you denounce the Anglo-Saxon plot or American strategies here and there, the French system has no doubt collapsed because it no longer corresponds to today's demands.' Citing the example of France's independent line in Yugoslavia, he argues that the country simply did not have sufficient resources to implement François Mitterrand's vision to prevent the break-up of the country; nor did it have the power to bring others round to its point of view.

The fact is that France is – albeit belatedly – adjusting its foreign policy in Africa, as it has been in other parts of the world. Far more than François Mitterrand, Jacques Chirac has made great strides in economic diplomacy. He sandwiched the two-day Hanoi *francophonie* summit between meetings with business leaders in south-east Asia, for instance, and he regularly takes a group of corporate chief executives with him on his travels. It is true that France may have a less than glorious record of colonial and post-colonial rule. The tense legacy lives on today in its awkward relationship with Algeria, its role in Middle Eastern diplomacy and in the immigrant groups that help shape its domestic politics. The country may remain involved in a whole series of political and economic manipulations beyond its own borders which are far from praiseworthy. But are these any worse than the 'dirty tricks' of the US in Central and South America, or the aggressive attempts to win foreign markets by a number of its leading rival trading partners?

What remains of France's exception in maintaining an independent role in international diplomacy is in many ways healthy. It provides some form of counterbalance to US hegemony, questioning conventional wisdom at a time of general conformism by other Western powers, of incoherence in the former Soviet bloc and weakness among many of the non-aligned nations. Its role in the negotiations over Iraq and Kosovo in 1999 showed that it was valued as an alternative power. Its hardline stance towards Russia about human rights abuses in the breakaway North Caucasus republic of Chechnya in 1999 and 2000 stood in stark contrast to the weak words of Tony Blair and other Western politicians who flocked to meet President Vladimir Putin and came out of their meetings in awe. At the same time, France has maintained a loyalty on fundamental issues to the West. The real challenge lies not with its policies abroad, but with its tensions at home.

Notable exceptions

Why should the fact that France does things differently matter to the rest of the world? Every country has its own 'exceptions', its distinguishing marks which make it stand out in one way or another. But few have intellectualized and politicized them to the same degree as the French. *L'exception française* is not simply incidental. It has been grasped by many of the country's decision-makers as the basis for a unique approach in the world, the bedrock of their philosophy of a model that sets it apart from its peers. It has become a cult, a phrase that crops up hundreds of times a year in newspaper articles, political speeches and policy papers.

French exceptions have become too visible, too powerful and too distinctive to be ignored. Too visible, if only because France is the world's most popular tourist destination, attracting 73 million visitors in 2000 alone. Too powerful, because it maintains a huge cultural and social influence internationally, and because it is still a major industrial player, ranking among the world's top five largest economies – as large as the UK and bigger than Italy. And too distinctive, because it dares to use its weight in a way that does not always entirely tally with the views of the world's other powerhouses. Among the leading G7 states, it is often difficult to find many fundamental distinctions in ideology or foreign policy between the US, Canada and the UK. Germany, Japan and Italy remain relatively timid and conformist – particularly on military matters – in the wake of their wartime defeats. That leaves only France in a rather more ambiguous position: on the winning side, but also with a determination to stand apart.

In short, the principal reason to examine French exceptionalism – and the main weakness of any argument that is too critical about its system and culture – is quite simply that it works. Whatever its faults, France remains a force to be reckoned with internationally. It remains as solid a democracy as its counterparts, with little danger of collapsing in spite of its internal problems. And its influence cannot be simply waived aside. That is why it can prove a source of admiration and inspiration; or be a thorn in the side of so many other nations. Its exceptions demand attention.

There is no shortage of examples of France's original stance. There is the practice of *priorité à droite* on the roads – forcing speeding traffic to grind to a halt to allow in an occasional car from a side street; the substitution of a comma for the decimal point when writing numbers; or the positioning of the table of contents at the back rather than the front of its books. Any selection is inevitably limited and open to criticism. But it is perhaps most revealing to pick examples of national achievements or disgraces, selecting varied themes which reflect broader trends and have a message about the way in which the society was formed, and how it operates as a whole.

The exceptions chosen cover politics and business, trade unions and the civil service, culture and regional policy, technology and the media. They often focus on particular events or tangible projects. They are examples which may often be cited as strengths, but in fact often have a weak underbelly; or those which may be seen as shameful, yet have a more positive message. Above all, they are examples which in nearly every case also bear the mark of particular powerful interests groups or elites. These cliques are behind many of the most visible signs of change – and conservatism – in contemporary

France. All countries have their own elites, of course. The UK has its class system, with power and influence still strongly influenced by birth. In the US, family origin may be far less relevant, but money has become the criterion of reference – the tool to be elected to Congress, the benchmark by which success is achieved, and the way to progress and ensure your children do the same. French society is distinctive because it remains far more meritocratic, with the judgement of individuals based far more on intellectual achievement. At the heart of the system is education. With very few exceptions, all the top pupils attend state schools, which also provide the best training for those with lower levels of achievement. Access to the top *grandes écoles* – just like recruitment into the civil service – comes initially through competitive and anonymous exams or *concours*. The approach is not foolproof. A school in the 5th *arrondissement* of Paris does not bring the same results as one in the troubled suburb of Seine St-Denis. Parents and relatives play a determining role; classmates and teachers too. But merit has a strong place. And like money or class, it also has its limitations.

There is little point in dwelling for too long on some of the exceptions that are most positive in France – notably the quality of life sought by so many contented holidaymakers, the wine, the countryside or the enormous cultural heritage. They have been analysed countless times before, and to a large extent they speak for themselves. In many ways, the extremes and above all the negative exceptions are far more revealing. They show the limits to which the society can be stretched, the excesses which it creates or tolerates. It is there that the pressure points of contemporary French society lie, providing perhaps the best clues to its future evolution.

Language and culture seem a good place to start. It was Jack Lang, the long-serving Socialist minister of culture under François Mitterrand during the 1980s and early 1990s, who was as responsible as anyone for the origin of the phrase *l'exception française*, which has since become a form of common currency if not an article of faith among many national policy-makers and opinion-formers today. It was originally coined in the form of *l'exception culturelle*, to justify a special status given to culture to protect it from the vagaries of free market forces. It has expanded over time and has been appropriated by many others to form a far broader corpus of sacrosanct French-style policies and approaches. But how far have the cultural elites who control the country's unique system of linguistic regulation at the Académie française – or those in charge of rules and supports for cinema – helped boost its global position and influence?

If *l'exception française* had its origins in culture, it rapidly took on a broader meaning in the 1990s. Most notably, it has become a catch-all designed to describe a distinctive French economic model. It is a vague philosophy, more a label than a meaningful or coherent approach. One that is defined less by what it is, and more by opposition to what it is not: the supposedly ultra-liberal Anglo-Saxon model. But at its core it boils down to the enormous influence of the state and the public sector on French life, centred on its capital city. There are the long-standing caricatures of centralization and *dirigisme*. And there is the preferred contemporary scapegoat of the *enarque*, the graduate of the elite civil service training school – the Ecole Nationale d'Administration – who best symbolizes the supposedly technocratic decisions made by individuals based in Paris, far removed from the realities of daily existence. How centralized is France, and has the system proved a force for good?

Concorde, Ariane, the TGV, Minitel, nuclear power: France's postwar technological achievements are among its most admired assets. They combined vision with technical expertise and pragmatism. Building on the country's long-standing engineering prowess, they were rooted in a strong spirit of *volontarisme* or active interventionism. They reflected the power and influence of a small group of impressive and highly trained public servants functioning at the peak of their capacities – notably the top graduates of the Ecole Polytechnique, recruited into the state's most prestigious technical administrative *grands corps*, the Mines and the Ponts et Chaussées. They employed a technocratic approach, with little tolerance for other opinions and with an unstoppable momentum of their own. What is their future today?

If France is characterized by a centralization of power from the top, what effect has that had on the development of strong counterbalances capable of holding decision-makers in check or of keeping them accountable? The judiciary, regulatory bodies, consumer groups, independent watchdogs or other brakes on excess have often proved weak in the face of political power. And the parliament was in the past equally feeble, emasculated when successive presidents passed controversial legislation by decree. To analyse the French media is a way to broach a range of far broader questions about political and corporate patronage and influence-peddling, about intellectual traditions, the role of the press and the broadcast sector in society, as well as to examine attitudes towards privacy and the personal lives of public figures.

As anyone stranded for days on the country's motorway system as a result of a truckers' strike will testify, one of France's most eye-catching exceptions is the continued strength of its labour elites. They seem to reflect an extremely rigid society in which smooth and regular negotiation between management and employees has proved impossible. 1968 remains a nostalgic battle-cry, and long after cities in eastern Europe have been de-Sovietized, Paris still has a metro stop called Kremlin Bicêtre and there are many an Avenue Lenin in the 'red suburbs' around the capital. But how typical are such outbursts and manifestations of left-wing belief? What do they say about the power of the state in balancing different interest groups? And how far are their gains those of a selfish, largely public-sector, unionized minority?

There is no better illustration of what the French have dubbed *déresponsabilisation* than Crédit Lyonnais, the state-owned bank that swelled to become one of the largest financial institutions in the world in the early 1990s, only to come speedily crashing down with a bill for the taxpayer likely to run to more than Ffr150 billion. The story of the bank's downfall highlights the influence of the tight-knit super-elite of *inspecteurs des finances*, who became top civil servants, regulators and business executives. No one wanted to claim responsibility when things went wrong. But who was really to blame? And were the bank's experiences unique, or did it reflect a broader pattern across the management of public-sector – and even private-sector – companies?

The extreme right-wing National Front has won up to 15 per cent of the vote in the presidential elections, and in 1995 gained control of three towns of significant size in the south of France. Its influence is explained in part by racism. But the causes are far more complex. An analysis of the party's success helps to understand the broader nature of the current crisis and to explore the internal tensions and failures of the nation's political elites. It also provides a way to consider the very distinctive approach to identity and citizenship, and to new immigrants and how best to integrate them. In short, what it means to be French today.

Although France's foreign policy in Europe, Africa and elsewhere around the world may attract much comment, its influence is far more significant and measurable in its own former 'colonies'. It is perhaps most revealing of all to look at its closest 'colony' – or the furthest part of the 'mainland' – the Mediterranean island of Corsica, which has been scarred by separatist violence for the past quarter of a century. Studying the operation of the state in a region with its own fiercely guarded identity provides a way to understand the outcomes of French-style governance. While in some ways unique, Corsica helps analyse the ultimate limits of French society.

2

The closing of the French mind

Every Thursday morning, a group of aged men and women files into a magnificent ancient stone building overlooking the River Seine to fulfil a curious but solemn duty. They are continuing a task entrusted to their predecessors more than 360 years ago. Hobbling into a meeting room next to a large amphitheatre capped by a gilded cupola, they take their usual places and prepare for the challenging task ahead. Their deliberations say much about the operation of French society, and their decisions still carry considerable influence to this day.

These are the 'immortals' of the Académie Française, whose number is strictly limited to 40 and whose average age is well over 70. Despite the title, death has taken its inevitable toll, but only just over 300 people have assumed the venerable role over the centuries. Their task, the sole obligation with which each of them is charged when elected, has remained unchanged since the institution was first created by Cardinal de Richelieu in 1635: 'To give clear rules to our language and make it pure, eloquent and capable of handling the arts and the sciences'.

Perhaps even more than the construction of the TGV railway

lines in the 1980s or the financial destruction of the bank Crédit Lyonnais in the early 1990s, the French language itself is one of best and most long-standing examples of *l'exception française* with all its ambiguities. It both reflects and has proved a powerful tool in shaping a culture with a worldwide reputation for literary, artistic and intellectual achievements. The Académie Française has been its guardian-in-chief, spawning imitators in other countries such as Turkey and Russia. And its approach has been aped in other spheres in recent years, notably in the efforts to protect French cinema.

Contemporary French is in part the result of the firm but increasingly futile efforts to control the national tongue by a small linguistic elite with strong political backing. Their rulings are often made in defiance of the evolutions in the spoken and written language that are taking place around them. The watchdogs of the Académie make every effort to impose their views of how the language should be expressed by the broader population. They reflect a powerful example of the French desire to codify and control, to regulate and restrict at all costs. They have contributed to a closing of the French mind to the outside world.

Insistent on secrecy, the Académie has only extremely rarely allowed its Thursday meetings to be observed by outsiders. The occasional exceptions have been for curious visiting monarchs and crown princes, appropriately enough for an institution which has survived equal periods under regal and republican rule. However, the fruits of the immortals' discussions soon draw public attention, in the form of regular published extracts of the latest edition of their official dictionary, which lays down what it judges to be acceptable among words, spelling and syntax.

Not that productivity has been the strong point of the immortals in the past. The first edition of the dictionary was published in 1694, and the eighth and most recent in 1935. Labouring at length over such delicate subjects as whether *chariot* can be permitted to be spelt with a single 'r' given that its Latin root has two, it was only two months into 2000 that they got as far as preliminary debates around the word *millénaire*. Later in the same year, they managed to publish the second volume of the revised dictionary, which ended with *mappemonde*, and one immortal in an article in *Le Monde* estimated that they might get round to finishing their work by as soon as 2010.

Maurice Samuel Roger Charles Druon, Grand Officier de la légion d'honneur, described in *Who's Who* as a 'man of letters', plans to change all that. He seems perfectly suited to the role of chief advocate and defender of French linguistic purity. The 'perpetual secretary' of the Académie until late 1999, sitting in his book-lined study up a winding staircase just behind the cupola, is elegantly dressed, with a monocle dangling around his neck and donnish tufts of white hair adding to his authority. No one can doubt his credentials. He is the author of around 30 books and three plays. A Commander of Arts and Letters, he was a wartime companion of General de Gaulle while in exile in London during the second world war, a minister of culture, and was elected to the Académie in 1966 at the almost obscenely youthful age of 48. Twenty years later, he took up his current role, and has pledged to accelerate the production of the current and future editions of the dictionary in an effort to prevent French from wriggling free of the immortals' grasp.

'I am not an adversary of the English language,' he says. 'I would like English to be the first language of all francophones.' But he grimaces as he warns of the encroachment of 'the language of the dollar' and of 'Anglo-rican' expressions incompatible with French syntax. 'The language of a people is its soul. My fear is that in French – and in English – that is being lost. The language of the elite should become the language of the people.' It is a phrase that sums up both the strengths and the weaknesses of French today – and by extension, many broader aspects of France itself.

French as a mirror of France

A weighty dark green volume stands as testament to the energetic recent labours of the Académie under Druon. Published in 1994, it covers the first part of the latest dictionary, which runs all the way from *A* to *Enzyme*. In a sign of the immortals' proof of imagination, it includes such ground-breaking new words as *baladeur*, remarkably similar to the name of the patrician Gaullist politician Edouard Balladur, who was prime minister at the time of publication. It might have drawn on a fifteenth-century word for fraudster, but its latest definition was: 'a radio, cassette or compact disk player with earphones, small and carried around with one. *Should be preferred to the English walkman*'.

Who can fault a language and a supporting culture which has such originality? Which has created so many internationally recognized words and accompanying ideas as *renaissance* or *laissez-faire*, even if their influence is perhaps rather less strong in contemporary France? With a humanist, secular tradition that has coined in place of 'illegitimate child' the far more pleasant and less value-laden *enfant naturel*? And which has given English *bon vivant* and *savoir vivre*, and even lent to Vietnamese *xa phong* (savon or soap) and *ba te* (pâté)?

Or more recently, a language which has given birth to such original phrases as *vrai-faux* (real-false), used in such contexts as the supposed husband-and-wife team of secret service agents employed to blow up the Greenpeace ship *Rainbow Warrior*, and subsequently applied to the passport secretly sanctioned by Balladur's interior minister Charles Pasqua allowing the secret agent Yves Challier to flee the country under a false name and avoid scandal? Even if we do have to wait another decade before the Académie makes it far enough through the alphabet to judge whether or not the phrase is in their view considered acceptable.

If the French have a justified reputation for inventiveness, it is clearly reflected in their language. Other national attributes are equally well mirrored. None more so than that greatest of Gallic characteristics: a passion for food. There is often different slang for phrases which exist in other languages but which maintain the culinary references. 'He has lots on his plate' becomes *il a du pain sur la planche*. 'The big cheese' becomes *la grosse légume*, even if some speakers have also been heard to re-adapt the English version more directly and talk about a *Camembert* (a word that also means a pie chart). Money can be referred to as *blé* (bread), but also as *une galette* (a type of cake). And the Bank of France is even sometimes called *La Grande Boulange* (the big bakery).

But French gastronomic argot is far richer still. *La bonne poire* or pear is a sucker; *un pépin* or seed is a problem; *un cornichon* or gherkin is an idiot; *un navet* or turnip is a bad film; *une prune* is a parking ticket. To *faire monter la mayonnaise* is to provoke; *se faire rouler dans la farine* is to be ripped off; *cracher dans la soupe* is to soil your own nest; *aller à la soupe* is to act in your own self-interest; and *manger à tous les rateliers* is to take advantage of everyone. Not that most of these examples would pass muster with the Académie.

Far more powerful cultural elements are at work alongside the immortals to mould the language, often in ways that are not terribly positive. For example, those who argue that there are strong racist aspects to French culture – or at least that there is intolerance towards foreign influence – can point to the use of the word *nègre* (literally, negro) for someone who ghost-writes a book; to the chocolate-coated sweet and variety of mushroom both called a *tête de nègre*; or to the colloquial expression *travail d'arabe* to mean a task poorly carried out. Not to mention *filer à l'anglaise*, even if the British return the caricature with their equivalent: to take French leave.

Simone de Beauvoir may have been an early feminist, but those who believe women's rights still have a long way to go in France need look no further than the battle over the gender of certain words. As Josette Rey-Debove, a linguist who heads the editorial department of the dictionary-publishing group Robert points out, popular usage and the Académie alike appeared to have no difficulty in accepting the feminized *cuisinière* (cook) or *épicière* (grocer). But tensions arise when women start to occupy positions of power, becoming ministers or presidents and threatening to feminize these words too. She argues that while *doctoresse* formally exists in French, few women doctors would dare refer to themselves as such for fear of losing male clients. There are, incidentally, just two women immortals.

Those who see French society as intensely intellectual can point to literary references such as the phrase *un choix cornélien* for a difficult choice. Equally, there is the enormous number of Latin phrases dropped into everyday usage far more casually and widely than in other tongues: *ex nihilo, a priori, quid, grosso modo, de facto, nec plus ultra ... ad infinitum.* And for those who regard France as a highly stratified and hierarchical country, there is also plenty of supportive ammunition in the language. There is the obsession with titles, with great emphasis placed on referring to *monsieur le ministre* or *monsieur le président*, for instance, even if the individual in question has long since ceased to hold that office. There is a large number of written forms of address to be mastered, notably at the beginning and the end of a letter, if protocol is to be obeyed, and important nuances depending on whether the recipient is male or female.

Above all, there is the distinction between the plural or formal word for 'you', *vous*, and its singular or informal equivalent, *tu*. The former serves to create a clear distance between superiors and inferiors, at work or even – as with Balladur and his wife, or between many French parents and their children in the past – within the family. The *tu* form, by contrast, serves to create bonds between friends and colleagues from the same elite (often of very different ages). To add to the confusion, they may well refer to each other as *tu* in private, but switch to *vous* in a more public forum to re-establish their (self-) importance when others are watching. Since the 1960s, growing informality has diminished the use of *vous*, making the distinction all the more pointed when it is employed today.

But perhaps no aspect of the French character is better mirrored by its language than the constant attempts at centralization, classification and regulation exemplified by the efforts of the Académie. Might not the immortals' attacks on the encroachment of anglicisms and other foreign words seem at best creative, and at worst to be rather harmless and archaic fun? Surely the views of such a small group of linguistic purists and prudes barely echo against the walls of the adjacent Paris mint, let alone make it to the Louvre on the far side of the Seine, permeating into the heads of passers-by on the way?

In fact, their collective pronouncements have a resonance unmatched by the concerns of their like-minded counterparts in other countries. The Académie is taken extremely seriously in France. *Le Monde* religiously reprints at full and exhaustive length (typically a double page of tightly spaced text running to several thousand words) the inaugural speech of each new immortal, which takes the form of an eulogy to his or her departed predecessor. Leading national figures, such as the recently deceased ocean explorer Jacques-Yves Cousteau, not to mention the likes of Voltaire, Pasteur and Victor Hugo in their time, have been delighted to assume the role.

Equally, the Académie's deliberations are widely discussed. Take, for instance, the 9 January 1998 issue of *Le Figaro*, the conservative newspaper which is among the most widely read in the country. It was a day on which the Socialist government of Lionel Jospin was facing one of its most serious crises since its election, over protests by the unemployed. Claude Allègre, the education minister, had just launched an ambitious consultation exercise on reforms to the high school curriculum. Statistics released for the year had highlighted an escalating trend in urban violence.

Yet *Le Figaro* found room for an extensive article on its front page about the latest salvo from Druon. In the full letter, reproduced inside, the perpetual secretary and two fellow immortals wrote to President Jacques Chirac in his role as 'protector' of the Académie, to intervene in 'an affair from on-high in the state, which threatens the French language'. His concern? That 'certain of the women who have the honour of being part of the current government have decided to call themselves Madame LA ministre' in spite of the fact that their official nomination decrees gave them no authority to 'modify on their own behalf French grammar and the uses of the language'. As a 1996 decree most recently stipulated, it was the Académie that acted as the reference on 'matters of terminology and neology'. Resisting demagogy and maintaining a uniform written and spoken language in all francophone countries was what ensured that French remained universal, warned Mr Druon. Had not [all two of] the Académie's female members agreed that they should be referred to as *académiciens* and not *académiciennes*?

Wasting no time in efforts to show its own support for the views expressed in the letter, *Le Figaro*'s front-page editorial on the rather more significant subject of the demonstrations by the unemployed pointedly referred to the obligations of Martine Aubry, *Madame LE ministre* for employment and solidarity. But such concern with linguistic pride is not limited to the right-wing press, nor to France's more conservative citizens. The left-wing daily paper *Libération* rapidly caught up with its rival and reported Mr Druon's remarks, albeit with a rather more sceptical eye. *Le Monde* devoted news stories, two guest editorials and two columns to the debate over several subsequent days.

It was no surprise when the historian Hélène Carrère d'Encausse, who replaced Mr Druon in October 1999, chose to refer to herself as Madame LE secrétaire perpétuel.

The Académie's views have rubbed off on others. In April 2000, union pressure swiftly forced Air France to withdraw a

rule that pilots speak English to air traffic controllers at Paris's
Charles de Gaulle airport.

The obsession with language

It was not a football match or even a pop concert that inaugu-
rated the Stade de France, the hugely expensive stadium built in
the northern Parisian suburbs to host the summer 1998 World
Cup championship. Hundreds gathered, and many tens of thousands more watched, as France 3 broadcast a prime-time television programme from the site in January 1998. It was the annual
'Dicos d'or': a dictation contest in which Bernard Pivot, the
country's leading cultural journalist, solemnly reads out
intensely complicated phrases to the contestants in an attempt to
test their ability to spell the most obscure of words. His questions are slavishly reported in the following day's newspapers –
another sign that language matters passionately in France.

Few are currently as insistent on the choice of their words
and the manipulation of their understanding as Jospin. On the
satirical television puppet show *Les Guignols*, he is frequently
ridiculed for his interjections in response to interviewers: 'I
don't like your choice of the word …' Jospin, the Socialist
leader, called during the 1997 general election campaign for an
end to privatizations and a halt to proposals for private pension
funds. He winced at the suggestion of labour market 'flexibility'
as a way to help cut unemployment, and condemned the *pensée
unique* of a group of like-minded technocrats in the centre-right
government who were supposedly pushing for monetary union
at any price.

Jospin, the prime minister, has edged around his rather different policies by reverting to some extraordinarily agile linguistic gymnastics. France Telecom was not privatized, for
example; its share capital was 'partially opened'. Pension funds

are set to go ahead eventually, but they must be called *épargne retraite* (retirement savings) schemes. After pan-European discussions about employment, Mr Jospin may have approved the need to tweak the labour market, but he emphasized that the measures adopted should help *souplesse* and not the dreaded *flexibilité*. Speaking about a difference of opinion between the Socialist party and its young members' division, he took pains to stress that everyone was talking 'not two languages but with a *unité de pensée*' rather than, of course, the horrifying *pensée unique*. When he wants to condemn policy initiatives from other countries, Jospin and his ministers condemn them as *ultra-liberal*. No more moderate a description appears to exist for the approaches taken in the US or even the UK. He has also repeatedly insisted on the importance of preserving *service public à la française* as a way of maintaining the railways, utilities and other assets in the state's hands. Yet he has offered no precise definition of the concept.

Such scrupulousness by the French for their language often translates into the need for extreme caution in the face of foreign influence. When Allègre addressed the summer school of French Socialist party militants in La Rochelle in August 1997, his periodic use of such anglicisms as 'software' drew sharp intakes of breath from the audience. When he snapped back that 'English is no longer a foreign language' and that to fight against it was 'something completely obsolete', he was strongly hissed.

Even this minister's more liberal attitude has its limits, however. In January 1998, he felt obliged to issue a formal denial of 'a false rumour' that he was considering making the teaching of English compulsory in schools, even if 87 per cent of secondary school pupils opted to learn the language. There was no reason that such a policy should be implemented, of course, but was it necessary for the education department to put out a widely distributed statement to stress that 'the minister wants to leave the choice to parents who can choose another important European language or Arabic, which will reinforce the strength of our country in an effort to fight against everything being in English'?

If the Académie stood alone in issuing linguistic edicts, and a minority of militants were isolated voices which supported its views, both could probably be safely ignored. But there is a far larger mechanism with extensive historical roots. François I first made the use of French compulsory in official documents with the Villers-Coterêts edict of 1539. That excluded the use of Latin, but also Occitan, Picard and other regional languages. The Académie got to work on its first dictionary in 1639, but by 1673 it was also calling for a standardized system of spelling and of pronunciation.

As the linguist Henriette Walter explains, the French Revolution only enhanced the fervent desire to standardize and control the language. The Convention decided that local languages smacked of the *ancien régime* and threatened the influence of revolutionary propaganda. In 1791, the calls began to establish 'primary' schools (the word dates from that year) in each commune around the country, 100 years before a similar system existed in the UK. As the Bishop of Autun wrote in his report to the Constituent Assembly, the schools would 'finally put an end to this bizarre inequality: they will teach the language of the Constitution and the laws to all, and that horde of corrupt dialects, the last remnant of feudalism, will be forced to disappear'.

Four years later, the schools were established by law, and debate began around the creation of Ecoles Normales (stressing the importance of the 'norm') to instruct primary teachers. The pioneering Ecole Normale Supérieure in Paris, for secondary-school teachers, was also founded in 1794. And a separate law passed in the same year required all legislation to be written in French, under pain for the transgressors of six months' imprisonment and being stripped of public office.

The new language police

The last thing Edmond Delpal needed was a new source of trouble. A gravelly voiced, grey-haired businessman, he had been long locked into a struggle with the corporate headquarters of the Body Shop, the UK-based cosmetics chain, over the conditions imposed and the financial projections given to him for his struggling local franchise outlet in the Alpine town of Chambéry. But when government inspectors paid him a visit in November 1995, it was for an entirely different matter. The local office of the department for competition, consumer affairs and the suppression of fraud had been tipped off by irate customers. They identified ten products on the shelves of his shop – including pineapple facial wash, bubble bath and body spray – which were labelled in English. By the following January, a local court had fined him Ffr1,000 and ordered him to immediately cease selling those items which did not carry labels in French.

Efforts to control the use of the language continue to this day, and have become in some ways tougher over time. The 1975 Bas-Lauriol law made French obligatory in all written and spoken advertising, and on instructions on packages. Much to the chagrin of the Basques, Bretons, Corsicans and other regionalists, the constitution of the Fifth Republic, approved in 1958, was amended as recently as 1992 under a Socialist parliament to add to Article 2: 'the language of the republic is French'. France long stood apart from its neighbours in refusing to sign the Council of Europe's charter on minority languages, and has done relatively little to support its distinctive regional cultures. In summer 1998, even as the Jospin government was again considering whether to ratify the charter, the deputy prefect of the Luberon region ordered Pierre Pessemesse, the mayor of Buoux, to withdraw from sale admission tickets to the local fort that had been printed in Provençal.

However, none of the recent regulatory measures has

acquired more notoriety than that introduced in 1994 by Jacques Toubon, the Gaullist minister of culture. The national constitutional council diluted some of his more extreme proposals, arguing that they ran against the principle of freedom of expression enshrined in the declaration of human rights. But in its residual form, the law still obliged civil servants and those involved in carrying out a public service to operate in French – and a French that it judged acceptable. Existing measures would be toughened, and compliance mechanisms installed through the surveillance of activists in five separate associations for the defence of the language.

Swiftly dubbed by the French 'Jack Allgood', his name translated literally into English, Toubon became a source of national mockery. But work on implementing the measures soon got under way. If the action against Edmond Delpal's Body Shop outlet was one of the first such high-profile attacks, several dozen prosecutions were successfully brought by the language defenders during 1996 alone. One in October of that year targeted Georgia Tech Lorraine, a French teaching off-shoot of the US-based Georgia Institute of Technology. It was pursued in the courts for distributing information in English on its Internet computer site, in spite of the fact that it was aimed at students who were required to attend classes in English; and it was accused of breaching rules on linguistic protec-tion because of its connections to its main site based in the US. In 1999, the French authorities carried out a record total of 9,573 linguistic inspections, issued 725 warnings, sent 282 cases to the public prosecutor and won 98 rulings that had made it to court. That included four that had gone to appeal and one which went as far as the supreme court.

After the Toubon laws came into force, travellers on the Parisian metro noticed that posters containing simple English phrases – even those advertising language tuition – were also obliged to carry French translations in the small print. Viewers of Friday evening television were surprised when the presenters suddenly (and albeit briefly) started wishing them *bon congé de fin de semaine* (end-of-week holiday), in an effort to avoid the taboo English word 'weekend'. The CSA, the national audio-visual regulator, also sees itself as part of the language police. Its widely circulated monthly newsletter contains regular articles on abuses of French. Among the items in the October 1997 edition was a warning on the use of sub-titles. 'In spite of the recommendations of the CSA, television stations continue to use the English abbreviation system, when all of the written press respects French usage,' it scolded. 'So it is right to recall that French does not use a full-stop when the abbreviation is the final letter of the word: Dr (and not Dr.) for doctor.' Or its January 1998 missive: 'Liaison is incorrect after a singular noun which ends with a silent consonant. Le Credit T'Agricole sears the ears.'

State intervention in broadcasting goes much further than reprimands over style and grammar, however. Since the start of 1996, all music radio stations in the country have been obliged to ensure that 40 per cent of the songs they play are French and half of these must be new releases – that despite complaints from listeners, concerns over liberty of expression and practical objections that there simply are not sufficient high-quality domestically-produced songs to go around. Not to mention anomalies such as the fact that Khaled and Youssou N'Dour, two extremely popular singers, do not count towards the quotas. They may be 'francophone', produced by French record companies, often resident and best known within France, but one is Arab and the other African. And they do not always sing in French.

Elitism and insularity

If the Académie recognizes the term *démocratie* in its dictionary, it certainly does not apply it to its own mode of operation. *Elitisme* is another case entirely. For the institution could not have done more to limit the degree to which it reflects the society over which it casts its collective ears and eyes. Not only are most of the immmortals male, white and well past retirement age, but they are also a shamelessly self-selecting elite. In spite of their immense intellectual and practical achievements, few can claim any formal expertise in linguistics or grammar. And Druon waves a dismissive hand at the suggestion that journalists and broadcasters, those immersed daily in the written and spoken language, might ever be immortalized. He calls them 'agents of degradation'.

The institution has certainly often failed in the past to reflect changes in France in its composition, or to select those whom history has ultimately judged to be among the most distinguished and memorable citizens. The holders of its non-existent so-called '41st seat' who were never accepted is embarrassingly extensive: Balzac, Descartes, Dumas, Flaubert, Gide, Molière, Pascal, Proust, Rousseau, Stendhal. Not to mention Zola, who was feted as a hero in 1998, 100 years after his letter to the president, '*J'accuse*', helped sway public opinion in the Dreyfus affair, but whose application was rejected many times.

This sense of being out of touch is exemplified by but certainly not limited to the Académie. It might seem strange, for instance, that France's newspapers sometimes refer to their own citizens as *Frenchies*, implying that the word is understood and regularly employed by the residents of London or Washington when they talk about their counterparts in Paris. The fact that it would draw a frown of incomprehension from anyone outside the country's own borders symbolizes a certain isolation from the rest of the world. A senior executive responsible for the academic publishing arm of Havas, a French media group, laments the role of the 'ayatollahs' in the ministry of education who periodically demand that scientific papers he issues in journals should be produced in French. The result is to limit their circulation to certain markets, or reduce their influence because of the additional costs of paying for bilingual journals that are twice the size. A similar dissuasive effect comes with the insistence in the Toubon law that conferences held in France must offer translation into the national language as at least an option.

Such closure to the outside world is also highlighted by the experience of Alan Sokal, an American theoretical physicist who began discovering with horror the elementary errors in the pseudo-science written by a number of philosophers and other intellectuals, many of whom were French. When he responded with a parody published in a US academic journal in 1996, he created a stir in the academic communities of many countries – with the exception of France itself. It took many months before the first waves of response finally hit the French press. It was only when he produced an expanded book-length analysis in 1997 (purposely published in French first, as a way of avoiding accusations that he was simply another foreigner indulging in a little 'French-bashing') that he provoked much reaction. And then it came mainly in the form of insults rather than serious responses from those he had criticized.

While the French have proved to be great creators in many fields, their language has meant that others have often been more effective at capitalizing on their work. That is an indictment above all of the narrow-mindedness of other cultures, notably American, which have proved all but impermeable to works in French. But it has economic costs, and it has helped reduce the potential influence of their culture on other countries. 'My Way', for example, was a song composed by Claude François, but it was popularized by Frank Sinatra. Films from *La Cage Aux Folles* to *Un Indien Dans La Ville* have been made in

French but then profitably remade by US producers in English. The children's television programme 'The Magic Roundabout' was devised by a Frenchman, but who remembers him? No surprise that among the most successful 'French' films in recent years have been *Léon* and *The Fifth Element*, made by the French director Luc Besson, but both produced in English with a largely American cast. And should it be a shock that, according to the National Music Export Bureau, the French songs which sell best in other countries are those in English, or which are predominantly instrumental?

For Luc Sante, a Belgian writer who now lives in New York, the attempts to restrict the development of French over the centuries have left a language that remains 'a seventeenth-century cadaver'. If words and grammar substantially reflect the French of several hundred years ago, spelling is still largely determined by pronunciation during the same period. The author Jean-Pierre Ceton argues that French needs to be liberated from a range of forms that are 'bizarre (masculine words ending in 'e'), anachronistic (letters which are not pronounced) or very complicated (multiple and uncertain exceptions to the rules)'. Not only do existing rules of grammar and spelling run against the supposedly dominant logical Cartesian framework of which the French are so proud. They have also put off many foreigners from attempting to learn the language.

The strict application of often needlessly complicated and sometimes contradictory rules has above all made French a language of the elite, acting to distinguish rather than help unite different groups. In business meetings, top executives sometimes use language as a weapon, interrupting and humiliating a speaker by correcting their use of the subjunctive or some other fine point of expression. Indeed, in an all too typical incident, Jean Mattéoli, the head of the Economic and Social Council, apologized at a press conference for using the slang word *rigoler* after it rolled irresponsibly off his tongue, even though it is a widely understood word meaning 'to laugh'.

In short, French has become a tool which risks being used to establish or broaden a gap between the more and the less well trained and educated. It is difficult, frustrating and humiliating enough for foreign journalists who telephone a government department or a company to be asked to send their requests in writing, knowing that grammatical slips or poor expression risk making them look stupid. Imagine the intimidation and the handicap presented to an immigrant in France who is required to apply for a job or to seek approval for a work permit from an unsympathetic public official.

Given such complexities and subtleties in the language, it is perhaps not surprising that the French adult literacy rate is relatively low. An OECD study published in 1995 analysed the ability to understand everyday texts, respond to written information and carry out simple arithmetical operations among citizens in eight countries. Having participated and contributed Ffr7 million to the three-year project, French officials discovered with horror that they ranked second lowest, just ahead of Poland, and behind such other countries as the US. They demanded that all references to France should be purged from the final version of the published report. When details of the figures subsequently leaked out anyway, they claimed that the methodology was faulty.

A losing battle

Perhaps the most important criterion for judging the Académie and the other regulatory attempts to police the language is to assess whether they work. Has French become stronger and more widely used? The answer appears to be no. France may be the world's fifth largest economy, but with an estimated 131 million speakers, French ranks only in ninth place. Among languages spoken in more than one continent, it lags behind English, with 594 million speakers, but also after Spanish, Arabic and Portuguese. As a first language, it ranks only eleventh with some 70 million speakers. France may still be one of the most influential member states in the European Union, but French is also losing ground as a leading working language despite aggressive efforts to maintain its role. A recent survey showed that out of more than 1 billion documents translated by the European Commission, 42 per cent were from English and 40 per cent from French. Another study estimated that 85 per cent of international organizations use English as one of their working languages, against 49 per cent for French.

Of course, most of this declining influence has nothing to do with language regulation, and much to do with the waning international political and commercial influence of France from at least as early as the start of the nineteenth century. By the time of the Treaty of Versailles in 1919, which was drafted in English, French lost its pre-eminent role in diplomacy, and it continued to fade thereafter in the shadow of its commercial rival. These are factors well beyond the reach of the immortals convened near the River Seine in Paris. All other languages have suffered against the ever-growing dominance of English. What has made the French special is their attempt to maintain a global role and fight against the trend. But their efforts seem often to have been misdirected. Training in foreign languages has until recently not been a top priority for the Quai d'Orsay, France's ministry of foreign affairs, for instance. Many of its diplomats are posted abroad with no preparation in the language of the country to which they are sent – or are expected to pay for lessons themselves. They have traditionally considered that their own tongue was the one in which discussions would take place.

Have the efforts of the language police even been effective in restricting the evolution of French? While reinforcement may have increased in recent years, so too has the ingenuity of those seeking to get round the rules. French radio stations, for example, have attempted to bend the letter of their quota regulations by playing all 40 per cent of their required weekly French songs at low-listening periods such as Sunday evening, or by broadcasting techno and other word-free music which is unclassifiable. It is clear that the Académie, legislation and the associations defending the French language do not have it all their own way. The vigorous debate over *madame la ministre* that followed Mr Druon's remarks showed just how many opposing views and forces exist. The pervasive and growing influence of the mass media in the second half of the twentieth century has also diluted the power of the immortals' missives. And pressures beyond national control are also building. The European Union has permitted foreign cable and satellite television broadcasters to transmit within France without having to comply with the quotas that apply to domestic media groups, for example. Such unequal competition is likely to erode the restrictions still further over time.

Even if it is against the wishes of the guardians of a 'pure' form of the language, French has evolved considerably over time. The Académie itself has tolerated such encroachments as *gangster* in its latest dictionary. Ironically, many of the richest influences for change have come less from English than from the country's own former colonies. Take the widespread use of *verlan* or backslang, which splits words in two and reverses their order. It owes its origins largely to the *beurs* (*arabes*, or those of North African origin), but it has become a firmly established part of the language, most famously endorsed by François Mitterrand's remark about being *chébran* (*branché* or trendy). Or there is the unorthodox French style of Patrick Chamoiseau from Martinique, who won the prestigious Goncourt literary prize in 1992.

Like the widespread popularity of Algerian *raï* music, and the high volume of foreign novels translated into French, these examples suggest that France has been able to absorb different ideas and to adapt over time in spite of the efforts of the linguistic and political elite to put their language into a straitjacket. But how much energy has been wasted, which could have been far better used to consider ways to simplify and adapt the language, to make it easier to learn, or even to encourage greater use of foreign languages in order to better preserve and export French ideas and culture? The cartoonist Plantu perhaps best expressed how skewed the national priorities can be in a drawing for the front page of *Le Monde*, on a day when educational reform and juvenile delinquency were both national news in 1998. A teacher pointed to a blackboard on which was written the declensions of 'I, you and he/she want to burn a car'. She warned her class 'and the first one who forgets the circumflex accent on *brûler* [to burn] will get it from me.'

The broader picture: French cinema policy

A star-studded cast had come to speak at the hall in central Paris. From film-makers to politicians, they lined the stage for the debate in spring 1998 triggered by the new Multilateral Investment Agreement, which threatened (though hardly as its primary purpose) to attack the unusual package of aid provided to French cinema. Hervé Bourges, head of the CSA audiovisual regulatory body, set the tone with a speech defending the status quo, and expressing delight at the variety of speakers who would follow him in making their diverse views known. But what diversity? Over several hours, it would have been difficult to squeeze a strip of celluloid between the differences. From Gaullist to Socialist alike, not to mention those holding far more extremist views, there was firm support for the welter of quotas, subsidies and policies that make up France's most distinctive cultural exception. There was more consensus than at the average

Supreme Soviet meeting in years gone by. Here was the *pensée unique* in all its glory. While the Académie and the *loi Toubon* may provoke sharp criticism and at the very least raise sniggers, the role of the state in protecting French films is far more serious and tolerates little dissent.

Conventional wisdom has it that this system, built up over many years, has created a flourishing French film industry while its counterparts across most of the rest of Europe have all but withered away in the face of the growing giant of Hollywood. It was vigorously defended during the European Union's 'television without frontiers' discussions, the GATT round of World Trade Organization talks and the OECD talks on investment. On a first viewing, it is hard to disagree with its success. In 1999, there were 181 French films produced, half of which were first or second films made by young directors. American films account for the overwhelming majority of cinema entries in the UK and most of continental Europe. Yet – while *The Titanic* may have been the most popular film ever in France – total US films represented just 54 per cent in that year, against 34 per cent for French films. And recent French films and actors have had some notable successes abroad, maintaining something of the international standing once held by Godard and Truffaut, not to mention the pioneering Lumière brothers a century ago.

The figures are the result of government policies begun as early as the 1950s, enhanced under the Socialists in the 1980s, but made more protectionist still by successive centre-right administrations. That is not to say that other European countries have not indulged in similar defensive approaches. Indeed, even before the decision of Tony Blair's government to introduce funding through the National Lottery for films, other subsidies came through the considerable aid to the BBC, and there were demands even on independent broadcasters to produce original material. But the system has reached its limits in France. There are some 80 types of subsidy in total, ranging from support for cinemas and tax exemptions for individuals who invest, to a levy on cinema entries. The bulk of the system is financed through television broadcasters, who are obliged to invest a proportion of their turnover in French production companies. At least 40 per cent of their total programming must be French-made, and 50 per cent of the films they show must be French-speaking. Yet at the same time, to protect cinemas, there are limits on how many films TV can show each year and the times at which they can be broadcast (never in the early evening of Wednesday when new releases come out, or on Saturday afternoons, for instance). 'You need a doctorate to understand it all,' says Patrick Le Lay, the chairman of TF1, France's largest commercial channel.

The system is vigorously defended by most representatives of the film industry itself, of course. Nicolas Seydoux, chairman of Gaumont, the film production company, argues forcefully: 'You can't just treat culture like tarmac or other products. It is essential that Europe preserves its cultural diversity. When you realize that children spend more time in front of the television than with their teachers, you have to encourage audio-visual creation. The Americans already have half the market. We just ask that we can keep the remainder.' He suggests that without quotas, US programmes would rapidly come to dominate because with their costs already covered in their own domestic market they can be cheaply 'dumped' at highly attractive prices with European broadcasters, squeezing out local production. Jack Lang, the Socialists' long-standing minister of culture in the 1980s and early 1990s, argues: 'Culture is something fragile. It needs attention and tenderness. The notion of time is important. The traditional market system cannot always assure the necessary financing.'

Yet the reality is less simple. Patrick Messerlin, an academic economist based in Paris, is a rare voice in France with an alternative view. He attacks the statistics on the number of French films each year as nothing short of 'lies'. The definition is decided by the state-controlled Centre National de la Cinématographie, based simply on whether or not it has provided funding. But the prospect of gaining access to the organization's money brings the temptation to indulge in considerable rule-bending. To be classified as 'French', a film does not have to be in the French language, controlled by a French director nor even use French actors or technicians. Many foreign backers are perfectly happy to see their film labelled as French, in exchange for a slice of French taxpayers' or cinema-goers' money. Messerlin cites the example of Milos Forman's *Valmont*, a 'French' film made in English, under a British co-production, using seven American and two British actors. But it involved one French actress, was based on a French novel and had a few scenes shot in the country. 'With such criteria, the Walt Disney film *The Hunchback of Notre-Dame* would probably pass the test', he argues. *Valmont* was, incidentally, both a critical and commercial flop compared with its less US costly direct competitor *Dangerous Liaisons*, which was released almost simultaneously.

He calculates that a more pure definition of truly French films would cut the total annual numbers in half, excluding in the process many of the more critically acclaimed recent releases, including the Polish director Kieslowski's trilogy *Three Colours: Blue, White, Red* (what better way to suggest that they are French than to refer to the tricolore?). He concludes that over the period 1978–94 the volume of French films has been dropping towards the levels of production in other European countries, and that their market share relative to US films within France has also been steadily falling. Equally, while France has the highest density of cinemas per head in the world – 4,655 in 1997 with nearly 1 million seats – it does not top the league for attendance. Even with broadcasting quotas that are designed to push people away from watching the television and go instead to their nearest cinema, France sold an average of less than 2.5 tickets per head in 1996. That was only just ahead of Belgium, UK and the European average, and significantly less than the levels in Spain and Ireland. And way behind the US which, with 4.6 tickets per head, clearly showed its ability to entice the public into cinemas.

Messerlin argues that the French system has had a number of perverse effects. The consequence of limiting the amount of US-sourced programmes that can be broadcast has been to encourage imitation US-style productions (of often even poorer quality) by French companies, hence accelerating the Americanization of French television still further. The tax levied on cinema tickets has meant that US films have helped subsidize the upkeep of cinemas to show their works, while the more popular French films have made a contribution to subsidizing less successful films. The result, combined with other subsidies to domestic film-makers, is to create an industry sheltered from competition, which does not need to export because its losses are partially made good by the state. No surprise that cinema is referred to in France as the 'seventh art' and is supervised by the Ministry of Culture, rather than being seen as a form of commerce that could generate funding and raise France's image in the world – on the basis of the vulgar capitalist criterion of popularity.

If the overall result of the protectionist French system was a cinema that was a commercial failure but a critical success, there would at least be some compensation. But in his analysis, Messerlin shows that the number of prizes at leading international cinema festivals won by French films – even on the most generous definition – dropped steadily over the period 1978–94. As the British academic Guy Austin suggests, while French government policy and funding during much of the 1980s and early 1990s paternalistically encouraged the development of high-cost prestige 'heritage' films such as *Germinal*, focused on the adaptation of French literary classics, many of the most popular films in practice turned out to be low-budget popular comedies, from *Les Visiteurs* and *Trois hommes et un couffin* to *Gazon maudit* and *Marius et Jeannette*.

There is no reason why French films should be judged purely by their commercial success, and less still by how they do outside national borders. There is also little doubt that state intervention has helped sustain an industry that has all but disappeared in neighbouring European countries. But the policies adopted have not always been the right ones, targeted at the most deserving films. Some observers have also pointed out the connection between substantial state funding in France and the apparent reluctance of film-makers to attack established power, politics, corruption or even social policy in the way that their counterparts in the UK and the US have done. While the recent success of the British film industry has been largely built on the drama of unemployment and those living on the margins of conventional society, and dozens of American films have attacked the judiciary, the media and politicians alike, such subjects remain all but taboo in France. The national system set up to support French cinema may ultimately have ended up undermining both its critical ability and its commercial viability at a time of growing competition. If so, its decision-making elites will have served the cause of foreign interests by weakening rather than reinforcing French culture.

3

The pull of Paris

From the outside, the large green gates of the building on the Rue de l'Université in Paris's chic 7th *arrondissement* look imposing enough. But behind them lies one of the most powerful institutions in France: the Ecole Nationale d'Administration. It is not by accident that ENA, the training school for France's future top civil servants, is just a few minutes' walk from the prime minister's office, the National Assembly and more than a dozen government departments and public organizations. Its graduates have dominated the top positions in the state for half a century.

The *quartier* reflects the huge concentration of power and wealth that is focused in the French capital. Paris has historically monopolized decision-making in the public and private sectors alike. From ministries to corporate headquarters, from the choice of 'o1' as its telephone prefix to the high-speed railway and the motorway networks that radiate outwards from it like spokes from a hub, the city has dominated and controlled. It was a system that had clear advantages in the past, whether in creating a unified and egalitarian education system or in overseeing industrial reconstruction after the second world war.

But it is one that is posing increasing problems in a fast-moving, complex and competitive world. And one which has come under growing criticism in the last few years. For many, the problem begins with ENA itself. In a remark picked up with relish by the French press, Alain Madelin, the former right-wing economics minister, told one gathering in 1997: 'Ireland has the IRA, Spain ETA, Italy the mafia and France ENA.' Senior civil servants were soon bristling with anger and – in a sign that he recognized the risks of crossing them – Madelin was swiftly forced to issue a retraction.

There is little doubt that a small group of *enarques* and other similar elites have come to dominate top positions in many public institutions and even a number of private-sector companies. While highly intelligent, their academic-based selection and training leads to a certain conformism, and gives them a head start in careers in both the public and the private sectors. Their subsequent advancement is often owed at least as much to personal contacts and political patronage as to management ability, with wasteful and increasingly damaging consequences.

But it is all too easy to criticize *enarques*. Alain Madelin may not be one, but many others who have periodically attacked such technocrats are, including President Jacques Chirac himself. Most graduates of ENA are devoted, well trained and highly ethical civil servants who remain firmly under the control of their ministers. They serve as convenient scapegoats for politicians and others who are themselves ultimately at least as responsible for a range of poorly conceived or implemented actions.

The public sector poses a number of far broader challenges, starting with its enormous size, which creates a huge financing burden for taxpayers. But – in contrast to many other countries – its enormous influence on French society has created a 'nobility of the state', in the words of the sociologist Pierre Bourdieu, with its own rules and systems of protection at the expense of those in the private sector or other parts of the economy.

It is also intimately linked to a desire to exercise and to centralize power, which is translated into an enormous volume of regulations, legislation and administrative acts that attempt to control but which are often far removed from the day-to-day realities of life in the country. Power is not simply exercised from the top and meekly implemented, of course, but reinterpreted by 'little chiefs' and 'barons' at every level, making the situation still more complicated.

While most government departments have remained firmly rooted in Paris, considerable power has been decentralized over the past two decades. But much has been in the form of sharing administrative burdens rather than decision-making, in a system that has created new levels of complexity and duplication.

Life ends at 20: the power of ENA

A weighty and closely guarded 700-page reference work sits on the shelves of many of France's most influential people. With its dozens of glossy advertisements for such companies as the management consultancy McKinsey, the engineering group Alstom and the bank Société Générale, it might easily be mistaken for a graduate recruitment brochure for one of the country's leading business schools. But it is in fact the comprehensive list of alumni of ENA, which has become a hallmark of the French public administration and the envy of the world. The institution was created in 1945 to nurture a new public-sector elite of future leaders of the nation who would be untarnished by the Vichy era. They would enter the most prestigious *grands corps* of the state in a style that was far more meritocratic than the traditional system based on contacts.

A flick through the pages of the directory reveals just how successfully ENA has met its aims. The book is a *Who's Who* of the country's leading decision-makers in almost every field. In just 50 years, the institution has established a near stranglehold on top public-sector jobs. Pick a top government official, and the odds are that they have passed through the same 'mould': from Jean-Claude Trichet, governor of the Bank of France and future head of the new European Central Bank, to Marc Tessier, head of France Television. But ENA's influence stretches well beyond such positions. Most of the country's leading politicians attended, from Chirac to Lionel Jospin, the prime minister, and many of his cabinet colleagues – not to mention their policy advisers. And, as the advertisements in the alumni list suggest, *enarques* are also strongly represented in the corporate sector. There are those who run public enterprises, such as Michel Bon, the chairman of France Telecom, and Jean-Cyril Spinetta, head of Air France. But there are also many in charge of companies in the private sector, such as Gérard Mestrallet, chief executive of the utilities group Suez-Lyonnaise des Eaux, and Jean Drucker, head of the television channel M6. So well-placed have *enarques* become that it sometimes seems by the time they have entered ENA as young as their early 20s, their career success has already been guaranteed and all doors will be opened for them in the future. In a culture which has an ambivalent attitude towards money, it is *enarques* far more than financial traders who are the 'masters of the universe'.

With its rituals, its jargon and courses, ENA provides an intense and shared experience that helps bind its graduates together into a tight and loyal network that serves them in the years to come – often regardless of their different political views. To enter, they have all performed well in academic exams, and been forced to endure a *grand oral* during which they make a presentation and are questioned by independent examiners for 20 minutes timed on a unique four-faced clock. They spend a first year on practical assignments in government departments, before coming together for an initiation weekend during which they choose the class name by which their 'promotion' will be

known in the future. At the conclusion of their 14 months of
class-work, they gather at an *amphi-garnison* to stand up one by
one to announce their choice of career in an order determined
by their final grade. The top 15 or 20 have the pick of the prestigious *grands corps*: the Inspection des Finances, the Conseil d'E-
tat and the Cour des Comptes. The others choose from a range
of different positions, from the Quai d'Orsay or ministry of foreign affairs, to the *préfecture*. While many countries have their
own systems of training elites – the thousands of students at the
Ivy League of the US, or Oxford and Cambridge in the UK –
ENA is far more selective: it takes in just 100 pupils a year.

There are considerable compensations for their efforts. From
the moment they enter ENA, the super-elite of the state is paid
to study. Like other civil servants, they have the guarantee of
lifetime employment and the possibility of spending six or more
lucrative years in other organizations or the private sector with
the assurance of being able to return to a job working for the
state at an equivalent level and salary to that when they left. But
more than their fellow civil servants, the *crème* that attends ENA
can expect generous additional bonuses, kept highly confidential, that often add substantially to their base salary and which
are exempt from social security contributions. Some have extra
benefits such as low-rent apartments. 'I met one adviser to a prefect who looked about 19, but already had a chauffeur-driven
car and accommodation that was paid for,' says one foreign
diplomat. 'Those are perks that you might get at about 57 in my
country.' ENA has failed on at least one of its founding principles as a result. Rather than breaking down the power and influence of the *grands corps*, it has helped reinforce them, even if
entrance is more meritocratic than it was before.

Above all, *enarques* carry the calling card of their institution
and the network of contacts that it has helped them build. In a
culture obsessed with secrecy, the ENA alumni directory carries
the home addresses and phone numbers of nearly all of its grad-

uates for their exclusive and mutual use – right up to the contact details for Chirac himself. They automatically use the familiar *tu* form of address when speaking to members of their own
class, even if they have not been in touch for years, and easily
adopt it for those in other promotions. It was unusual enough to
be widely reported that when in 1998 Ernest-Antoine Seillière,
the head of the French holding company CGIP, became president of the CNPF (now called MEDEF), the employers' federation, he said that he would no longer *tutoie* his former
classmate from the Stendhal promotion of 1965, a certain Lionel
Jospin. The same class, far from incidentally, also contained
Jacques Toubon, successively Gaullist minister of justice and of
the interior, and his left-wing replacement in 1997, Jean-Pierre
Chevènement.

The ENA system brings considerable advantages. The civil
service in the US has rarely managed to lure the best and the
brightest for long-term careers, and the image of the public sector has been degrading for years in the UK. But the continued
importance and prestige of the state in France meant that at least
until recently it remained the preferred option for many of the
country's top students. ENA's approach to selection, drawing
from the best products of the excellent state school system, has
given a primacy to merit that permits an intake from a far
broader social background than its equivalents in many other
countries. Even if, as one young *enarque* concedes, 'More than
ever you need money to live in the right areas to get your children into the catchment areas of good schools.' Or that excellence in foreign languages, an important distinguishing factor in
the fiercely competitive race to be first, may be considerably
enhanced for those students whose parents can afford to send
them abroad for extended periods in order to practise. ENA has
helped build a class of leading civil servants who are intelligent,
cultivated and highly ethical. The system of secondment helps
give them a rounded experience of different public- and often

also private-sector organizations. While plenty of French politicians have been investigated in recent years for corruption, *enarque* civil servants have rarely been placed under suspicion.

The perils of *parachutage*

When Edmond Alphandéry abruptly 'quit' his job as chairman of Electricité de France (EdF) in summer 1998, the identity of his replacement caused considerable head-scratching. François Roussely hardly seemed to have an appropriate background to run one of the country's largest enterprises, as it geared up for a painful period of restructuring in the face of growing questions over its dominant strategy of nuclear generation, not to mention the liberalization of the electricity market and the prospect of tough competition. A 53-year-old civil servant, Roussely had been 'parachuted' in to the new job although he had never worked in the power industry, had no engineering background and had not even operated in a commercial business environment. But he was an *enarque*, and had distinguished himself over the years as a loyal ally of the Socialist party, working successively for Gaston Defferre, Pierre Joxe and most recently as head of the private office of Alain Richard, the defence minister. His nomination was a classic case of the highly political way in which so many French appointments take place.

It would be wrong to imagine that his nomination was purely part of a recent story of Socialist governments favouring their own kind. The political right is at least as guilty of the same game. After all, Alphandéry, a former centre-right economics minister, had been in turn nominated to EdF by the previous Gaullist prime minister, Alain Juppé. More intriguingly still, Alphandéry's consolation prize shows just how much cross-party complicity exists in the system. For while *Les Echos*, the French daily business newspaper, saw fit to raise questions over the highly political nature of the decision to give the EdF job to Roussely, it considered Alphandéry's new role as head of the Caisse Nationale de Prévoyance, a state-owned life insurance group, to be a 'very honourable' choice. Not a bad reward for someone with a mercurial temper who had helped trigger a huge internal management crisis at EdF, who had overseen a costly rescue package for the bank Crédit Lyonnais that considerably boosted the total bill for taxpayers, and whose own experience of the commercial sector was extremely limited.

Talk to former senior civil servants today, and few will disagree that the upper echelons of the public sector have become highly political in France. That is not to say that they are corrupt. Most have shown proof of enormous integrity and talents as 'all-rounders' capable of handling many different challenges. Indeed, they are often fascinating company, and love to pontificate about the broadest range of subjects, to write articles, to participate in conferences – in short, to do almost anything but concentrate on running their business. No surprise, since they have done so many other things in the past, and probably count on resting only a short time before changing jobs again. Their specific competence for the job has often featured far less as a criterion for their selection than their loyalty to one or another politician or party, or simply to the state itself. Jacques Friedmann, a classmate of Chirac at ENA, ran the state-owned insurer UAP in the mid-1990s, for example, yet was incapable of responding to a journalist's question at a press conference in 1996 on his group's 'return on equity', an elementary financial ratio.

The only divergence of view among those who have worked within the system is when the trend towards politicisation started. 'It really began with Mitterrand,' says one *inspecteur des finances* who left the public sector at the start of the 1980s. 'It started with Giscard d'Estaing,' says another who left in the early 1970s. 'It was already under way with de Gaulle,' says a third.

Appointments based on political fidelity have no doubt always played some role. But after the long-standing 'dictatorship' of Charles de Gaulle, the change was noticeable with the arrival of Giscard d'Estaing and his distinctive centre-right political family. It became more pronounced still with the election of François Mitterrand, bringing the left to power for the first time in a quarter of a century. And it took on a far greater amplitude from the start of the 1980s, if only because the nationalizations he undertook created a wave of new posts to be filled which came under his control. 'We were suddenly asked to train 36 people to run banks,' recalls one former senior civil servant, in the wake of the takeover of a series of privately-owned financial institutions. 'Some of them didn't even know what a bank was. We wrote to the Treasury warning them. But we were over-ruled. It was a political decision.' As one Socialist from the time recalls: 'There was a feeling that we've been kept away from the buffet for ages. Now we're going to stuff ourselves.'

It is not simply attending ENA that creates the essential network for future career success. The personal connections that will be called into use in later life can begin earlier, with many students studying at Science Po, the Institute of Political Science in Paris, before going to ENA, and sometimes forging friend-ships during military service. Many *enarques* have at best mixed emotions about ENA itself, with its competitive environment in the struggle to come out top often limiting camaraderie. But friendships are nonetheless made and subsequently reinforced when the graduates work together within the administrative corps to which they are recruited. Above all, it is the dozen or more advisers who work at any one time in each ministerial cabinet who are exposed to politicians and who acquire the patronage that helps them to succeed. ENA certainly helps.

Take the students in the promotion named in honour of de Gaulle, which graduated in 1972. Their career histories highlight the successive barriers and trampolines posed by their political connections and the compensatory influence of friendships forged in the classroom. It encompassed students of many different political beliefs, and many with none at all – or with ideologies that would change considerably over time. A few would enter political life directly: Juppé (who became prime minister in 1995) and Dominique Perben (who joined his government as minister for the public sector) on the right; Christian Pierret (the junior industry minister appointed to Jospin's cabinet in 1997) on the left. Others would remain in the public sector, but would be firmly marked by their political allegiances. Didier Bargas, clad in a leather jacket and still carrying the aura of 1968 with him, was a Communist party militant who is now an inspector at the ministry of education. 'It was unimaginable to give responsibility to someone with my [political] engagement in the 1970s,' he says. His fortunes changed sharply with the arrival of the left to power. 'In 1981, I had the choice of working in four different ministerial cabinets.' Once the Communists quit the left-wing ruling coalition of the time, and he became critical of his own party's line, he swiftly fell back out of favour.

Jérôme Clément, supported by the ministry of culture, was a candidate for a top job at the Musée d'Orsay in 1978, but says he was vetoed by the right-wing presidential staff at the time in view of his past work for the Socialist Pierre Mauroy. But as his classmates rose to positions of influence, he would fare better in future years. Named head of the Franco-German public television station Arte, he would successfully lobby Juppé and Perben to ensure that his mandate was renewed. During the time of Juppé's administration, Raphaël Alomar, another classmate, would be named head of the Council of Europe's social development fund. And when Juppé needed someone to run the SNCF, the state railway company, in 1996, he would call on Louis Gallois, a former left-wing 'opponent' from the same promotion at ENA, who had a reputation among all his peers for enormous integrity (to the point of even travelling in economy class for domestic flights in his previous job as chairman of the aircraft group Aérospatiale). Gallois, in turn, would summon another member of his promotion, Paul Mingasson, to become his secretary general.

ENA is not the only springboard for such elevations to high office. Graduates of the prestigious Ecole Polytechnique, who have gone on to join France's leading 'technical' administrative corps, the *Ponts et Chaussées* and the *Mines*, also benefit. Still other *parachutages* owe nothing to a civil service training and much more to pure political favour-mongering. Alphandéry did not attend ENA, for example, but he was looking for a job after Edouard Balladur's cabinet was dissolved in 1995. Nor did Pierre Habib-Deloncle, the chairman appointed in 1996 to Marseillaise de Crédit, a state-owned regional bank whose small size was compensated by its substantial financial losses. But Habib-Deloncle happened to be treasurer of the Association of the Friends of Jacques Chirac, and the son of a close ally of the French president, whose say was instrumental in his appointment. In the following two years, Habib-Deloncle did little to restructure the bank or to achieve his stated mission to swiftly privatize it. Even though his successor in 1998, the Socialist-leaning Patrick Careil, an *enarque*, managed the sell-off in less than six months while simultaneously holding down his other job as chairman of the state-owned Banque Hervet.

Accelerated promotions within the civil service for those with party affiliations have sometimes led to inexperienced individuals too rapidly gaining power beyond their capacities. They have also demoralized others who have been bypassed and end up by quitting. 'There is no point in staying here in the long term,' says one bright young employee who works in a regulatory division of the ministry of finance. 'I am not an *inspecteur des finances*, so I have no chance of making it to a senior position.' His *enarque* boss gave him the name of a classmate who had become a senior executive at a large French bank. Use of the name swiftly delivered him an interview with the man in question. For others who are out of favour during political alternances but who choose not to quit, the system has created enormous waste. Catherine Bersani, an *enarque* who became associated with the political right, says that with the election of the Socialists in 1997, she joined the 'elephants' graveyard' of over 500 members of the *corps des Ponts et Chaussées* who have been *placardé* or put into a cupboard to gather dust. 'I consider it completely scandalous that more and more top civil servants are *placardé*. Given the quality of people that exists and how much we are paid, we are not used enough.'

ENA may be good at selecting individuals who are academically talented and have good oratorial skills when they are in their early 20s. But at its extremes, it becomes a pass-key for all subsequent career advancement, which might more suitably be determined by such different talents as the ability to manage others. There is a danger that such skills have been given too little attention when considering promotion, and that 'late developers' who never attended ENA but have all the necessary attributes to be good civil servants are pushed to one side. Joël Lebeschu, one of the highest-ranked students in the ENA promotion of 1972 who spurned the *grands corps* for the *préfecture*, says: 'ENA does not train people. It ranks them not by intelligence but by conformity. Those who go into the *grands corps* progress rapidly, without ever managing more than one person. That's the big problem with French technocracy.' In public-sector organizations and even in many companies, they enter at top levels into a hierarchy modelled on the civil service and often distant from the daily realities of management. Aided by what they call the 'tyranny of the first diploma', the French sociologists Michel Bauer and Benedicte Bertin-Mourot found that a third of the top managers in the 200 leading companies were drawn from the *grands corps*.

The result of the politicization of nominations has been to

create two streams of candidates for *parachutage*: those who are in favour with the government of the day and are entrusted with jobs in organizations and enterprises linked to the state; and those who are fed up and want to leave. Neither movement has proved healthy for the reputation or the effectiveness of the civil service. After all, how objective can a senior civil servant be when employed as a regulator scrutinizing a company run by a former colleague or boss? Particularly if he or she hopes to use that connection to seek a job in the future? And – even with the legislative restrictions that have been imposed over the last few years – how is it ever fully possible to avoid conflicts of interest and the transfer of sensitive information when passing out of the state sector into a company, when that company is hiring in part precisely because the former civil servant has sensitive information and contacts that it seeks to tap?

Parachutage has in many ways proved even more catastrophic for the enterprises to which civil servants and other political allies are sent. Nominating inexperienced or inappropriately qualified outsiders to top jobs has sent a very strong demotivating message to long-standing employees working within these organizations. Will the best ever be willing to stay and invest all their energies, knowing that they will almost never have a chance to become number one? It is also a highly costly way of giving something to individuals to do while they wait for something better, particularly since many large companies with links to the state take the precaution of hiring a few of each political persuasion as an insurance for future changes of government. The privatized Banque Nationale de Paris, full of *enarques* at the most senior levels and a chairman who preaches in favour of the free market, became almost an antechamber for power, providing in the space of a few weeks from among its ranks the new more left-wing heads of the state's Commissariat du Plan and of its Caisse des Dépôts after the election of the 1997 left-wing administration.

But *parachutage* has also led to devastating decisions. Traditionally, former senior civil servants from the finance ministry were named to unchallenging top positions such as 'governor' of Crédit Foncier, a property lender controlled by the state, which offered healthy salaries, luxurious low-rent apartments, chauffeur-driven cars and access to one of the best wine cellars of Paris for their lunch tables as they moved gently towards retirement. But increasingly over the last few years, they have chosen to abandon their simple role as figureheads and attempted to interfere more directly – often with disastrous consequences. It might have been reasons of necessity – such as the economic crisis, restructuring and growing competition of the 1990s – which led Crédit Foncier's executives to embark on the financing of property speculation that went sour; or for more ideological reasons, in the wake of the nationalizations of the 1980s. Jean Matouk, a former professor who was appointed chairman of the bank Marseillaise de Crédit by the left, for example, decided to begin offering loans to local companies at below-market interest rates. His aim was to help support small businesses and job creation. The result was to distort competition and further entrench losses at the bank, helping trigger the need for successive state rescue plans totalling over Ffr3 billion.

The nomination of Roussely to Electricité de France is in a somewhat different category. In some ways, he was a good choice of candidate, given his political connections and his impressive inside knowledge of the French administration. After all, the culture and organization of EdF mirrors that of a civil service department much more than that of a private-sector enterprise. His experience in handling the unions at a time of radical restructuring, similar to the changes he helped implement with the professionalization of the armed forces, should prove useful. The appointment nonetheless represents the continuation of a French penchant for its public-sector elites and a style of operations reminiscent of the past, which is arguably far less appropriate for the challenges facing EdF in the years to come.

The weight of the state

It sits like a gigantic UFO on the bank of the River Seine in eastern Paris, engulfing the tiny eighteenth-century customs house that today serves merely as its main entrance gate. The futuristic glass and stone 'Bercy' complex is more of a city than a mere office building, with its 8,000 inhabitants, its numerous cafés and auditoria, its post office and even its own heli-pad and speedboat. In a country that supposedly has a free market system, and which has privatized and considerably deregulated its economy over the past decade, Bercy remains an incredible monolith and a testament to the continued desire by the state to try to interfere in almost every aspect of its citizens' daily lives. It is the nerve centre of the powerful ministry of economics, finance and industry, which employs a total of 180,000 staff around the country, in over 3,800 offices. Its luxurious modern facade is a reminder of just how important successive governments of all political persuasions consider it to be.

Across Paris, unwieldy government departments bear testimony to a distinctive French obsession with a very large state sector, highlighting a problem not simply with a small number of powerful *enarques*, but rather with the sheer bulk of the entire civil service. The size of the public sector in France is staggering. Between national and local government, hospitals and public enterprises such as the Post Office, there are over 6 million employees – or a quarter of the total national labour force. According to a study by the Organisation of Economic Cooperation and Development, the state represents 27 per cent of the workforce, more than in all the world's other industrialized countries except for Finland, Sweden and Denmark. The cost is equally substantial: some Ffr670 billion a year in salaries and pensions. The nationalizations of 1982 added 670,000 new employees to the public sector at a stroke. While many have since been shifted back to the private sector, the total wage bill has continued to rise. Over the last decade, public-sector salaries have risen faster than those in the private sector, creating an ever-increasing financing burden for taxpayers. Taxes and social security contributions were 45.7 per cent of GDP in 1999, a record for France and one of the highest in the industrialized world. Government spending was 52.4 per cent of GDP, also very high compared with its peers. And there is little sign of that changing. When Juppé talked about 'the bad fat' (*mauvaise graisse*) of the state sector in 1996, he triggered a sharp outcry. His plans for a reduction in civil servant numbers – simply by 'natural wastage' or not replacing all those who retire – got no further than those of his predecessors. Jospin has promised nothing more than to keep public-sector employment at its current levels.

Nor has there been much attempt to reorganize the way in which public servants are employed. Time and again, the French practice has been to add new institutions without removing or rationalizing the old ones. Take the ministry of war veterans, an independent government department which still employs over 2,300 staff to manage a rapidly diminishing number of pension-ers, now down to just 550,000. Or the ministry of agriculture, which has increased its workforce by 3 per cent over the past decade to 30,000 even as the total number of farmers fell by over 500,000 in the same period. Successive governments have created so many parastatal *observatoires* to analyse different issues seizing public attention at any one time, and which are never abolished or integrated into mainstream organizations, that the *Canard Enchaîné* newspaper joked there would soon be the need for an *observatoire des observatoires*. Yet ironically, many of these bodies have been set up precisely because there is a belief that they will be more independent and objective than the state in carrying out the same functions.

That is not to say that French civil servants are unproductive. The country's teachers, its health service employees and its engineers have a very high reputation for quality and ethical standards, for example. The investment represented by their salaries is not wasted. But there are limits to the country's financing capacities. And such a mass of people imposes a distinctive set of cultural and ideological values on the entire country, including on politicians, most of whom themselves have little direct experience of the private sector. According to a survey by the magazine *Le Revenu Français*, 57 per cent of the French adult population are either civil servants or the parents, children or spouses of one. That creates a huge vested interest in opposing any significant reform of the state. But it also triggers hostility, suspicion or simply ignorance of the problems facing the commercial sector of the economy. There is even a monthly magazine called *Devenir Fonctionnaire*, designed to help people who want to join the ranks of those most sought-after jobs in the country: those in the public sector.

Such *parti pris* against the private sector is illustrated by the reaction to Colette Patonnier, a French hairdresser from the south-eastern city of Valence. Fed up with paying substantial pension and health care contributions, she registered her business under the name of 'Hair CC Limited' in the UK, slipping out of the net of the French system. Her action triggered other small traders in the region, from bakers to electricians, to do the same. The publicity gathered by their action brought swift warnings that it was illegal from the ministry of finance and the ministry of social affairs, and derogatory articles in the national media about the organization behind the protest, a maverick shopkeepers' association described variously by the left-wing *Libération* as *poujadiste* and the right-wing *Le Figaro* as close to the National Front. But such attacks did little to address the reality that France's shopkeepers make large payments for their health and retirement benefits into a social security system which provides them with little in return. It is the worst combination of public and private: compulsory and monopolistic on the one hand, and yet individualistically focused on their own profession on the other. Since shopkeepers are shrinking in numbers and ageing fast, the monthly contributions for those who remain are rising while the reimbursements they receive diminish. Civil servants, by contrast, pay contributions at a lower rate than those in the private sector and receive more generous benefits in exchange, underwritten by the taxpayer.

The size and the power of the state has also created a class of people all but removed from the risk of unemployment, and relatively immune from the need to respond to their clients. While French politicians often defend the *service public* offered by such state-owned monopolies as Electricité de France and the SNCF, it is tempting to suggest that if there is plenty of *public*, there is often not much accompanying *service*. Challenge a parking ticket in Paris, for example, and you are likely to get back a form letter stating that it was 'not possible' to change the decision and that you should pay up, with no further explanation and not even a telephone number allowing you to protest further or simply to ask for information. Secrecy and high-handedness by the administration often appear to go together. No surprise that the mediator of the French republic deals with 50,000 complaints each year, with a further 100,000 going to the social security tribunal and the same number again to the administrative tribunal, an entire legal system reserved exclusively for matters relating to the public sector, and distinct from the civil and criminal courts. It is revealing that some of the best service in France comes from a system at the opposite end of the spectrum from the regulated state: the *arabes* or corner stores run by immigrants, who are friendly, offer a wide variety of goods and are open long hours.

The imperial instinct

When Chirac decided to boost his popularity in 1996, he

indulged in a bit of bank-bashing. Seizing a populist theme, he blamed the country's lenders for their meanness, arguing that they imposed excessive interest rates and unreasonably tough conditions on borrowers and were responsible in the process for destroying many struggling small businesses. His proffered solution was to get prefects around the country to 'convoke' the bankers in their region with an invitation that they would be strongly advised to accept, and thrash out together a strategy of how to extend additional financial support.

It was just one manifestation of a continued impulse to control power from the centre that has long historical roots in France. Under the *ancien régime*, it was reflected in the decision by Louis XIV to hold the aristocracy under control by keeping them in the gilded cage of Versailles. Napoleon's greatest contribution came in 1800, when he created the network of prefects that remains in place today. Appointed by the government, they played a key role in a rigidly hierarchical system which allowed little scope for local autonomy or even expression. One was appointed for each department with the remit of representing Paris in the provinces. Even today, they are housed in elaborate palaces with gilded and mirrored reception rooms that resemble foreign embassies more than domestic departments of the state. As the parliamentary reporter put it at the start of the last century when the law was introduced to create the system, the objective was 'an uninterrupted chain of execution from the ministry to the administered [which] transmits the law and the orders of government ... at the speed of electric current'.

Centralization fits just as easily with the more modern Republican notion of ensuring equality and democracy through uniformity. It is an approach that can prove highly successful. Without the steamroller of the Parisian administration to push them through, the development of the high-speed rail lines and other *grands projets* would have been all but impossible – or at the very least they would have taken much longer to complete and been marred by much more compromise. And in a country of individualists, centralized power exercised by the state can be necessary to bring about change or useful to ensure stability. During the mid-1990s, for example, the *préfecture* in Toulouse in the south-west of France played an essential role in helping to protect the local economy. Airbus, the aeroplane manufacturer, was suffering from the effects of the economic downturn. Its role as employer, taxpayer and customer for dozens of subcontractors in the region was immense. The prefect had the authority to convene a series of meetings to bring together representatives from the business community with the local administration, the tax and social security authorities and bankers. Between them, they successfully worked out a plan to waive or defer taxes, provide state-backed financial support and extend the terms of commercial loans to companies threatened by the short-term crisis. They also unanimously agreed not to seek the support or endorsement of the authorities in Paris, fearing that the bureaucracy, politics and publicity would all jeopardize the scheme.

But modern France is at times imprisoned by its obsession with centralization. DATAR, a government agency charged with regional development, has its headquarters in no more far-flung a destination than at the foot of the Eiffel Tower. The Institute of Decentralization, set up to promote the delegation of greater power to France's regions, has managed to locate its offices no further out of Paris than Boulogne-Billancourt, the closest suburb to the west. No institution better symbolizes the continued desire for the state to plan and control from Paris than the Commissariat Général du Plan. It sits in the crumbling nineteenth-century Hôtel de Vogüé in the 7th *arrondissement*, with gently fading 1960s Vasarély art decorating its walls. While Gosplan has long ceased to exist in Russia, France still holds on to the entity which emerged after the second world war to coordinate the reconstruction of the country. Its four- and five-year plans were a tightly integrated part of government decision-making. It was only after the elections of 1993 that the 11th plan, destined to cover the period 1993–97, was formally renounced by the government. Yet no politician has had the courage to axe the Plan itself, and Jospin gave it a new lease of life in 1998 when he made it directly accountable to his office and charged it to undertake a number of new studies.

Accompanying the institutions, as part of the same tendency, is extensive legislation. It is no accident that the room where the National Assembly's finance commission gathers today is called the Salle Colbert, after Louis XIV's finance minister, an idol who is still revered by many top *enarques*. Jacques Pelletier, the mediator of the Republic until 1998, says: 'We codify too much in France. We are throttled by regulations. The law cannot antic-ipate everything. Fewer rules would create greater flexibility.' Take the system for launching new businesses. According to a 1998 study by the accountants Arthur Andersen and the French Agency for Business Creation, the rate of start-ups of new com-panies is significantly lower than other countries including the UK and the US. It highlighted 1,800 separate types of aid that exist for French entrepreneurs launching their own companies. Successive governments have each added their own new initia-tives while doing nothing to hone or rationalize those that already exist, nor much to reduce the heavy tax and social secu-rity burdens that are imposed on business.

In a different field, companies were required to submit redundancy plans to the local prefect for approval at the start of the 1990s. Now it is local judges who examine them, frequently delaying lay-offs. It is something which may seem desirable for the local workforce, but can have a devastating effect on com-panies' future survival, and tempt them simply to open new factories in other less constrained countries. The process can also reach surreal extremes, like the court ruling that a company re-employ someone long after the entire factory in which they worked had been shut down. Or consider the tight state controls surrounding pharmacies. The prefect decides whether a new one can be opened, in a decision based partly on the size of the local population. There is a ban on anyone owning more than one shop, restricting the investment that can be made and the potential economies of scale. In exchange, pharmacists are granted a monopoly on the sale of drugs even including aspirin (and until a few years ago, nappies and mineral water). All done in the name of public health and safety, of course. But the result is a form of protectionism generating healthy profits for the pharmacists. And allowing them to sell products legitimized by their professional image which may be safe but which – like homeopathy – have far from proven medicinal value.

The imperial instinct of control from the top has also had the paradoxical effect of undermining the structures that lie below it. Every seven years, for example, France goes through an extra-ordinary and disconcerting ritual as the presidential election draws near. There is a growing number of road accidents as dri-vers exceed the speed limit, a sharp jump in the number of peo-ple who park in defiance of traffic restrictions, and an increase in fare-dodging on public transport. The reason is the 'traditional' amnesty, under which successive presidents have deigned to waive legal proceedings against the perpetrators of a wide range of misdemeanours. It is a practice mirrored on a more minor scale every year with the pardons dispensed on 14 July. In a ges-ture more reminiscent of the *ancien régime* than the egalitarian spirit of the republic, the president reduces the sentences given to prisoners. But while there were only seven people left to be liberated from the Bastille in 1789, nearly 4,000 inmates had one in every four weeks knocked off their time in prison in 1997, up to a maximum of four months in total remission. Successive presidents have used the practice in a way that shows little more regard than the country's former monarchs and emperors for the autonomy of the judicial system or respect for the laws which it so loves to pass.

The courts – like other counterbalances to such an imperialistic exercise of power – operate in a system which risks favouritism and co-optation, with top officials nominated directly by the incumbent political administration. The French system of checks and balances also has some curious ways of dealing with those that it does pursue and finds guilty of transgressions. Unveiling the annual report of the Cour des Comptes in 1998, for example, Joxe, a former Socialist minister who is its president, contrasted his current calm to his youthful indignation as an inspector at the punishment meted out to a civil servant behind a corruption scandal. Instead of being fired, the man was sent into 'internal exile', by being appointed several months later as head of an obscure research institute. A reprimand in the eyes of his closest peers, perhaps, but hardly a harsh measure in absolute terms, nor a way for outsiders to be assured that justice was being done.

The ineffective state

There is an easy way to tell whether the show-offs driving flashy convertible sports cars through the streets of Monaco are as wealthy as they like to make out: look at the number plates. If the last two digits, those signifying the region in which a car is registered, are 51, the chances are that the occupants have rented while leaving their own rather more modest vehicle in the garage at home. Since the mid-1980s, local regions have gained considerable extra autonomy, including the right to set certain taxes such as vehicle registration fees. And Marne, a department in north-eastern France, has long set its rates at the lowest level in the country, tempting rental companies and other organizations with large vehicle fleets to save considerable sums by setting up 'letter-box' headquarters there from which to register all their cars.

The approach illustrates simultaneously the ability of the regions to resist the unifying pressures of Paris, and the proclivity and inventiveness of the French for circumventing legislation. It also highlights the reluctance of national politicians and civil servants to delegate power, since the government intervened in 1998 as news of the 51 number plate 'scam' emerged, in an effort to curb the trend. All three traits have long historical precedents. For as long as the country's rulers have attempted to exert power over their subjects, they have met firm and individualistic resistance: from the troublesome fictional village of Gauls fighting the Romans in the Asterix cartoon books, to General de Gaulle's famous complaint that it was impossible to manage a country that produced more than 250 varieties of cheese.

To some, modern law, rooted in the Napoleonic tradition, is necessary because France has traditionally been a culture based more on codification than on trust. Civic consciousness is certainly often lacking. For proof, you need do no more than step into a Parisian street and you encounter one of the most unpleasant of French exceptions: the copious quantities of dog dirt on the pavement. It demonstrates the selfishness and individualism of the city's hundreds of thousands of dog-owners. It also illustrates the ineffectiveness of the state, which spends large amounts on cleaning up the mess each day with specially-devised *moto-crottes* or 'pooper-scoopers', but is incapable of an enforcement of the ban on such canine activities in the street.

Introducing legislation has frequently done little to change mentalities in France. For confirmation, simply try peering through the murky atmosphere of any respectable café or restaurant in search of the 'non-smoking section' sign obscured by cigarette smoke. The French have proved as ingenious as any race at getting around the rules. Why do so many companies have 49 or fewer employees? Because they stop hiring or split into separate entities to avoid transgressing the threshold of 50 beyond which they are required to set up works councils for staff. Why are there no five-star hotels in the country? Because a law introducing a higher luxury rate of value-added tax on the top category of accommodation encouraged owners to re-label themselves as 'four-star de luxe' establishments instead. Ask a professional caterer for a quote for a dinner, and it will come with the suggestion that 'independent' serving staff are hired directly (and in cash) by the client: a way for everyone involved to avoid paying substantial social security charges and a higher rate of value-added tax to boot.

The situation has got to such absurd extremes that even the French state itself bends the rules. When the government was forced in 1993 to put together a rescue plan for the Comptoir des Entrepreneurs, a troubled bank controlled by successive political appointees, it set up a financing mechanism based in an offshore trust – a concept that does not even exist in French law – as part of a rather handy tax-avoidance mechanism. It used similar structures in the Cayman Islands to create 'quasi-capital' for state-owned companies in the early 1990s so they could raise money from private investors while getting round Mitterrand's stated policy of '*ni-ni*' – neither nationalization nor privatization – which ruled out selling conventional shares with voting rights. Or take the example of a social security office in the Paris suburbs that indulges in practices which would hardly be endorsed by its ministers: hiring staff on low-wage, short-term contracts and discouraging them from taking the exams that would open the way to them becoming permanent employees. Not to mention the envelopes stuffed with cash which are handed to top civil servants in ministerial cabinets each month as undeclared additional salary. The examples may be an amusing tribute to creativity, but they also suggest that in many areas the system is not working, and the efforts necessary to get around it are cumbersome and wasteful.

The criticisms of the centralization of the state and its excessive involvement in citizens' lives are as old as the process itself. Early in the nineteenth century, the journalist Joseph Fiévée was already condemning the 'slavery' of French communes under Napoleonic rule, and calling for urban regions to counterbalance the dominance of the central government. He should have known. He was a former prefect himself. In 1858, the political analyst Alexis de Tocqueville wrote to a friend telling him that he was 'crushed by the weight' of the examples he had amassed of centralization.

There is little doubt that the grip of Paris has loosened in recent years. In 1982 Mitterrand pushed through a radical law on decentralization. In a process seen by some as a settling of accounts between the ministry of the interior and prefects, the prefect's role was reduced to examining decisions made *a posteriori* by local politicians to ensure that they were legal, rather than approving them *a priori* before they could be implemented. The construction and maintenance of educational establishments, and environmental services were among those aspects farmed out. Infrastructure investment, alliances between regional centres, and crossborder links with mayors in neighbouring European countries have all helped forge identities that are less dependent on the French capital and the national administration.

But the link between Paris and the regions remains very tight. After all, Mitterrand himself was never keen on relinquishing his imperial powers, and he supported the idea only under pressure from such regional Socialist 'barons' as Gaston Defferre in Marseille and Pierre Mauroy in Lille, who were long-standing advocates of acquiring greater autonomy. The result was a form of extremely centralized decentralization. By accumulating local and national elected offices, many politicians remain intimately linked to the capital. Indeed, as Yvon Ollivier, the civil servant who prepared the 1982 law, openly admits: 'Decentralization is an administrative and not a political reform.

The primary idea was to allow the state to shed its secondary roles and allow it to concentrate on the essential ones.'

The delegation of powers was not accompanied by a corresponding increase in funding by the state to local authorities, creating an ever-widening financing gap. And regions are still obliged to obtain approval from Paris before seeking funding from the European Community. Yet they were given more freedom than their European counterparts to set taxes, for example, in a move which has led to some extraordinarily un-egalitarian multiples between the property and business rates in different regions. Control mechanisms were also initially limited, with little attempt to cut down on conflicts of interest. The result was many incidents of corruption and favouritism in the award of public contracts and in local government job appointments. Nor was much thought given to rationalization of the different administrative levels. Instead, the principle was to sprinkle a few additional powers at each existing level without fundamentally disrupting the balance, a way of perpetuating a form of 'divide and rule'. Hence, in a rather arbitrary way, communes take responsibility for primary schools, regions for secondary schools, and the state for universities. That is despite a growing debate about what purpose is served by France's nearly 37,000 communes, a unit originally defined as a stretch of land that could be covered on foot in a day. There is similar questioning of the role of departments, whose old-fashioned boundaries were defined in the past as the reasonable daily limit of travel on horseback from the local administrative centre.

The result today, according to Hugues Portelly, an academic and mayor of a small commune north of Paris, is less a conflict between Paris and the local district, and more a form of permanent tension between all the multiple political and administrative layers, which have little clear hierarchical distinction. Many decisions require hugely complex negotiations between communes, towns, districts and regions, not to mention the unelected inter-communal and metropolitan councils that have sprung up over the past few years. It is a process that adds to costs and reduces the speed of decision-making. 'Thanks to the French principle of uniformity, a mayor of a village of 100 people has the same powers as one in a city with a million,' he says. But while the larger centre has the funds and expertise to use its powers, the smaller ones instead seek the help of the local prefect. Yet France's prefects, stripped of their past autonomy and facing the tensions of conflicting political pressures from the different local levels of government, increasingly take shelter behind written procedures. And their civil service staff, often now paid less than those in local authorities, are demoralized. Meanwhile, Parisian ministries, with their authority over the regions reduced, increasingly resort to regulations and circulars. The consequence is a form of legislative sclerosis mixed with baronial feuding. No surprise that there is a growing discussion about the 'recentralization' taking place in France.

No gesture better symbolizes the half-hearted French approach to decentralization than a snap decision taken by Edith Cresson shortly after her appointment as prime minister in 1992. A rare recent example of a senior politician who was not an *enarque*, she wrought her revenge by deciding without consultation to relocate ENA itself from Paris to Strasbourg in the east of France near the German border, home to the Council of Europe and one of the sites of the European Parliament. A bold idea in theory, but something which required Ffr170 million in one-off funding and has added 50 per cent to the school's annual operating costs, since it relies on regular guest lectures from civil servants and other outsiders. Pupils and teachers now spend much time and expense shuttling between under-used buildings in the two cities, generating far higher bills for the taxpayer. Perhaps Cresson should have consulted a few *enarques* first, for they were certainly opposed to the idea.

Full speed ahead

It is a good thing, as François Mitterrand once quipped, that the green countryside of Kent is attractive. Because passengers on the high-speed Eurostar rail link between London and Paris certainly have a disproportionate amount of time to look at it. The sleek blue and yellow trains systematically pull out of the Gare du Nord in the French capital on time, rapidly reach their maximum speed and within 90 minutes are halfway through the Channel tunnel. They have already covered well over two-thirds of the route, but will take at least as long again to reach the British capital as they slow down on reaching English soil and often come to a halt behind local trains using the same track.

Time and again, passengers impressed by the achievements of the French rail system are jolted back to earth by the British side of the Eurostar joint venture. Those who begin their journey in London, by contrast, seem to be propelled into another, more advanced era as they pass out of the tunnel and at ever-increasing speed into France. For if the British are not renowned for their mastery of the French language – let alone of French acronyms – there is one exception: the TGV or *train à grande vitesse*, the high-speed train of which Eurostar is one of the most recent and sophisticated manifestations. Three letters which are,

significantly, probably better known in the UK than the country's own nearest equivalent, the abortive APT or Advanced Passenger Train.

Seized by the mood of euphoria following France's victory
in the football World Cup in summer 1998, the magazine *Marianne* asked foreign journalists what they considered to be the
(other) national successes. The answers were as predictable as
they were unanimous. Apart from the 'theme park' quality-of-
life assets – the food and wine, the monuments and the countryside – it was technology that was cited above everything else.
There was Concorde, Airbus and the Ariane space-rocket. But
highest of all, there was the TGV, symbol of France's technical
and engineering prowess, which has carried more than 500 million passengers since the first of its lines opened in 1981.

The true history behind the TGV, like these other prominent
technological achievements and still more such as the nuclear
programme or the Minitel phone-based information system, is
not as close to certain perceptions of the French as might be
imagined. There was no single centralized decision taken at the
highest political levels in Paris to launch the project, and there
was considerable dissent at different levels of power which
meant the outcome was far from certain. The TGV did not represent a considerable technological leap forward, but was rather
a victory for pragmatism over any obsession with the uncertainties of excessive innovation. And, while France may be
renowned for its overbearing state, the high-speed programme
was not even financed directly by the government, but instead
by the financial markets with a close eye kept by officials on the
costs and potential returns.

Yet the TGV and its bedfellows are the fruits of a distinctive
French approach. They reflect a national belief in and support
for ambitious projects, built on the solid base of a strong techni-
cally-focused education system, the graduates of which form a
powerful and tightly unified elite. These same projects also

represent another side of a national character, with a highly effective machinery for implementation once a decision has been made, frequently in a manner that is ruthless and offers little scope for democracy. They have allowed France to catch up with the progress made in other countries and to overtake them – whatever the cost. It is an approach that has allowed France to maintain a strong technological reputation, but has periodically proved expensive, and led to a momentum which has subsequently proved difficult to hold in check.

The brakes on the TGV

France may be one of the countries most closely associated with sophisticated modern railways today, but it long struggled to catch up with its neighbours near and far. It was the Briton George Stephenson who invented steam locomotion in 1814, and the German Werner von Siemens who pioneered the electric engine in 1879. After a period during which the world speed title was held by the Americans, it was the Germans who broke the world speed record at 210 km/hour in 1903, in an achievement that was not surpassed by France until 1955. And it was the Japanese who introduced the pioneering high-speed Shinkansen 'bullet train' service in 1964. Only in 1981 did the first orange TGV trains begin service between Paris and Lyon, followed in 1989 by a second line stretching towards the Atlantic coast via forks to Le Mans and Tours. The third, to Lille and onwards towards Brussels with a connection to the Channel tunnel, opened in 1993.

The German historian Babette Nieder argues that the development of the TGV in some ways disproves a common stereotypical view of the French. In a detailed comparison with Germany, which took a decade longer than France to develop a high-speed train programme conceived around the same time, she highlights that even by the late 1960s there was little sign of interest in the railways from senior politicians. In his famous inaugural 'new society' speech in September 1969, Jacques Chaban-Delmas, the prime minister appointed in the wake of the student troubles of 1968, talked about motorways, telecoms, nuclear energy and other ambitious infrastructure projects. But 'there was not a word about the railways,' Nieder writes.

For Philippe Essig, a former head of the SNCF, the French railway operator, one problem that played against the development of high-speed trains was a tragic train accident in Dijon in 1962 that left 45 people dead. There were also more technical and financial objections. Michel Walrave, who headed the economics division of the newly created SNCF research department, recalls the gloomy conclusions of a fact-finding group that visited Japan in the mid-1960s. 'They said that Japan was very different, with a high population density, and that the idea wouldn't work in France.' He recalls a far broader hostility expressed by politicians, top civil servants and the SNCF's own hierarchy alike. 'They thought railways were something from the past,' he says. 'The SNCF had heavy deficits and its technology had not evolved since the war. The attitude was that the future lay with motorways, and the railways should simply be given jabs of morphine to help them to die.'

With an eye on the evolutions that had already taken place in the US, many of the most senior executives of the SNCF believed that passenger traffic was doomed and that the future lay with freight. Others, including some of the organization's own engineers and the head of DATAR, the state regional economic development agency, were favourable to the high-speed rail programme. But they argued for more advanced, experimental technology, pushing for alternatives to electric traction such as locomotives powered by gas turbines and other aeronautic techniques.

Political opinion was strongly split, and support did not

come from some of the quarters from which it might have been expected. Valéry Giscard d'Estaing symbolized the new generation of youthful, fast-rising post-war technocrats who had turned to politics. A graduate of both the prestigious Ecole Polytechnique and the Ecole Nationale d'Administration, he could have perfectly captured the modernist spirit that the TGV would come to represent. He was willing to support investment in roads, and lent his support to the financing and construction of a luxurious and costly motorway that would open up the Auvergne, his own isolated rural electoral region in central France. The empty black tarmac remains today far more in evidence than the occasional car using the multi-lane *autoroute*. But Giscard was defiantly hostile to the new high-speed rail programme.

In part, he was playing his role as minister of finance, with a brief to block or prune back large-scale public sector projects. Overruled by President Georges Pompidou, who authorized the development in principle of a first TGV line in 1971, Giscard did not renege on the commitment when he became president in 1974. But he used all his powers to block future progress. One SNCF official remembers receiving a call at midnight in 1977 with the purpose of definitively stopping the second proposed TGV, the Atlantic route, which would have passed close to Giscard's château in the Loire. And he continued to manifest his personal opposition right to the end. Offered the chance to exploit the political opportunities of inaugurating the Paris-Lyon line in the build-up to the presidential election in 1981, Giscard turned it down, making it clear that only a junior minister would attend the ceremony.

Some politicians, by contrast, were strong advocates from the start. Edgar Pisani, the infrastructure minister, was urging the SNCF to develop its high-speed programme from as early as 1966, drawing unfavourable comparisons with the progress being made in other countries. Others, including most importantly Pompidou, who took over as president from General de Gaulle, were won over to the cause. External factors, notably the oil shock of the early 1970s that rekindled interest in public transport and other energy-saving approaches, also certainly helped sway opinion in favour of high-speed trains. But there was another, internal, factor that played an essential and ultimately successful part.

The rule of the *polytechniciens*

The development of the TGV – and of France's other technological projects – is in large part due to the role played by a small but highly influential and well trained technological elite. They are the top graduates of a single institution whose members move smoothly between the political, administrative and corporate worlds. They cultivate and caress a potent personal network – their all-important *carnet d'adresses* or address book – and provide continuity, often working on the same long-term projects or subjects over the years in a series of different jobs. They were able to sway decision-making on the high-speed rail programme, often operating in spite of rather than in cooperation with senior politicians. They periodically kept decisions secret, used arguments designed to please rather than those based on fact, and pushed ahead rapidly with implementation to limit the possibility of any subsequent change of opinion.

For over 200 years, the Ecole Polytechnique has been a central pillar of the French education system. As recently as 1970, a law reasserting its vocation could not have put it more explicitly: 'To train men with the aptitude to become, after specialization, the top managers of the Nation'. The institution, along with several dozen other *grandes écoles* including the Ecole Nationale d'Administration, is intensely selective. Thousands of students each year compete for a small number of places in an extremely tough exam, after typically spending two years preparing for it in *prépa* classes. It is an exceptional institution in many ways. Controlled by the ministry of defence, its students have a uniform, including a sword and a distinctive two-cornered hat. They march in the annual 14 July Bastille Day parade in Paris, and undertake a year's compulsory military service at the start of the three-year course. They are paid throughout their studies, in exchange for a commitment to work for the state afterwards. And they benefit from extremely generous teaching resources, with some 250 teachers for just 600 students.

There is an extraordinary mystique, a series of special practices and a private language that all help bind those who have attended 'X'. The letter is a nickname which some suggest is derived from the crossed swords, the symbol of the artillery which was still the most popular destination for graduates in the nineteenth century. But it could equally reflect the French intellectual passion for Greek. Or for mathematical equations, since the Polytechnique's entrance exam is heavily focused on maths: in a mathematical joke, the *taupins* (moles) who study for its *prépa* are known as *trois demis* in their second year and *cinq demis* if they have to spend a third year before passing the exam that allows them to 'integrate' into the institution. French executives and civil servants often reveal their mathematical training by talking about the 'delta' (∂) rather than simply the 'change' or 'difference' between two events.

If Polytechnique is at the pinnacle of a French obsession with science and engineering, its teaching is also regarded as abstract, theoretical and generalist. Many graduates thus go on afterwards to attend one of a number of 'application schools'. But just a handful of the top students enter as salaried members of the state administrative corps that operates within each one, of which the most prestigious are the *corps des Mines* and the *corps des Ponts et Chaussées*. Their members are all but guaranteed a successful career. If many of the top positions in France's privatized and state-owned financial sector are held by top graduates of the Ecole Nationale d'Administration who went on to be *inspecteurs des finances*, it is the top graduates of the Ecole Polytechnique turned *X-Mines* and *X-Ponts* who dominate French industry. The SNCF has a good smattering of them, but so do many other enterprises from the chairman down: Francis Mer at Usinor, the steel group, Thierry Desmarest of TotalFina Elf, the oil and gas giant, Jean-Louis Beffa at Saint-Gobain, the glass manufacturer, and Jean-Pierre Rodier at Pechiney, are all *X-Mines*, for example. And each corps selfishly protects its turf. When Philippe Jaffré, an *inspecteur des finances*, was proposed as the new chairman of Elf, the petroleum group, in 1993, it triggered enormous – though ultimately fruitless – angry pressure from the *Mines* who had traditionally controlled the top job.

This small elite has also been at the heart of most of France's ambitious post-war engineering projects. At the SNCF, Walrave is a case in point. A graduate of the Ecole Polytechnique, and a member of the *corps des Ponts et Chaussées*, he spent most of his career working for the railways, in the company of many senior colleagues who had taken a similar route. Unlike in some countries such as Britain, his primary training as an engineer proved to be no handicap to career advancement. On the contrary, he rose from a job in charge of economic research in the TGV unit to executive vice-president of the SNCF. He began his career at the Atomic Energy Commission, and had a taste of direct government administration at the ministry of public works and transport. He also spent two years as a technical adviser to Pierre Mauroy, the Socialist French prime minister, in 1981–83. Another example is Jean-Marie Metzler, a *Ponts* project director for the Lyon and Atlantic TGVs, who also worked at the engineering group Schneider at the time of its merger with Alsthom, the principal contractor of TGV rolling stock. There are many more among those who helped contribute to the high-speed project, including Bernard Esambert, an *X-Mines* who was adviser to Pompidou. Or Philippe Essig, a *Ponts* who headed the SNCF in 1985–88. Not to mention the men after whom two separate reports were named, recommending to the government that the TGV programme should go ahead: Le Vert and Coquand. Both were members of the *corps des Ponts*.

It was 'an elite of generalists with technological ambitions', as Nieder argues. 'Even if … they were imbued with maths and science, they did not have a career in research but in management. Their decisions were influenced by personal relations as much as logical deduction, they reacted more than invented.' Unlike their counterparts in some other countries, they did not get excessively bogged down in technical detail and ambition, opting instead for well-established technology. They were also capable of considerable cunning. Orders for prototype rolling stock were being placed even ahead of the official announcement of the decision to go ahead with a high-speed line in December 1969. The prime minister and the finance minister were initially deliberately kept in the dark. The SNCF increasingly began to justify the need for the TGV in terms of lack of capacity on existing routes in order to please the new infrastructure minister, although that had never been part of its original rationale. As the project advanced in the mid-1970s, against the backdrop of austerity measures threatened by Raymond Barre, the prime minister, rail executives encouraged rapid expenditure 'so that we would have something to show, and to demonstrate that it would be too costly to cancel', according to Walrave. He adds: 'It was a period when we had a very powerful administration – or what some would call a technocracy – with limited political interference.'

The elite that he represented had a capacity to conceive and implement large-scale technological projects, a strong, self-willed *volontarisme*, and an enthusiasm that it shared with – or was able to transmit to – many others who had not had any engineering background. After all, it was Pompidou – a literary graduate – who approved the TGV programme. And it was Mitterrand, who also prided himself on being a man of letters and who always dreamed of ambitious projects, who happily exploited the political opportunity spurned by Giscard by inaugurating the Paris-Lyon TGV line in 1981. But it was Walrave, who in preparing the new president's speech while working for Mauroy, took care to insert a new-found expression of support for the second, Atlantic rail line as well as renewed interest in the Channel tunnel project – in one swoop overriding Giscard's wishes.

Riding roughshod:
the crushing of opposition

It may be the orange and white or blue and silver TGV trains that most catch the eye of the user. But it is the less glamorous railway tracks on which they run that are at the heart of the success of the French high-speed train programme. In terms of cost alone, the track represented one-third of the Ffr18 billion spent on the most recent TGV line heading north from Paris, for example. The SNCF concluded early on that it was impractical to operate a high-speed service without the construction of new lines dedicated to passenger traffic. Not only would separation from existing tracks reduce the risk of congestion. It would also allow for the construction of lines that hugged the countryside, taking a trajectory far closer to the shortest direct route between destinations on gradients far too steep for freight and other conventional trains to use.

The choice of routes would not be without conflict. There was no question, naturally, that the starting point would be anywhere other than Paris, maintaining its firmly established historical role as the hub from which all the nation's transport – and much else besides – radiates. But from the late 1960s, some proponents of the TGV had argued that the first line should run northwards from the French capital, already with an eye on the possible digging of the Channel tunnel and a connection to the UK. They included Mauroy, then the mayor of Lille, who was keen to foster economic development in his depressed region. Others, such as DATAR, were keen to promote a line to the relatively impoverished west of the country.

Walrave and others pushed instead for Paris-Lyon. 'It was the busiest and the most profitable route,' he says. 'I argued that the TGV was a complex project and it was important to get it right.' The potential for improvement was significant. In the late 1960s, the fastest train between Paris and Lyon, the 'Mistral', took three and three-quarter hours, and ran just once or twice a day. Ordinary trains took four and a quarter hours or more. With the inauguration of the full TGV line, the journey – with a far more frequent service – would be cut to just two hours, far quicker than was possible by car on the motorway, and highly competitive with the aeroplane connection.

While others lobbied hard for their alternative routes, there was an intriguingly vocal opposition – as ironic as it was impotent – which came from Lyon itself. The mayor himself, Louis Pradel, was against the TGV, as was the local Chamber of Commerce, which had recently invested substantial sums in building a regional airport at Satolas to the east of the city. Others were in favour of the general direction, but wanted to introduce modifications to serve their own interests, such as Robert Poujade, the mayor of Dijon and minister of the environment, who pushed hard for the TGV to stop in his town. And there were individual objectors too, including Péron-Magnan, the owner of a forest which would be cut in two by the new railway line, threatening his game hunting. He employed a range of dissuasive tactics, from greeting the contractors with a shotgun, to forming an association of environmental groups (self-interestedly funded by Air Inter, the domestic airline that flew between

Paris and Lyon) which eventually launched an appeal with the Conseil d'Etat, the court which judges matters of public law.

In spite of these sporadic protests, two elements are striking. First, there were relatively few objectors. The environmental movement throughout Europe was still in its infancy in the 1970s, and France was hardly known for its place in the vanguard. The TGV route also passed through largely rural areas with a low population density, thus minimizing the risks of conflict. Second, those who did attempt to block or change the path of the TGV had little more chance of success than if they had stood in front of it as it approached at full speed. Ahead of the decentralization of power in the 1980s under Mitterrand, even local politicians with the considerable presence of Mauroy still had only limited weight. Perhaps given his additional influence in Paris as a government minister, Poujade won a concession, albeit modest: a branch-line providing Dijon with several TGVs each day. For the rest, their protests would be as futile as that of the mayor of a commune in Picardy, who attempted to place a clause in his will to lay his grave where the Atlantic TGV line was to pass. His effort failed.

There had been fierce fights over whether to go ahead with the TGV, how to resolve the choice of technology and which route to select. But once a consensus was achieved, the centralized state kicked in at its strongest. If the tight links between the *polytechnicien* technocrats helped forge the concept, they would leave little room for tolerance of alternative views or objections once the principal decisions had been taken. As Babette Nieder shows, the SNCF created a department for the TGV 'Paris-South East' line in October 1974, and by March 1975 it had already launched a request for bids for TGV contractors, two months ahead of the start of a public inquiry. It ordered 87 TGVs in February 1976, a month ahead of the official decision to declare the project of 'public interest'. Construction got under way in spite of Péron-Magnan's legal action. And it was no surprise that the Conseil d'Etat ultimately ruled against him, arguing that the advantages to the public interest of the TGV far outweighed the inconveniences. The various government departments involved had long sorted out their differences, cutting down on any infighting. And – even though the TGV cut across numerous regions – a single prefect was delegated to coordinate the public inquiry, ensuring that the entire project would be approved with a single decision. No outsider was going to be allowed to get in the way.

A momentum of its own

Chain-smoking nervously and sweating profusely in the ornate gilded and mirror-lined reception room, Jean-Claude Gayssot frowned in response to the question. He had talked for 30 minutes about the new east-bound TGV service from Paris towards Strasbourg for which he had authorized funding in February 1998. A former train-driver turned Communist party apparatchik, he had been promoted into the left-wing coalition government of Lionel Jospin as transport minister. He could barely contain his excitement as he explained how the 'tilting trains' to be brought into service would work. But he seemed surprised to be asked how long it would be before the money invested by the state would be reimbursed. 'You're just trying to discourage us,' he finally said with a smile. His technical adviser had little more to add. 'It's paid for by the taxpayer,' she said with a shrug. It was a remark that highlighted the apparent lack of concern over the true costs or benefits of the high-speed rail programme by the government today. It had acquired a dangerous momentum of its own.

It would be wrong to assume that costs have never been taken into account in the assessment of France's technological projects. On the contrary, from its early stages the TGV was subject to detailed economic analysis. Walrave cites the Nobel prize-winning economist Maurice Allais as a strong personal influence on him. He had attended his seminars and specialized in economics during his studies. He spent most of his time in the period 1967–81, while the TGV was being developed, in a range of senior research jobs at the SNCF. He carried out tests which supported the economic case for the choice of electric traction over gas turbines and capacity studies that indicated the profitability of the Paris–Lyon route. Radically, the SNCF did not turn to the state but opted for the use of external financing of the TGV programme by issuing bonds. That provided the necessary discipline to help ensure a good return on its investment.

But by choosing the most financially attractive Paris–Lyon stretch as the pioneer, the subsequent lines were condemned from the start to offer more disappointing financial returns. Pierre Lubek, a director of the SNCF, argues that Paris–Lyon offered the attraction of high capacity combined with low costs of construction, with not a single tunnel and few environmental pressures for landscaping. During the 1980s, competition from alternative forms of transport in the years before airline deregulation was limited. Inflation was also high, rapidly eroding the cost of borrowing. 'The TGV was financed in 1975–80 francs and repaid in 1983–88 francs,' says Philippe Essig. While he was chairman of the SNCF, he pushed for the idea of a European high-speed network to be constructed gradually over 25 years. But he argues that the government moved too quickly. By 1987, it had agreed in principle to an extension of the Lyon line to Marseille, the Atlantic coast route, and TGVs to the north and the east. 'The state put on pressure to act straightaway, and the SNCF wanted to show off its technical skills,' he says. Regions across France were clamouring for TGV lines, but without any serious consideration of how they would be financed.

The SNCF's debt for the entire TGV programme today is

Ffr125 billion. And there is little sign that it can be rapidly repaid. If the Atlantic line, the second to open, still benefited from some of the favourable conditions of the Paris-Lyon stretch, the situation changed radically in the following years. Airline and other forms of transport competition put new pressure on fares. Growing environmental pressures, and the more urbanized regions through which the TGVs passed, added to costs. The economic boom of the late 1980s, combined with significant price-rigging, pushed up constructors' bills. And by the time the new lines came into service, the economic downturn of the early 1990s had begun to eat into the long-standing increase in annual passenger traffic. A scathing report from the Cour des Comptes, the public-sector watchdog, concluded that the estimates of travellers on the northern TGV line had been heavily overestimated, used outdated information, omitted key information and were not adequately scrutinized. Even Lubek concedes that there was 'an excessive optimism' by those at the SNCF, whom he says were not sufficiently independent in their assessment of a project that was 'dear to their hearts'. A report by government inspectors in autumn 1997 concluded that the new TGV-Est, at a construction cost of Ffr66 million per kilometre, 'could not be supported on economic grounds' given the difference between the 670,000 passengers currently using the route each year and the estimated 9 million required for it to break even.

The Channel tunnel:
French vision versus British scepticism

From William the Conqueror to Napoleon, and from Nicolas Desmarets to Francis Bouygues, there has nearly always been one thing in common about those who shared the vision of a cross-Channel link. While they may have a reputation for being inward-looking, in the history of the Channel tunnel it has always been the French who have been in favour and the British who have consistently proved their insularity; the French who have come up repeatedly with proposals and funding, and the British who have stalled and vetoed. What was a dream for the former nation over the centuries was a nightmare for the latter. Like the TGV, of which it was in many ways an extension, the experience of the tunnel illustrates the importance of the French engineering tradition and its taste for ambitious projects – at whatever the price.

Among the engineers and the scientists, it was the geologist Nicolas Desmarets who raised the idea of reconnecting the UK to the continent at a conference in 1750, and Albert Mathieu-Favier who proposed the idea of a tunnel in 1801. Aimé Thomé de Gamond, in many ways the father of the present tunnel, first suggested a rail link in 1833. He went as far as diving naked in 33 metres of water weighed down by stones to carry out the first systematic geological and hydrological surveys of the Channel, complaining in the process that he had been attacked by malevolent fish. Many of the potential contractors and financiers for the tunnel in the past were also French. Ferdinand de Lesseps, the man behind the Suez and Panama canals, wrote with enthusiasm about a cross-Channel link in 1882. The Compagnie de Suez, constructor and operator of the canal until it was nationalized by President Nasser of Egypt in 1956, helped form GETM, a study group on the tunnel under the Channel, in the following year. It would prove instrumental in the project which began excavations in 1973. And Francis Bouygues, head of the engineering group with the same name, would be among its leading advocates.

The British always proved rather cooler. Queen Victoria initially expressed enthusiasm – if only because she saw in the tunnel a way to avoid her problem of sea-sickness. But she would later change her mind. Economically, the UK was more interested in its commercial and colonial exploits around the world than in promoting tighter links with the rest of Europe. Military considerations weighed heavily. The first Franco-British company launched in the 1870s to carry out excavations could only proceed after the British parliament had delayed the project over concerns that there was insufficient British capital involved. Work was halted definitively in 1883, in the wake of a lobbying campaign masterminded by the soldier Sir Garnet Wolseley, which whipped up fears of invasion, cholera and cheap imports. It was only in 1955 that the British ministry of defence finally lifted its embargo based on the belief that a tunnel posed a strategic danger, clearing the way for a second serious attempt at construction. But military concerns would soon be replaced by economic ones. With work already well under way, the Labour government called a halt to the tunnelling in 1975 under the pressure of an economic crisis.

It was France once more, under the new prime minister Mauroy, that would relaunch the idea of a cross-Channel link again after the Socialists' victory in 1981. Urged on by Walrave, who had been recruited to his private office, and with rekindled interest in the economic impact on his de-industrializing region, Mauroy placed the idea of the tunnel on the agenda of the first Anglo-French summit with Margaret Thatcher later that year. It would lead to a historic compromise of French visionary engineering ambitions and British pragmatic management. With the problems of state-funding highlighted by the previous fiasco of the 1970s, as well as her own ideological beliefs, Thatcher agreed on condition that 'not a public penny' would go towards the project. According to Sir Nicholas Henderson, chairman of the Channel Tunnel Group, she was motivated by a desire to encourage a major industrial enterprise and to make a positive move towards Western Europe.

In spite of the stereotype of the French as reluctant, risk-averse investors in the private sector, it was they who would also prove most enthusiastic in coming up with money. The French bankers came forward more easily to provide initial funding than the British, who had to be strongly encouraged by the Bank of England. 'The British bankers did it for the business,' says one French banker involved at the time. 'The French were part of the same elite mould as the engineers.' And when Euro-tunnel, the operator of the project, was floated, it was again French shareholders who soon became by far the majority holders of the capital, with painful consequences following the company's financial crisis in the 1990s. Recklessly urged on by investment advisers, their motivation was often far less the result of cool-headed reflection on future profits than a deep-seated belief in the intellectual concept of the tunnel. 'I thought it was fabulous. It was like the building of the pyramids. It was the pro-ject of the century,' says Mireille Giovine, a retired singer who, egged on by friends and her banker, invested Ffr300,000 in the project. That represented all her savings: a life insurance policy, gold coins inherited from her father and her share of the pro-ceeds when the family house was sold.

If the French public was strongly in favour, so too were the politicians. The national proclivity to steamroller through pro-jects stood in stark contrast to the more rebellious tactics of the British. The Canterbury Treaty, giving the go-ahead by both governments, was signed in February 1986. The general elec-tions in France later that year, which created the delicate prece-dent of a *cohabitation* of the new centre-right government operating with a Socialist president, could well have derailed the affair. But the new Gaullist prime minister, Jacques Chirac, was quick to endorse the Channel tunnel. By contrast, what should have been a less turbulent re-election of the Conservatives in Britain in June 1987 was a source of greater friction. The French National Assembly and Senate passed the Channel Tunnel Act in the space of just a few weeks and by unanimous votes. The British parliament took six months, with the need for a casting vote by the chairman of the transport committee, such was opinion split: all that against a backdrop of lobby groups funded by the cross-Channel ferry companies fighting against the project, and British paranoia over fears of everything from foreign invasions to rabid foxes balanced on the bumpers of trains coming through the tunnel.

The project would ultimately be completed and the service opened to traffic at the end of 1994, well behind schedule and at a cost more than double the original estimate: Ffr101 billion, against the Ffr48 billion announced in 1987. It is difficult to argue that the blame – any more than the credit for finally completing the tunnel – was principally the result of one or other of the national cultures. Both Britain and France were represented among the contractors, the operator, the railway services and the regulators alike. But it seems clear that the British dogmatic insistence on forbidding public funding handicapped the project. It is probably impossible to fund such a large-scale infrastructure project without state aid, as the problems with the construction of the high-speed link between the tunnel and London have subsequently demonstrated. It seems equally clear that the French were far more prepared to invest, in the TGV line and in motorway connections to the tunnel alike; and that, to the extent that their technological culture held sway, they bear some fault for the escalating costs. For Essig, at least, who was briefly chairman of the Channel Tunnel Group, it represented 'the triumph of engineers over managers'.

Ringing the changes: the Minitel

A strange-looking chunky brown plastic object sits on millions of shelves and desks in homes and offices all across France. It is as mysterious to foreign eyes as the curious four-digit number '3615' on posters and television adverts that portray everything from beautiful couples in passionate embraces to puzzled employees wondering if their company is in financial difficulties. They are all marks of the Minitel, the telephone-based information system that helped give the country a substantial technological advance around the world for a decade, but which has more recently threatened to leave it far behind in the information revolution of the late twentieth century.

Placed alongside the typical modern personal computer, the Minitel terminal seems extraordinarily antiquated today. It is impotent when disconnected from the telephone line, offering none of the usual advantages of the PC, from word processing and spreadsheets to computer games. Even when online, the services it offers appear crude: it is extremely slow, and its small, low-resolution black-and-white screen is unsophisticated with little possibility to show graphics. Its simple keyboard has tiny, impractical keys. Within three months of his election as prime minister in 1997, even Jospin found time out from the struggle of more mainstream battles against unemployment and inequality to warn: 'the Minitel could end up hindering the development of new and promising applications of information technology. We are determined to close the gap ... because it could soon have serious repercussions on competitiveness and employment.'

His words echoed the situation of the country 30 years before. In the late 1960s, France appeared to be well behind in the development of its telecoms system. Customers had to wait months, and pay considerable fees, before getting telephones installed. And the network itself was old-fashioned, based on the electromagnetic system. In a parallel with the development of the TGV, the youthful economics minister turned president Giscard d'Estaing was opposed to significant investment in upgrading. 'He thought that the phone was a gadget for the *bourgeoisie* to call one another and chat,' says Bernard Esambert, an adviser to Pompidou. He managed to apply pressure for a bold increase in investment by the state: from an annual increase in the budget of 1.5 per cent in the late 1960s, it would leap to 30 per cent a year. Substantial money was also raised from private investors, through a series of companies set up to finance new telephone exchanges that operated on the pioneering digital system. As a result, France would catch up and overtake other countries over the next few years. Between 1974 and 1988, the number of phones jumped from 6 million to 28 million.

The Minitel itself represented a similar example of tardy but extremely successful imitation. The US, Japan and the UK, with its Prestel system, were all experimenting with screen-based information systems connected to the phone network in the late 1970s. Gérard Théry, a senior civil servant who headed the department that would become France Telecom, recalls meeting his counterparts in other countries to see how their systems worked and what lessons could be learned. 'I was convinced that there could be a rather large market from the start,' he says. While the equivalents elsewhere languished and faded away, the Minitel would come up from behind and become a huge commercial success. The first terminals were distributed in 1981, and there are now just under 6.5 million installed around the country, covering an estimated two-thirds of all households and one-third of businesses. Others can consult them in post offices and airports.

An estimated 35 million users a year use the Minitel, hooking in to 25,000 different services. You can check times and reserve tickets for the train and the plane, consult weather conditions or the depth of snow on the ski slopes, hunt for jobs and apartments, or examine your own bank balance or the annual published accounts of companies. You can bet on horse races, order jam produced in monasteries, send faxes or consult your horoscope. The so-called Minitel 'pink' services, erotic chat-lines and dating services, attract many users. One ingenious version even has a function called 'my wife is coming', that swiftly replaces the task in hand with a table of serious-looking statistics. But the most popular service remains the national telephone directory. Users can tap in a name and address – or even the address without the name – and rapidly find the phone number they are seeking. There are countless tales of how families and friends separated during the war found each other again thanks to the Minitel. The service was designed to save France Telecom huge amounts in continually printing and distributing paper directories that rapidly went out of date, although the tomes continue to be produced today. Long before the Internet was available, millions of the French were able to carry out simply and effectively operations only available in far more tortuous and cumbersome ways to citizens of other countries.

One reason behind the success was design expertise. At a time when the microcomputer barely existed, French engineers in the late 1970s developed simple terminals that were sturdy, reliable and easy to use and to produce. Like the TGV, they were not state of the art systems, nor were they intimidating for people to operate or liable to break down. And they cost just Ffr600 each to manufacture. But the principal reason behind the take-off of the Minitel was financial. Even though more sophisticated terminals are available for rent, the vast majority in use are the basic model handed out free by France Telecom. It was a policy that has since come under attack, but which provided lucrative production contracts to help support the French manufacturers Thomson, Alcatel and Matra.

Théry argues that the entire Minitel operation had been paid for by 1985, with the investment quickly recouped by income from phone calls. Apart from the first three minutes' use of the electronic phone directory, all use is charged, often at substantial premium rates. The beauty of the system for companies providing services is that France Telecom handles all the collection of money for them through its normal billing system. It then simply passes on the fees, after taking the substantial cut of 50 per cent for itself. The result has been huge revenues, which totalled nearly Ffr6 billion in 1999. While the Internet was still being described recently as 'the biggest zero billion dollar industry' in the world, the Minitel had long been offering a very concrete model of how successful electronic commerce could be.

External analysts are less convinced about the system's overall profitability, however. The Cour des Comptes concluded in 1989 that the Minitel had cost Ffr8.3 billion up to the end of 1987, against revenues of Ffr2.9 billion. It argued that the future profitability of the programme was uncertain and that the demand had been 'artificially created'. Even a consultant brought in to reply for France Telecom argued that with all financing costs taken into account, Minitel would only reach full break-even in 1998, 20 years after work first began on the project. As one prominent civil servant turned businessman puts it: 'France Telecom had the cash to fund the Minitel and the technology that allowed them to do it. It was a typical example of the French approach of defining the concept and not the market.'

If the return on the investment made in the system in the past is open to question, there is also a more serious contemporary concern: whether the Minitel has helped brake France's progress towards the Internet and other new technologies. In many ways, the two systems are diametrically opposed: the former tightly controlled, expensive and hierarchical; the latter cheaper and more 'democratic' with less scope for control by a central authority and the possibility for consumers to also become providers of information. France Telecom, swelled by the substantial income that the Minitel provided, had little economic incentive to encourage a shift to an alternative system. Its first meaningful moves towards the Internet only began in 1997, and have tried to combine the newer technology with that of the Minitel. There has equally been little incentive to change by the so-called 'Minitel mafia' of service providers such as the SNCF, which receives not only the payment for the rail tickets it sells but also a cut of the phone charges. At the same time, the fact that free Minitel terminals were available and that so many services existed – albeit at premium rates – may have helped dissuade the French from acquiring personal computers and from plugging into the Internet.

Successive French governments did little to help modify the situation until recently. By maintaining France Telecom's monopoly on phone services until 1998, they provided no competition to help reduce the cost of phone calls, one factor which repeated opinion polls have suggested has dissuaded the French from using the Internet. It was only in that same year that the authorities circulated a consultation document with the objective of reducing its extremely tight controls on cryptography, an essential step to encourage individuals to transmit sensitive information like credit card numbers by phone. The regulations in force, designed to ensure that the police and intelligence services can intercept and decode communications, put France on an unflattering par with a handful of other regimes including Iraq and North Korea.

The Jospin government unveiled a series of measures at the start of 1998 designed to encourage the creation of new information services and investment in high-speed data transmission lines, and to put the administration online. It also supported an 'Internet fête' in March of that year, one of the attractions of which, characteristically, was a serious debate between young lawyers. After lengthy deliberation, they 'condemned' the Internet to be disconnected, with a suspended sentence for the coming five years to give it time to respect national regulations, develop an ethics code and train its users in appropriate behaviour. Such intellectualizing may have had little effect, any more than government policy. But if they had a late start, the French themselves were not immune to the Internet revolution taking place elsewhere. Minitel revenues started dropping in the second half of the 1990s, and – while lagging behind other countries – ownership of home personal computers rose sharply to 23 per cent of households by mid-1999 and 7 per cent of households had an Internet connection. Five million people claimed to be surfing the web.

A shade of green

It had expanded almost as rapidly and powerfully as a nuclear reaction itself. In a quarter of a century, France's nuclear programme had propelled it from the experimental development of the atom bomb in the late 1950s to being one of the world's leaders in civil nuclear power generation today. In 1970, all of the country's electricity came from conventional sources. By the mid-1990s, 80 per cent was generated by nuclear fission through a network of 56 stations. As with the TGV, the Minitel or so many other bold French technological projects, nuclear power followed a characteristic pattern. There was a powerful vision, a ruthless determination to implement, and an effective result – with little thought to the views of opponents or the ultimate costs involved. Once started, the momentum was difficult to brake.

In the early 1970s, the decision to go nuclear had made considerable sense. France had next to no oil supplies, and its dependence on energy imports at a time of fast-rising prices made it keen to find a home-grown alternative. Its wealth of engineers and scientists gave it a good technological base, and under the presidency of Giscard d'Estaing, a political consensus was created to go ahead in earnest. But once started, it was difficult to stop. Environmental concerns were brushed aside, to the extent that when the Three Mile Island leakage in the US took place, Giscard accelerated the rhythm of his programme. Time and again, concerns about health were minimized and information was kept secret. When the Chernobyl reactor burnt in 1996, officials claimed that the radioactive particles it emitted mysteriously stopped at the French border. None of the health precautions issued in neighbouring countries were provided, offering one of the strongest explanations for the far higher incidence of cancer in subsequent years in the regions most touched by the radioactive cloud, such as Corsica.

As with the Minitel and other *grands projets*, it has been a mixture of self-destruction and external shocks that has ultimately brought about change. The pace of construction of nuclear power stations slowed with the election in 1981 of Mitterrand, partly as a result of the new president's electoral concessions to the green movement. A shift in world opinion, with the realization of the huge potential health risks, aided. But it was the huge cost which helped finally bring about a consensus for serious change in France. 'By 1983, we were building five nuclear power stations a year,' says one civil servant. 'Everyone knew it was ruinous, and that all we would do was to produce subsidized electricity for the UK, Sweden and elsewhere.'

The growth during the 1980s and 1990s of environmental concerns across Europe did not leave France untouched. Outbursts by a newly emerged minority, aggressive protesters attempting to block tunnel and road construction, were matched by increasingly vocal concerns by the more passive majority worried about health issues and landscape. It was reflected in the election of members of the Green party to parliament in 1997, and in the decision of Jospin to appoint its leader, Dominique Voynet, as his environment minister. That raised a new prospect of a counterbalance to France's more technocratic projects. She did not disappoint. She swiftly put a stop to a number of motorway projects.

Voynet's colleagues in the regional government of Alsace fought to prevent the most recent eastbound TGV service from reaching as far as Strasbourg. She herself began openly denouncing the policy of 'all-TGV'. She argues that the high-speed train has come to dominate transport policy at the expense of greater investment in conventional passenger and freight traffic by rail. 'The TGV is a showpiece,' she says. 'It is used by executives who travel first-class, don't pay for themselves and don't realize the cost for more modest families. We want more regional rail transport that is used by a greater number of people, and those who don't have cars.' Her arguments are backed up by a survey in 1997, which concluded that more than half of the users of the TGV had incomes above the national average, and 44 per cent lived in the Paris region. Voynet stresses that the TGV has served to further 'deform' the map of France, marked for many centuries by centralization. 'Should we be encouraging Le Mans, Dijon and Lille to be less than one hour from Paris and turning them into suburbs? Maybe we should be helping to make the connections between Rennes and Brest quicker rather than cutting the time between Rennes and Paris.' While her contribution to the intellectual debate has been influential, again it has probably been the escalating costs of TGV projects more than anything which have slowed down the expansion of France's high-speed rail programme, matched with a continued ambivalence by other European countries towards the development of a network across the continent.

Just as controversially, Voynet called for the closure of the Superphénix nuclear fast reactor near Lyon, the ultimate symbol of France's nuclear prowess. Plagued by technical failures over the years, the plant had proved enormously costly and had been unable to operate during much of its lifetime. But the project's backers were strong: the Communist party, also in Jospin's ruling left-wing coalition, and the CGT trade union, which has a firm hold over employees in the nuclear industry. The closure was repeatedly stalled. One of the biggest shocks may prove again to have been external: with the election of the social democrats in Germany in 1998, the greens gained political influence and demanded an immediate halt to their country's nuclear industry. That included ceasing to export nuclear waste to France, an important source of income. The decision, although delayed, throws into question the delicate economics of the nuclear industry, even ahead of the huge and so far unknown costs of decommissioning of nuclear plants over the next few years.

5

Cheques and imbalances

When the glossy magazine *Paris Match* published a world exclusive revealing the existence of François Mitterrand's illegitimate daughter Mazarine, it sparked enormous interest from the media around the world. The photograph of the French president and the young woman with a striking resemblance to him outside a Parisian restaurant was widely discussed, except in one country – France.

Such relative indifference might seem more than a little surprising. So might the timing. For while more than a few within France, including numerous journalists, had been aware of Mazarine over more than a decade, it was only in late 1994 that the press deigned to report the existence of the then 20-year-old to the public. The apparent respect for privacy appeared in many ways healthy compared to the excesses elsewhere. Yet the precise story of how and why the information was kept quiet, and how it was ultimately revealed, also says much about the weaknesses of French broadcasters and writers, their complicity with political and corporate power, and their failure in many ways to act as an effective counterbalance.

There is little doubt that the French media have enormous strengths. There is a tremendous number and rich variety of

titles – in newspapers, magazines and radio and television broadcasts – that is almost unparalleled elsewhere. They cater to a
broad range of political and personal beliefs, from the daily *l'Humanité*, run by the Communist party, and the Catholic *La Croix*,
through to *Minute* and *National Hebdo*, associated with the
extreme right-wing National Front. The regional press has a
strong presence, including *Ouest France*, the highest-circulation
daily paper in the country. France also has one of the largest
magazine readerships in the world.

In a reflection of the dominance of the interests of the elite
in print media, there is an absence of the mass market, enter-
tainment-driven tabloid press found in the UK, US and some
other countries. Even newspapers in tabloid format, such as
Aujourd'hui, or others aimed more explicitly at a popular readership, such as *France Soir*, tend to avoid the xenophobic nationalist sentiment and scandal-mongering of some of their
equivalents abroad.

At the other end of the spectrum, newspapers such as *Le
Monde* remain references around the world, with an extraordinary intellectual depth and an impressive breadth of coverage. As
the nearest equivalents in the UK, the US and elsewhere 'dumb
down' and focus on parochial and sensationalist news, *Le Monde*
has if anything gone in the opposite direction. What other publication would devote pages over successive days to the academic debates of the day? There are also such innovative
publications as the weekly *Courrier International*, which translates
into French articles selected from newspapers and magazines
around the world on every topic imaginable.

But like the country's magistrates and regulatory bodies, its
parliament and local assemblies alike, French journalists have
often failed to act as effective counterbalances to hold the
excesses of power in check. They have frequently proved unable
or unwilling to probe too deeply with critical investigative
reporting and serious in-depth inquiries, and have succumbed

to flattery and even sometimes to financial temptations rather than acting as independent challenges to abuses of authority.

In a reflection of Gallic culture, the role of the serious press is not primarily seen as that of a source of objective information, of detailed investigative inquiries, 'scoops' or campaigning journalism which reveal scandals and attempt to destabilize the excesses of those in power. The articles it carries are often more about demonstrating literary style and flourish, airing intellectual debate, exploring the world of ideas. There can also be a fear of attacking the establishment, and an attempt to avoid asking too many sensitive questions, justified by overarching concerns about the violation of privacy.

Since the mid-1980s, the French media have started to play a growing role in exposing scandals. But their weight remains limited, and even when they do report, the consequences for those who are criticized are often far more limited than in other countries. They act far more as forums for discussions than as vehicles to bring about change.

Privacy and the public interest

When the sex scandal linking the US President Bill Clinton to his former White House aide Monica Lewinsky first began to gain wide media coverage in early 1998, Serge July, the publisher of the left-wing daily newspaper *Libération*, came forward on French television to give the time-honoured reaction of his countrymen. The reluctance of the more serious French publications to write about individuals' private lives was a healthy sign of one more *exception française*, he argued.

That ignored the fact that there was extensive reporting of the Clinton affair taking place in the French as well as the international press at the time, with a focus at least as much on its libidinous aspects as on the more marginal 'public interest' side of the scandal: that the US president allegedly lied to government investigators and encouraged Lewinsky to do likewise. Indeed, *Libération* itself took mischievous pleasure in probing American priests' views on fellatio to see whether they agreed with Clinton's denial of having sex – in the strict sense of the term – with his intern. It would also be among the papers that published substantial and salacious extracts from the Kenneth Starr report on the scandal later the same year.

There is no doubt that the French are as interested as any other nation in titillating gossip. It is a frequent subject in conversations between friends and colleagues, and whets the appetite of the consumers of newsprint. Why else does *Paris Match*, which sells over 1 million copies a week, let alone a growing number of other scandal-seeking publications such as *Voici* and *Gala*, do so well? After all, when the relatively serious current affairs magazine *Marianne* dared to break the taboo by publishing a lengthy article on the alleged extramarital antics of successive post-war French presidents in February 1998, it was rewarded by a significant jump in readership: 355,000 copies sold, up from 315,000 in the previous week.

It has to be said that the subject matter available for tabloid-style journalism is less present in France than in some other countries. The heady mixture of money, glamour, power and morality is relatively rare. The country's aristocrats have lost their wealth and influence; internationally-renowned 'stars' are in relatively short supply; and politicians tend to avoid parading their private lives and mores for electoral ends in the way that their American and British counterparts adore. Probably the most followed 'national' subjects in the French media are not French at all, but the members of the royal family of Monaco. Although one of the most sensational tabloid stories around the world for many years took place in Paris – and involved a pursuit by several French *paparazzi* – it covered the fateful car crash of Diana, the princess of Wales.

The intrusion into the private lives of stars by some publications – notably the British, Italian and American press – has no doubt gone too far. The degree of restraint practised by the more serious French publications, which is reinforced by some of the world's toughest privacy laws, may have benefits in protecting personal lives. It can also be periodically abused by litigation-happy personalities, such as the actress Catherine Deneuve, who regularly seeks damages from magazines that print photos of her, including in such public places as on the steps of the Palais des Festivals at Cannes (and fully clothed) during the annual film festival.

When it comes to scrutinizing the lives of those more closely associated with the French establishment, and in particular of those individuals linked to power rather than to show business, the national press often seems to have used the justification of the protection of privacy as an excuse for not probing into issues that arguably do have a strong public interest. That Mitterrand had one (or more) illegitimate children may not be a matter for anyone but him and his immediate relatives. That the French taxpayer may have been more than modestly required to contribute to financing his colourful secret life – with apartments, allowances, holidays, plane trips, security guards and assorted hefty costs for an extremely extended family – is a question that few have been willing even to pose, let alone attempt to answer.

That many other French power-brokers in government and business have mistresses who have been appointed to senior positions on a basis that had little to do with their professional qualifications, but which has led to costly and incompetent decisions, is certainly not something that should be left to the privacy of the boudoir. It is perhaps no surprise that the French equivalent of the 'casting couch' implies a technique that continues regularly over time and applies far beyond the field of acting: *promotion canapé*.

Christine Deviers-Joncour had already been placed in

preventive detention for over five months in 1998 in connection with the apartment, unlimited corporate credit card and large salary she received from the petroleum group Elf. It was only then that the French press finally stopped euphemistically referring to her as 'an acquaintance' of Roland Dumas, the former foreign affairs minister whom she was handsomely paid to lobby. She was, as they finally put it less coyly, his *amie* or mistress.

There is also another exception related to privacy which does not stop with the media at all. It has become a cliché that each time a British public figure resigns over a personal scandal, a French journalist is summoned to shrug in bemusement and to explain that no such reaction would occur in France. That is precisely the distinction: not that the press necessarily fails to report, but that the personality in question does not respond by quitting. When it relates to private behaviour that has no public significance, that is no doubt justified, and makes a welcome change from the brutally sanctimonious and effective witch-hunts of the UK tabloids. The danger is that a mute press and a disdain for public reaction creates a sense of impunity among public figures and the risk of their abuse of power.

The power of the president

Jean-Edern Hallier knew the secrets of Mitterrand's life sooner and better than most. A colourful writer, personality and left-wing activist with tight links to those in the president's circle of power, he had drafted an explosive book on the subject. It revealed not only the existence of Mazarine, but far more damaging information besides: the fact that Mitterrand had been diagnosed with cancer in 1981 despite his frequent denials, for example; not to mention his wartime association with the Vichy regime during the second world war. *The Lost Honour of François*

Mitterrand was ready by late 1983. But it would not finally be published for another decade, and only achieved wide circulation in an edition produced in 1996, in the weeks following the former president's burial and only a few months before the author's own sudden death.

The story behind the book reveals much about the manipulation of the French media by politicians. Frustrated at his exclusion from office after the victory of the Socialists in 1981, and troubled by substantial personal income tax demands, Hallier circulated his text to advisers in the Elysée Palace as a warning. It created 'a wave of panic', according to Paul Barril, the head of the secret political police force that Mitterrand had installed with him in the presidential palace. In his own book on the period, Barril tells of frequent meetings with and pressure on Hallier. Transcripts leaked to the French press show that the writer's telephone was bugged, and that by February 1984, Mitterrand had authorized taps on many others with whom he had contact and against whom there was little justification on national security grounds.

Surveillance swiftly led to action. The technical means at the disposal of the Elysée meant that the head of state was aware on 1 March 1984 that Hallier was to appear as a surprise guest the following lunchtime on the state-owned Antenne 2 television programme *Aujourd'hui la vie*, live and therefore uncensorable. Jean-Claude Colliard, the head of Mitterrand's private office, swiftly contacted the station. The broadcast was cancelled at the last minute, without explanation.

Over the subsequent years, Barril has argued that Hallier's reluctance to publish his revelations on Mitterrand was partly the result of his residual left-wing political beliefs and loyalties. But it seems that the writer also had financial incentives to remain quiet. For example, according to the *Canard Enchaîné* newspaper, it was only ten years later, after the centre-right government of Edouard Balladur came to power in 1993, that the budget minister Nicolas Sarkozy intervened and Hallier was again required to pay income tax.

Hallier himself cannot respond. Barril claims that the writer was subject to periodic threats and was in considerable danger. In an episode which serves only to further fuel the conspiracy theorists, he died suddenly at 60 from a heart problem while bicycling on the beach at Deauville in January 1997. Hallier was undoubtedly an erratic personality, who provoked widespread trouble with outspoken attacks on public figures, by engineering his own false kidnapping and even targeting bombs at those who had fallen out of his favour. But he had clearly done his homework on Mitterrand. And others, like him, held their silence for reasons that were just as questionable.

Take the case of Claude Gubler. He knew better than anyone the true state of Mitterrand's health, since he had been appointed as his personal physician at the time of the new president's election in 1981. In a book published in 1996 called *Le Grand Secret*, Gubler revealed that in Mitterrand's last few months in office, he was so smitten with illness that he was rendered all but incapable. A better title for the book would have been *The Big Lie*. For he had been diagnosed with prostate cancer by the end of 1981, and it was already at a sufficiently advanced stage that his doctors decided not to operate. Yet the new president, marked by the secrecy surrounding the cancer that struck Georges Pompidou, had already publicly announced that he would issue regular bulletins on the state of his health. Signed by Gubler and released every six months, none made any reference to the cancer. They were inaccurate from the start. It was only in 1992, four years after he had been re-elected as president, that Mitterrand chose himself to announce the news. He did so just when it suited him, in the days ahead of the referendum on the Maastricht Treaty that would pave the way to monetary union. It was a close-fought battle which Mitterrand was determined to win, and his statement triggered a burst of public sympathy that helped sway voters narrowly in his favour.

But the revelation did not leave Gubler with a free hand. When *Le Grand Secret* was finally published six years later, shortly after the president's death, it only remained on the bookshelves for a few hours. Mitterrand's family acted swiftly to have it withdrawn and pulped, pleading successfully in the courts that it represented a violation of privacy laws. (It was nevertheless distributed afterwards on the Internet, although in a way that backfired. The owner of the cyber café in Besançon who entered it on the Web attracted considerable publicity to himself, in the process being identified as someone who had abandoned his wife and child and disappeared without paying the maintenance allowances that he owed them.)

Why did so much information of potentially public interest surrounding Mitterrand take so long to be made public? On many occasions, because it was he himself who carefully controlled its release, deciding whether and when public knowledge of the information would best suit his interests. If it was the case for his cancer, it was equally so for the existence of Mazarine, as the president attempted to empty the private skeletons from the cupboard of his past in the last few months before his death. The timing is certainly not a coincidence. He clearly engineered the 'coming out' of his daughter, eating openly with her in a Parisian restaurant that he regularly frequented, whether or not he directly tipped off the photographers. *Paris Match* even admitted that it went to him with the photos it had obtained, and sought his permission to use them before publishing. In spite of his illness, the French president kept a firm grip on news management even during his final months.

The weakness of the press

For a country that is supposed to have a cultural hostility

towards business, France has an extraordinary number of publications on the subject. Where the UK and the US both get by with just a single general business daily newspaper each, France has three: *Les Echos, La Tribune* and *l'Agefi*. Where its 'Anglo-Saxon' competitors have a handful of weekly or monthly general magazines devoted to the subject, France has nearly a dozen. Not to mention many more specialist financial journals, and serious business sections in all the principal mainstream newspapers, as well as numerous radio and television broadcasts. Yet they do not follow the message of sound business management that they preach. The situation is unsustainable. *La Tribune* and *l'Agefi* have limped along, changing owners and formats periodically. The weekly *Nouvel Economiste* dabbled with a stock market offering, went into bankruptcy proceedings in 1996 and re-emerged as bi-weekly subject to considerable re-modelling.

The same difficulties exist for many more generalist publications. The French print media, and notably its national daily newspapers, face considerable financial pressures. There are simply too many titles chasing too few readers. The diversity is handy for consumers able to flit between the hundreds of titles squeezed into the racks of kiosks across the country. But they do not buy in sufficient numbers. The result is a form of divide-and-rule exerted by owners and subjects, readers and regulators, which limits the resources of the publications on offer to recruit and efficiently exploit a critical mass of journalists. The consequence is to threaten the media's independence, and dilute its role as a meaningful counterbalance.

Rare is the national daily newspaper title that has not run into financial difficulties over the past few years. Recent fatalities have included the *Quotidien de Paris*, and the short-lived *Info Matin*, a colour tabloid that collapsed after just two years. Others have gone through innumerable *nouvelles formules* or face-lifts, backed up by hefty capital injections. *Le Monde* underwent a substantial restructuring with the support of a number of

French companies in 1994. *Libération* followed a year later, saved by money provided by Jérôme Seydoux, a businessman with left-wing sympathies. It was forced to carry out a second operation a few months later. *Le Figaro* and *France Soir* struggled under the heavy – although never publicly published – debts of the media empire of their owner, Robert Hersant. *Le Figaro* received fresh money, a face-lift and a debt restructuring during 1999. And in 1999, *France Soir* was finally sold off. The Communist party's daily *l'Humanité* faced a continuing drop in its readers in line with its own falling membership, and re-launched its glossy Sunday magazine with corporate advertisements. In a sign of the times, even the Paris-based Centre for the Training of Journalists went bust in 1998.

Newspapers have proved adept at pleading for greater financial support from successive French governments. But few seem willing to question the economics of French newspapers and to draw some tough conclusions. The fact is that daily national newspaper readership, already low in France, is in long-term decline. Figures from the national statistical institute suggest that just 18 per cent of the French read a national daily newspaper in 1999, declining sharply from a decade earlier. The trend is echoed in other countries, but is particularly pronounced in France. An analysis by the agency Carat placed France lowest among the six principal European countries for penetration of national daily newspapers, at just 37.4 copies sold for every 1,000 inhabitants. A study by the World Newspaper Association suggested that in 1997, just 153 out of every 1,000 people read a daily newspaper in France, ranking it lowest among 22 industrialized nations.

Content no doubt plays a significant role in declining readership. In the past, *Le Monde* was a prime culprit among papers which gave the impression of being written more for their own journalists than for a broad public. There was a tortuous, intellectual style; sentences riddled with sub-clauses; lengthy articles on obscure subjects; tiny letters on densely packed text-filled pages; and quasi-academic dated citations of articles that had appeared in previous editions of the paper, as though readers would religiously guard all back issues ready to consult them. Since the mid-1990s, its style and clarity has improved considerably, and it has been rewarded with a modest rise in circulation. Yet at a time when other papers and magazines are introducing ever more sophisticated colour printing and graphics to help readers digest information in innovative ways, *Le Monde* still rarely even carries photographs.

There is also a question of price, which has helped contribute to a vicious circle of falling readership and revenues. French daily papers are very expensive, explained in part by high paper and distribution costs, an average of eight or more weeks' annual holiday for journalists, and a printing system dominated by the archaic closed-shop unions which hold the papers to ransom. The consequence is cover prices for most papers of Ffr7 or more a day, more than twice the cost in the US or UK. For two or three times that sum, readers can buy a weekly magazine that they can read at their leisure over the weekend, and which offers much of the same information presented more attractively. And they can buy the cheaper regional newspapers which provide them with information on their local communities rarely provided by the Parisian-dominated national press. Yet advertising rates in French newspapers are also among the most expensive in Europe. As circulation has dropped, advertisers have drifted away, further cutting income.

So it should be little surprise that a study in autumn 1997 by Insee, the national statistical agency, showed that between 1989 and 1995, turnover dropped by 5.7 per cent across the national generalist and political press. They made no profits during 1989–91, and reported losses thereafter. And while their investment needs were substantial, their ability to finance such expenditure was non-existent. With the economic upswing helping advertising revenues, and re-designs lifting circulation, the situation has improved since. But it is far from clear that the crisis is over. And nor does it apply simply to daily national newspapers. Other parts of the print media that might serve as counterbalances to power have also been affected. France has an apparently limitless appetite for specialist magazines, with publications on health, skiing and animal care – and above all numerous television listings magazines – which are thriving. Their substantial circulations are matched by healthy profits, even if the contents leave much to be desired. But for the country's weekly generalist publications, the situation is more bleak. Diversity is often not matched by profits. The left-wing weekly *l'Evènement du jeudi* periodically demands additional money and changes owners. Two of the other leading news weeklies, *l'Express* and *Le Point*, have long scraped along at little beyond break-even.

Such financial weakness leaves publications highly vulnerable to attack, and encourages a climate of excessive caution. Those which have dared to transgress have paid heavy and often barely sustainable consequences. The businessman Serge Dassault wasted no time in taking the newly launched weekly magazine *Marianne* to court in 1997 in reaction to an article critical of him. Dozens of branches of the Intermarché supermarket cooperative pursued the magazine *Capital* in their local courts in response to a strongly worded piece. And Pierre Suard, the former chairman of the engineering group Alcatel Alsthom, boycotted advertising in the business magazine *l'Expansion* after it published negative articles about him.

The problems of the French press have also led to frequent and sometimes controversial changes in ownership. The result is to trigger another distinctive national mechanism: the so-called 'conscience clause' which allows writers who are unhappy with the identity and beliefs of their new proprietor to resign on generous terms without losing their social security entitlements. It is in some ways a laudable response to journalistic integrity and independence, even if it is periodically abused by those who had long fancied leaving anyway. But it is also a rather worrying sign of the uncertainties and instabilities of the media.

Tellingly, there is one national newspaper in France which is so fiercely defensive of the threats to its independence that it accepts neither advertising nor external shareholders, living instead simply on readers' subscriptions and sales of one-off special reports. It is the weekly *Canard Enchaîné*, which mixes satire with hard-nosed investigative reporting. Its style is clear and concise, its subject material original and fresh. And, unusually amongst its peers, it publishes its financial results. They reveal that it is not only highly regarded and widely read, but also comfortably profitable.

The visible hand

If François Pinault expected to reap a quick profit when he bought the news magazine *Le Point* in late 1997, he would be sorely disappointed. In the previous three decades, the man who left school at the first opportunity had turned a modest timber business into a huge multinational retailing group, controlling such household names as the high street Printemps, La Redoute and FNAC chains. Yet his surprise media purchase was in an entirely different category. *Le Point* was a right-of-centre news magazine that has always been in the shadow of its longer-established rival *l'Express*. It keeps its head above water, but offers little potential to squeeze out extra dividends. It may be, of course, that Pinault had other things in mind than money, notably the protection of a magazine whose ideological line he shares. As Claude Imbert, the journal's founder and editor suggests: 'It's a bit like when he bought Château Latour [the vineyard]. It cost relatively little and provides a good image.'

Pinault is not alone. If vineyards and fashion houses were among the essential accessories for French businessmen in the

1980s, newspapers were the preferred trophies of the 1990s. Bernard Arnault, another member of France's entrepreneurial elite who has built up the LVMH luxury goods group through a similar strategy of aggressive acquisitions, owns the business daily *La Tribune*, the weekly *Investir* and until recently *l'Agefi*. Indeed, France boasts few successful publishing businesses in their own right. In other countries, self-standing media companies often dominate the market, such as Bertelsmann in Germany, Reed Elsevier in the Netherlands, and News International in the UK and much of the English-speaking world. Such large groups, spanning commercial interests in broadcasting and print media, can create important conflicts of interest. But the conflicts are much worse in France, since most of the country's best-known titles belong to business empires dominated instead by other activities. *Elle, Paris Match* and the *Journal du Dimanche* are owned by the defence and electronics group Lagardère. *l'Express, l'Expansion* and numerous other specialist titles are controlled by Vivendi, the utilities group. The women's magazine *Marie-Claire* has as principal shareholder l'Oréal, the cosmetics group. The current affairs magazine *Valeurs Actuelles* is owned by Dassault, the defence company.

Editorial control exerted by owners may sometimes take explicit – and not always predictable – forms. Many suggest that under the ownership of the press baron Robert Hersant, the right-wing establishment paper *Le Figaro* was curiously muted in its criticism of the Socialist Mitterrand, so much so that the former Gaullist prime minister Raymond Barre even nick-named the paper the 'New Pravda'. For example, during the 1981 presidential campaign, Hersant called up Max Clos, the editor at the time, who had already indicated his firm support for the rival candidature of the Gaullist Jacques Chirac, in order to prevent him from writing a new editorial on the subject. The reason was partly a long-standing complicity between Mitterrand and Hersant, both of them politicians of a certain generation. They had different ideologies but shared many common experiences, including the ambiguities of wartime Vichy, which prompted Hersant to mischievously say: 'I was the only man of my generation not to have been a hero of the Resistance'. There was also Hersant's apparent personal dislike of press campaigns and of attacks on individuals.

Other interference from owners in France has come more in the form of nepotism and favouritism. Take the edition of *Journal du Dimanche* of 25 January 1998. A large article dominating its books page was devoted to the review of a first novel by a certain Alain Genestar. Three-quarters of another page was taken up by a portrait of the obscure figure Frank Ténot and his friendship with Daniel Filipacchi. Ténot was a music producer and shareholder in Hachette, the media group controlled by Lagardère and presided over by the same Daniel Filipacchi, and which owns the *Journal du Dimanche*, a newspaper edited at the time by Alain Genestar – hardly the most disinterested choice of subjects.

The influence of the proprietor may also take more indirect forms. An internal memo from the head of *La Tribune* which was leaked to *Libération* in May 1998 argued: 'In no way are the relations with the shareholder normal ones. The interest of the shareholder should not be called into question by a newspaper which he controls.' The note came in the wake of critical articles that *La Tribune* had carried on the exposure of LVMH, its patron, to the Asian financial crisis. While downplayed by some senior journalists, it was sufficient to trigger a response from the internal staff association, which criticized what it perceived as an attempt to interfere in the way the company was reported. Whatever the facts of the case, there is a more pervasive but subtle pressure at work. As one journalist on the paper puts it: 'It's not a question of the need for censorship. It's more about self-censorship.'

Potential conflicts of interest triggered by the country's

complex system of media ownership are certainly not limited to the private sector. Perhaps the most blatant example of 'thought control' in newspapers is *l'Humanité*, the daily organ of the French Communist party, an institution not known for its tolerance of different viewpoints. The hammer-and-sickle logo which appeared on the red title page until early 1999 at least left the reader with little doubt about who is controlling the contents. Martine Bulard, editor of the Sunday magazine *Humanité Hebdo*, says that there was considerable internal conflict when in 1993 the publication dared to print the general election manifestos of other political parties alongside that of the Communists. And it was only in the days before his death in late 1997, and after he had already been replaced as secretary-general, that the paper began to place a subtle distance between itself and the long-standing leader of the party Georges Marchais, the man who had memorably defended the Soviet invasion of Afghanistan from Red Square.

If much financial assistance to support the media comes from the corporate world, the French state has also been heavily involved. There have been allegations of illicit funding, such as for the left-wing weekly magazine *Globe Hebdo*, which was patronised by the Elysée and openly funded by subsidiaries of the state-controlled GAN insurance group and Crédit Lyonnais bank. Up to Ffr20 million also came more tortuously via a Switzerland-based subsidiary of the state-run oil giant Elf, and became the subject of a judicial investigation. There is also far more transparent aid. Agence France Presse (AFP), the news wire agency which provides a valuable source of information for many other media organizations, has close links to the state. It vehemently stresses its independence, but the government has wielded its influence on the board in the past to determine the nomination of its chairman, and it provides a hefty subsidy by subscribing to a large number of the AFP computer terminals. For the print media, there is the direct funding granted each year to daily newspapers, with the justification that they receive limited advertising, notably to *l'Humanité* and *La Croix*. There are reduced postal tariffs for newspaper deliveries by mail. And there are tax breaks for journalists, amounting to a 30 per cent deduction on their tax bill, up to a maximum of Ffr50,000 a year, and long used as a justification by employers to maintain relatively low salaries. When the Juppé administration resolved to scrap these advantages as part of a rationalization of the extraordinarily complex tax code riddled with special advantages, journalists shamelessly used their columns and their access to politicians to lobby for the government to back down. Even when the government does not directly intervene, it keeps a close eye on the country's print media. Members of its intelligence service scan the leading publications each day before they are even printed and despatched to readers.

The excesses of *l'Express*

When Jean-Jacques Servan-Schreiber founded the weekly news magazine *l'Express* in 1953, his idea was to create a French equivalent of the highly influential *Time* of the US. But the project immediately took on a very Gallic twist. Dassault, the industrialist who founded the giant French aerospace and defence group, offered Servan-Schreiber 'a little cheque' and an offer of future support. When he saw the amount, Ffr5 million, the editor diplomatically refused. Rebuffed, Dassault went on to launch the glossy magazine *Jour de France*, which dominated French dentists' waiting rooms until the 1980s, inspired by the simple editorial dictum that it would only report good news.

It would be one of many incidents over the years which highlighted the heady mix of business and political interference in the French media, at the expense of purely objective reporting of events. Servan-Schreiber himself became increasingly involved in politics in the 1960s. When he decided to stand for election under the banner of the Radical party, *l'Express* became his vehicle. One notable cover story carried a picture of a young female candidate campaigning for votes in a district of Paris. Hardly the most important story of the week, except that the woman in question was Françoise Giraud, a writer for the magazine, a fellow Radical party candidate – and Servan-Schreiber's mistress.

Servan-Schreiber had early on recruited the journalist Claude Imbert, who had the mission of developing a strong news-driven approach in the magazine and pursuing scoops. But by the early 1970s, the growing use of *l'Express* for Servan-Schreiber's own political agenda was too much for Imbert, who left for *Paris Match*, before founding the rival *Le Point* in 1972. Imbert recalls obtaining an exclusive interview with the US car manufacturer Ford which revealed that it was to open a plant in Bordeaux. Believing that the scoop could provide ammunition for his political rival, Servan-Schreiber refused to publish the information.

L'Express subsequently went through a succession of owners, passing through the hands of the Anglo-French financier Jimmy Goldsmith, and Alcatel Alsthom, the engineering group, before the utilities group Vivendi, then called Générale des Eaux, gained control. But when Vivendi's recently appointed chairman, Jean-Marie Messier, decided to sell the magazine in 1997 as part of a broad strategy of disposals, Dassault's son Serge resolved to pursue the family tradition and put in a bid.

He was not alone. Jean-Marie Colombani, the editor of *Le Monde* who had been instrumental in restructuring the newspaper and had already discussed a partnership with *l'Express*, was seeking a new challenge. Transformed from journalist into mini-media magnate, he shamelessly used the columns of his own newspaper to argue his case. *Le Monde* published a series of articles denouncing the growing grip of industrial groups over the media, alongside editorials which criticized the high price being sought for *l'Express* and the 'political motivations at the expense of independence' which the paper claimed were driving Messier.

Sitting in his spacious, sparse modern office, Colombani says: 'We couldn't let ourselves be attacked without explaining our version of events. I don't have the feeling that we transgressed any ethical boundaries. We are the only newspaper that is transparent. We publish our accounts in the paper and all the details of our restructuring were printed. We have to apply the same openness at other times.' He believes that it was above all the hostility of Jacques Chirac and his entourage towards *Le Monde*, which had alienated the centre-right president, that played against his bid. 'Messier called me from New York to say "If I go any further with you, I'll get hell from the Elysée",' he says. 'He said he had been warned that there would be blood on the walls if *Le Monde* bought *l'Express*. Messier portrays himself as a young, modern capitalist, but this was an example of old French-style capitalism, with politics everywhere.'

Others suggest that Dominique Strauss-Kahn, the then Socialist economics, finance and industry minister, was equally keen to apply pressure in a different direction, to dissuade Serge Dassault, hardly known for his left-wing views, from gaining control of *l'Express*. Certainly Dassault would soon leave little doubt of his ultimate objective. In an interview in mid-November 1997 on the LCI cable news channel, he argued that an industrial group like his 'should have a newspaper or a magazine to express its opinion and perhaps also to respond to some journalists who have written in a disagreeable way'.

Messier will not comment on the political aspect of the negotiations. He simply says: '*l'Express* has a value of about Ffr500 million. That makes it worth about 1 per cent of our assets. And 99 per cent of our troubles.' Whatever the truth, Dassault allowed his offer to lapse just ahead of the deadline for

bids, even as the *l'Express* staff voted in favour of his bid in preference to that of *Le Monde*. Messier, who argues that the newspaper's bid was too low and risky, withdrew *l'Express* from sale.
The uncertainty of a change in ownership hanging over the
magazine may have been at least temporarily removed. But the
signs of attempts at influence-peddling in the French media
were as strong as ever.

Complacency and sycophancy

When the editors of *Trombinoscope*, the 'bible' of names and
address of France's political elite, asked a panel of the country's
most senior journalists to pick the 1997 politician of the year,
the choice of jury was as predictable as the winner of the prize.
The nine personalities, all well-known names drawn from television, radio and the press, selected none other than Lionel
Jospin. Opting for the man who had already been prime minister for six months seemed hardly the most inspired idea. Nor
was it original. Jospin also won the 'man of the year' award from
the magazine *Horizons Politiques*, among many others. But for a
group of journalists who could all expect to have considerable
contact with the man over the coming decade, it certainly made
some sense. And it served to highlight the dangerous complicity
between the national media and its leaders.

What applies to the political sphere is equally relevant in
other sectors. Many a 'businessman of the year' award by one of
the country's financial magazines has helped provide its journalists with access to a senior corporate executive, even if a few
years later, that same hero once feted for his distinctive *méthode*
or management style has been discredited by his successor or
overshadowed by a corruption investigation. Attend the annual
accounts presentation of many French companies, and at the
end a financial analyst will rise to his feet, make a speech of

thanks for the co-operativeness of the chairman, and lead off a round of applause. Access to information for those acting in the the interests of a company's shareholders (in other words, its owners) seems often to be considered less of a right than a privilege. Journalists too seem often to have to turn to sycophancy in order to gain an audience with those about whom they wish to write.

One reason is that journalists in France have a curious – and distinctly inferior – position to those about whom they report. In the UK, the most recent generations of reporters have often attended the same prestigious universities as business and political leaders, and are treated as intellectual and social – if not financial – equals. In the US, where a university degree is also now the norm for journalists, the sacred role of the 'fourth estate' has ensured that the media gains regular high-level access to decision-makers as a constitutional right. There is also a balance of power: while the media needs politicians, they in turn need journalists, and accept that they cannot dictate all the terms. In France, the situation is more complex. Until recently, few journalists attended the top educational establishments, whose graduates would never have dreamed of entering the media afterwards. Their ability to speak to the powerful is a question of delicate negotiations and relations. The situation is nothing new. As Balzac put it in his *Illusions Perdues*, journalism is an occupation from which it is no more possible to emerge pure than from a brothel. 'The fact is, newspapers in this country have always been seen as an instrument of propaganda,' says one civil servant, justifying the tortuous procedures necessary to win access to his minister.

In some other areas, France has caught up regrettably quickly with other countries and overtaken them. The 1980s and 1990s witnessed the growing use of public relations consultants, for example, who have been left freer than their counterparts elsewhere to act as 'gate-keepers' and to control information. Why is it that so many French newspapers and magazines carry enormously lengthy interviews with personalities who pontificate on a huge number of largely uninteresting subjects, and which contain perhaps just one or two phrases of interest? Because the space available to them has been negotiated in advance, and is allocated largely on the basis of what the interviewee and not the interviewer (let alone the reader) decides is worth saying. Why is it that so many of these articles take a question-and-answer format like an unedited transcript, rather than an article with quotes inserted into it? Because the answers – and very often the questions – have been tightly controlled. Rare is the interview with a prominent figure the themes of which have not been agreed in advance – if not the precise questions. Rarer still is the one in which the interview has not been faxed in draft form to the personality concerned ahead of publication to gain their approval, and often re-written either to make the person appear more eloquent or to remove comments that he or she may want to withdraw with hindsight. Agree to the conditions, or forget about future interviews.

This practice of 'thought control' is so widely accepted in France that the brothers Patrick and Philippe Chastenet, respectively an academic and a journalist, recount breathlessly in their biography of Hersant that after the media baron met the journalist Franz-Olivier Giesbert, he 'even refused to re-read the text of an interview ahead of publication as a way of expressing his confidence and esteem' for the man he would later appoint to edit *Le Figaro*. More generally, the preferred method of communication is informal briefings with a select group of 'friendly' journalists, where information can be dished out 'off the record', safe in the knowledge that it will remain anonymous – and often unverified. France boasts an endless succession of intimate clubs for diplomatic, economic, social affairs or other specialist journalists. Those excluded from such circles, each with their own rules, can find things difficult. When a Reuters reporter at a press conference of Charles Millon, the centre-right politician who was defence minister at the time, mischievously asked a taboo question – whether he had himself carried out military service – he received rebukes from his French colleagues.

While struggling against such blockages from others, French journalists have not always helped their own case or reputation with a certain sloppiness. When Jean-Michel Verne and André Rougeot, the latter from the *Canard Enchaîné*, wrote a book in 1997 alleging with the thinnest of veils that two national centre-right politicians had indirectly ordered the assassination of a rival in the Var region, their proof was thinner still. It ultimately cost them conviction in the libel courts. Yet the *Canard*'s (often very accurate) articles are frequently used as the basis for pieces written – without apparent further verification – by other newspapers. After *Libération* published an article questioning the recruitment of individuals in the European Commission close to the former prime minister Edith Cresson in 1998, *Le Monde* simply cited its rival's story two days later on its back page without carrying out any research of its own into the subject. It pooh-poohed the allegations, which would nonetheless lead to a vote of no confidence in the Commission by the European parliament in early 1999, and to its mass resignation. No surprise that just 48 per cent of the French quizzed in an opinion poll in January 1998 expressed confidence in the material published by the press, and 64 per cent believed that journalists were not independent of pressure from power, political parties and money.

But even when the country's journalists are doing their job 'properly', there is a marked lack of willingness to get their hands dirty with first-hand reporting. Although there have been improvements in recent years, the French press has far less of a tradition of investigative journalism than its counterparts elsewhere, including Germany. And there is a frequent tendency to mix fact and opinion in articles. 'When I was at journalism school, all that everyone wanted to be was a political commentator,' recalls one reporter. As the editor of *Le Monde* himself put it in 1997: 'In the past, anything other than politics was viewed with contempt by the journalists. It was a very arrogant view.'

The worst of all worlds: television

When Chirac made a rare extended television appearance in spring 1997, he and his advisers made all the decisions. They determined the theme: 'Year 2000: a chance for everyone', which concentrated on the problem of youth unemployment. They chose the venue: the Elysée Palace. But they also exercised their veto over the decor, the journalists, the producers and even the camera-crew. There were meetings between the president's staff and top executives at the television companies ahead of the programme. Chirac's responses could not be entirely controlled in advance, of course, but his selected interviewers were so unaggressive that by the time he had finished labouring through his lengthy answers without interruption, everyone had forgotten the original question. It symbolized what *Le Monde's* Jacques Buob dubbed the 'complex of deference'. In fact, the only thing over which the Elysée had no control was the public. It was perhaps no surprise that they voted with their remote control buttons, and that viewing figures were extremely low.

If the French media suffer from weaknesses that limit their role as a counterbalance to established power, the problems are multiplied tenfold with television. Financing is certainly less of a problem than for newspapers and magazines. As in other countries, the power of television images has drawn people in increasing numbers away from printed sources of information and entertainment. If French national newspapers can be criticized for being too intellectual at times, television has taken the opposite route also favoured in other countries, with highly populist programming which has drawn in large audiences and accompanying advertising revenue. It is no surprise that it has attracted considerable private sector interest.

But again, exceptionally in France, television ownership has been claimed by companies which are not essentially media groups. The controlling shareholder in TF1, the broadcaster that tops the viewing figures and was privatized in 1987, is Bouygues, the utilities group. The biggest investor in Canal Plus, the satellite and subscription TV operator, is its competitor Vivendi. A third rival, Suez Lyonnaise des Eaux, owns a large stake in the youth music channel M6, as well as a number of cable television operators. The French state also remains heavily involved, controlling the France 2 and France 3 national stations, as well as Arte and the Cinquième channel. It is also, via the public stations and through France Telecom, an important shareholder in TPS, one of the country's two satellite networks.

Such ownership links have resulted in a considerable vulnerability to influence peddling. Until the late 1960s, the government still played a major role in determining the news content for broadcasters, with editors meeting directly in the office of the minister of information to draw up their daily schedules. While the private sector is often criticized for encouraging short-termism, it is striking to see that TF1 has consistently maintained higher ratings for its prime-time evening news programme than its state-owned rivals. One explanation is the continuity of the privately owned chain's staff and programme format over the years. The state channels, by contrast, have suffered from frequent changes of government, which have often led to reshuffles among senior broadcast staff, with those out of favour put into 'cupboards' and new ones brought in to tinker around in unsettling ways.

Not that TF1 can claim to be more pure in other ways. Take the main TF1 evening television news on 26 December 1997, for example. It contained an item on a play in Paris followed by another on the boom in the sales of portable telephones ahead of Christmas. The play was sponsored by TF1, the principal shareholder of which, Bouygues, was one of France's three operators of portable phone networks. Two of the most important news subjects for viewers on that day, or commercial interests dominating over objective news judgement? On the other hand, TF1 did not consider important enough to report on its evening news bulletin of 7 November 1995 that its own chief executive, Patrick Le Lay, had been taken into police custody for questioning in relation to an investigation surrounding corruption allegations at Française des Jeux, the national lottery organization. Needless to say, rival media organizations did.

At Canal Plus, Karl Zéro, the bespectacled creator of the 'Vrai Journal', a weekly investigative and satirical programme broadcast on Sundays, put it more bluntly in a newspaper interview with *Le Monde*. He said that in the contract he signed when his series was launched, 'there were three subjects we could not investigate: football, cinema and Compagnie Générale des Eaux'. The first two because Canal Plus invests heavily in them and they provide the mainstay of the chain's output; the latter because it is the dominant shareholder in the company. 'This contract limits our ambitions a bit, but it's like that everywhere,' he added. True enough, except that the grounds for conflicts are enormous when the dominant shareholder has such diverse interests.

There are other interesting interpretations of journalistic ethics on France's television channels that would be unlikely to past muster in other countries. Patrick Poivre d'Arvor, the star TF1 news anchorman, has maintained his position over the years despite such episodes as his 'false' interview with Fidel Castro. He broadcast what appeared to be an exclusive chat with the Cuban leader, which turned out to have been a carefully edited selection of answers given at a press conference, many of which were not in response to the French journalist's questions at all. 'PPDA' was also condemned in 1996 by a court in Lyon for receiving free flights, accommodation and other gifts worth FFr535,000 from Pierre Botton, the son-in-law businessman of Michel Noir, the city's mayor at the time, whose campaign he had helped to fund. His suspended sentence was matched by a very brief absence from the small screen, long enough only to avoid the embarrassment of having to read out the details of his own conviction.

During the late 1980s, French viewers regularly had the pleasure of watching two of its leading political television journalists, Christine Ockrent and Anne Sinclair, interviewing members of the left-wing administration right up to Mitterrand. Yet both were the spouses of ministers in the Socialist government of the time. Ockrent was married to Bernard Kouchner, the minister of health. She continued to broadcast after the new election victory of the left in 1997, which led to his reappointment. Sinclair, long-time host of the prime-time Sunday evening '7 sur 7' political television interview on TF1, was married to Dominique Strauss-Kahn, a junior commerce minister at the time. In the same way as many set-piece interviews in French publications are carefully negotiated and screened, Sinclair would regularly have lunch with her Sunday guests – such as the prime minister Edouard Balladur – the day before the broadcast. Not a formula for engineering much spontaneity, nor for keeping a professional distance from her subjects.

There is often a complicity with those in power rather than a willingness to put people who should be held accountable on the spot. While in daily life the French often adopt a conflictual approach, their journalists go mute when faced with politicians. For example, the producers of 'France-Europe Express', a high-profile monthly television discussion programme, went as far as to seek out a British newspaper journalist (the author) to pose questions to Martine Aubry, the social affairs minister, in their first show in late 1997. They explained that they were keen for an interview that was *à l'anglaise*, meaning aggressive and something they considered alien to their own journalistic tradition.

Turning the page

It would be wrong to suggest that the French media were largely deficient, any more than to argue that they were not transforming over time. It is no bad thing that there is still a suspicion of and a reluctance to indulge in British-style tabloid journalism. The diversity of publications and broadcasts may create financial weaknesses, but it offers enormous choice to the consumer of information while it lasts. And there is an extraordinary space given to academic debate and discussion, which is probably unparalleled elsewhere in the world. It reflects the continuing powerful role of intellectualism in contemporary France.

French journalists have played an important part in reporting the scandals that have affected their country. The information may have been manipulated and selectively leaked to serve particular interest groups, but the national media have exposed everything from the *Rainbow Warrior* and the contaminated blood affair to phone-tapping abuses and corruption at Paris city hall. Many of the issues cited in this book have drawn on their reports. And certainly most newspapers some of the time have taken a hostile view to established power, even when that means attacking the governments with which their editorial line is most sympathetic.

There has also been growing debate around and recognition of the dangers of conflict of interest. While she did not consider them sufficiently important in the 1980s, Anne Sinclair cited such tensions as one reason why she decided to cease presenting the '7 sur 7' programme following the appointment in 1997 of her husband as the powerful minister for economics, finance and industry. There has also been a clampdown on *ménages* – the practice of moon-lighting by well-known journalists for commercial organizations. The taboo on reporting the public interest aspects of private lives has also started to crumble. *Paris Match* gave France its own 'Ffr 21,972 question' in August 2000 when it published the daily price of the luxurious suite on Mauritius occupied by President Chirac and his family each summer, along with photos.

In the self-critical French tradition, checks on abuses by the media are also coming from the media itself. The magazine *l'Evènement du jeudi* carried regular articles on abuses on television. *Le Monde* casts a periodic eye on the subject, and *Libération* does so regularly for both the print and broadcast world. There is also the excellent Sunday lunchtime television programme 'Arrêt Sur Images' that every week dissects the all too frequent inaccuracies and manipulations of others. Its messages are unfortunately not often taken to heart.

Those who think the era of media manipulation came to an end with the presidential reign of Mitterrand, or that it has become more difficult in the era of privately controlled broadcasters, would have been advised to watch an April 1998 broadcast of 'Public', a prime-time Sunday evening interview programme on TF1. For her mediocre first novel, Mazarine was granted the entire slot. Breaking with the rules that apply to all others, it was pre-recorded to allow greater scope for controlling her responses. The programme was co-produced by Betty Bialet and Bernard Barrault, the publishers of the book, as well as a book written by the sycophantic interviewer for the programme, Michel Field. These facts were widely and critically reported in the media over the following days. But no action was taken in response. The former president, a master at controlling journalists, may be no more. But his legacy, a mixture of complicity and impunity, clearly lives on at the turn of the century.

6

The spirit of '68

It may have echoed the youthful uprisings taking place in many other parts of the world, but the student troubles in France in May 1968 had a very distinctive twist. While their counterparts in Berkeley, Tokyo and London took to the streets motivated by the big political issues of the day, in Paris the movement that so marked contemporary history began instead around a very specific and rather different subject: that of sex.

There is no doubt that a social revolution, triggered by rising incomes, the demographic boom and the introduction of the pill, was taking place in many countries at the end of the 1960s. But perhaps more than most other societies drawn into the student protest movement, France was characterized by a rigidly hierarchical structure, marked by tough parental rule and symbolized politically by the near dictatorial presidency over the previous decade of Charles de Gaulle.

In terms of method, by contrast, the marches and clashes with police on the streets of Paris in 1968 represented in many ways less of a rupture than they did in other countries. They may have given a nod towards the revolutionary tradition glorified by Marx, Castro and Mao. But they were enshrined in a far longer-standing national historical reality in France, most notably in 1789, 1848 and 1871.

The troubles of 1968 gained further legitimacy in the eyes of some with the participation of the trade union movement. For the French Communist party, closely linked to the CGT union, had played a significant role during the second world war in the Resistance movement, leaving it with a strong grip on political power immediately afterwards. And while the student and union movements viewed each other with mutual hostility, they formed a pragmatic alliance that would turn the *évènements* into one of the largest general strikes the country had ever known, as well as its most important student demonstration.

The protests that took place were not by any means representative of the overwhelming view of the French population. But they left their mark on that youthful – and now rather ageing Viagra – generation, among those who participated on the streets on both sides of the barricades, and on many of the then relatively green politicians and civil servants who continue to govern the country today. May 1968 continues to be a reference – for good or bad – and its vocabulary (such as *ras-le-bol* or fed up to the brim) has entered the language.

In the same way as the explosive mixture of ideological rhetoric and violent action in Paris mirrored and inspired liberation struggles in different parts of the world, including the bloodshed in Northern Ireland and the troubles in the Middle East, it contributed in its own more modest way to such events as the birth of violent nationalism in the French Mediterranean island of Corsica, where the legacy of bombings and murders is still felt today.

Few of the *soixante-huitards* ('68-ers) maintained their belief in violent revolution and the overthrow of capitalism for very long. But the public protests, strikes and mass mobilizations of those who still take to the streets, matched by the sympathy felt by many of those who do not even participate, remain a very French form of political weapon today. They are in some ways healthy signs of a vibrant democracy, and an unusually effective way of exercising popular resistance against established order. They reflect an impressive degree of solidarity – particularly when someone else is perceived to be picking up the bill.

As illustrated by the strikes of autumn 1995 which helped destabilize the centre-right government of Alain Juppé, however, use of the 'street' can often also reinforce the legitimacy and power of self-interested, corporatist unions whose demands are in some ways dangerously removed from the economic and social realities of modern France. Like numerous truckers' strikes and farmers' protests, they highlight a state that is often willing to cede to pressure, and incapable or afraid of intervening in conflicts. The actions are symptomatic of a society that finds negotiating change extremely difficult, and heads instead into often painful conflict in its efforts to resolve tensions.

Youth wakes up

American students had the civil rights movement and conscription which threatened to drag them directly into the Vietnam war; the Czechs lived daily the oppression of Communism; and the Spanish had had 30 years of dictatorial rule by Franco. But for the youth of France, living on the cusp of the '30 glorious' years of postwar economic boom, their daily frustrations were rather more tame. As the commentator Pierre Viansson-Ponté put it bluntly in *Le Monde* in March 1968: 'The French are bored. They take no part, either at close range or from a distance, in the great dramas that are convulsing the world.'

One of the few conflicts to which he could point had not even taken place in Paris itself, but at the university of Nanterre, just to the west of the capital. A concrete campus completed in 1964, it had an initial intake of 2,000 students, but by 1968 it was teaching 15,000. On 8 January, François Missoffe, the minister for youth and sport, decided to pay a low-profile visit to see the new swimming pool that had just been completed. But in a taste of things to come, he found the way marked by impromptu signs inviting students to a 'gang-bang' at the pool. Daniel Cohn-Bendit, a Franco-German student, made his way up to the minister and asked for a light for his cigarette. Puffing away, he dismissed a report recently commissioned by the minister on French youth, a generation which, it concluded, was largely concerned by professional advancement so they could raise their children appropriately, while saving for a car or a dowry. Hardly the reactionary values to which most of those studying at Nanterre at the time would admit, at least in public.

'In 300 pages, there isn't a single word on the sexual problems of the young,' said Cohn-Bendit, mindful of the frustrations of his fellow students on campus. Rebuffing his persistent line of questioning, Missoffe riposted that in order to cool his ardour, 'I can't recommend strongly enough that you dive into the pool'. Cohn-Bendit replied: 'Now there's a response worthy of the Hitler Youth.' It was a comment that provoked the ire of the minister, and triggered the start of expulsion proceedings against him. 'Danny' quickly became a hero among his fellow students and a leading light in the political battles to come. He would co-ordinate the 'movement of 22 March', a campus sit-in triggered when a Trotskyist militant at Nanterre was arrested in connection with a bomb blast that destroyed the window of the American Express building in central Paris in a protest against the Vietnam war.

But the swimming pool incident, perhaps more than any of the subsequent protests, symbolized what 1968 was really about for most of the participants: the painful transition towards a different set of social values, of modified relations between parents and children, of the development of youth culture. Only 20 years after being given the vote, women still could not have abortions legally, nor even open a bank account without the permission of their husband. Less urbanized than other industrialized countries, France's conservative values reflected its traditional, rural roots. No surprise that some of the most memorable slogans of the period have less to do with politics than with liberty, such as *il est interdit d'interdire* (it is forbidden to forbid), *sous les pavés, les plages* (underneath the cobbles, the beach), or *jouissez sans entraves* (let it all hang out). Jérôme Clément, head of Arte, the Franco-German television channel and then a leftist militant who travelled to the US to escape the constraints of the society of the time, says: 'There was an enormous gap between the leaders of the Resistance and student lifestyles. There was a feeling that France was still too focused on its colonial past, was too bourgeois and conservative and not open enough. It seemed ill-adapted.'

Militants in the student movement would continue to be marked by their experiences in later life, and to carry out projects which bore the mark of the era. Some were instrumental in founding the left-wing anti-establishment daily newspaper *Libération*, which is still flourishing today with the support of many of the same – now ageing – readers. Even if it has long since abandoned its policies of accepting no advertising and maintaining very low differences in pay scales among its staff, not to mention being forced to accept outside control – by the media group Chargeurs (now renamed Pathé – itself partly owned by the giant utility Vivendi) – as a condition for its financial survival. Frustrated by the arid, abstract political debates in the comfort of Paris, Bernard Kouchner founded Médécins Sans Frontières. A young doctor who would become a Socialist-party politician and minister, he wanted a humanitarian organization that would break with the rigidly imposed neutrality of the Red Cross. After initially working in the Biafra conflict in Nigeria, the organization he created would never afterwards be willing simply to passively offer emergency medical treatment and logistical support. It has often instead bravely spoken out against injustices and criticized political regimes – at the price of periodically being evicted by disgruntled governments.

Even the pupils of the prestigious Ecole Nationale d'Administration, the finishing school for top civil servants, would eventually play a part in the uprising of 1968. Characteristically, their protest was late in coming and would not ultimately have much effect. But the 'Charles de Gaulle' promotion – which narrowly missed being called 'Commune de Paris' – made a gesture in 1971, with two-thirds of its 100 students pledging to reject the *grands corps*, the jobs in the administration that were traditionally ranked highest in the pecking order. Not all would keep their promises, but their gesture marked the extent to which the social uprising of the period had permeated through many different parts of French society.

More passively, the generation that lived through 1968 would form the basis for the new consumer society. Club Méditerranée, the much imitated French holiday village operator, may have already been in existence since the end of the 1940s, but it really came into its own in the late 1960s, with its communal style, informality and the chance for easy sex dovetailing perfectly into the era. Its clients would bring back into the workplace the habit of *tutoiement* or using the informal *tu* form when addressing their colleagues. And many of the *soixante-huitards* would conserve a political nostalgia for the period, contributing belatedly to the historic post-war victory of the Socialist party under François Mitterrand's presidency in 1981.

Looking back today, Cohn-Bendit, still a highly charismatic personality who is now a politician and leading member in the green movement in Germany and France, says: 'Politically, we lost. Our rhetoric was very retrograde. But our emotions, our calls for social equality and liberation, pointed to the future. The world has changed since and we were a factor. I'm very proud of that.'

The culture of confrontation

For a left-wing academic who played a leading role in May 1968, Henri Weber looks a little out of place in the creaking corridors of the French Senate, a bastion of rather more conservative values. Dressed in his leather jacket, his hair dishevelled, the Socialist senator argues that the results to come out of the *évènements* of 30 years ago were 'largely positive'. He cites the social gains of salary raises and union rights, but equally political and cultural tolerance, women's and gay rights, and a more open, less paternalistic form of democracy. What is striking is that many of the same advances took place over the same period in other countries – yet without an equivalent to the demonstrations on the streets of Paris in 1968.

The difference is that in France, conflict is part of the culture – not just in tense discussions between unions and employers, where expressions like *bras de fer* (a battle of strength) and *rapport de force* figure frequently. Go to many a Parisian restaurant and an extension of the same idea is under way. Clients address waiters haughtily, and waiters bark at clients and regard them disdainfully. The same applies in shops, especially those into which the customer has not previously trodden, or built up a strong prior relationship with the owner. It is not simply about impoliteness, but rather aggression as a style of communication. It is a near sacrosanct principle of French conversation that when three people get together, there will be at least two discussions taking place. Someone who has paused – often for many seconds – may suddenly resume their argument or anecdote as though nothing had happened, cutting directly across others who have started speaking in the meantime. And these parallel conversations may be lengthy, as each of the different speakers attempts to monopolize the attention of all potential listeners. When they have stopped, they can expect to be brutally contradicted by someone else: a form of discussion that seems rude and abrupt to the

British, whose circumlocutions the French consider hypocriti-
cal because they often prefer diplomacy to a candour that risks
triggering conflict.

The use of street protest is part of that same tradition, one
that perhaps reflects a belief that there is no other way for individuals to express their views effectively. It is reinforced by the
strong historical precedents for change brought about by protest
in France. The sociologist Michel Crozier, writing just two years
after the *évènements*, criticized Raymond Aron, the intellectual
who had denounced the 'revolutionary' ambitions of the
marchers of 1968. Crozier agreed that the demands of the students, who desperately and unsuccessfully tried to find someone
willing to take on and carry out the revolution for them, may
have been unrealistic. But he argued that their protests reflected
an underlying malaise in France, which he labelled as a 'blocked
society', rigidly hierarchical and stratified in social affairs and
equally in the workplace. In the wake of 1968, Antoine Riboud,
the head of the agro-food group Danone, earned the scorn of
many of his peers when he called in public on fellow company
bosses to adopt a more social style of management. For there is
little tradition in French companies of day-to-day discussion
and negotiation between unions and managers, making it all but
inevitable that there will be periodic explosions. In the words of
Bertrand Collomb, chairman of the building materials group
Lafarge, 'We have difficulty in France in maintaining a spirit of
discussion, because it has been killed by being formalized'.

If May 1968 in the popular imagination is most closely associated with students, it was also tightly linked to the trade union
movement. Georges Marchais, the long-standing and hardline
general secretary of the French Communist party, regarded the
students with deep suspicion. In a front page editorial in *l'Humanité*, the party's daily paper, on 3 May of that year, he
denounced 'the German anarchist Cohn-Bendit' and other
'pseudo-revolutionaries', whom he accused of serving the cause

of the Gaullists and of big business. The feeling was mutual. Many of the more politicized students at the time rejected the Communists as part of the political establishment, and were sharply critical of its links to the already discredited Soviet regime. They were far happier to be labelled Maoist, or to participate in the ideological debates of other, more obscure and extremist factions.

But the trade unions would quickly become associated with the movement, turning May 1968 into a far broader mobilization than in many other countries. The Communist-linked Confédération Générale du Travail (CGT) organized a march of its own in Paris on 1 May, and would soon be in the vanguard of launching a general strike that paralysed the country. By 20 May, up to 10 million people had stopped work, pushing the government into negotiating the so-called 'Grenelle agreements', named after the address of the ministry of social affairs where the talks took place. There was a 10 per cent increase in salaries, a 35 per cent rise in the minimum wage, and a series of commitments to training and union recognition. No surprise that the CGT's membership shot up afterwards – by 300,000 according to its own figures. And 'Grenelle' entered the history books, and would be cited again as a battle-cry nearly 30 years later in the roundtable talks between the government and unions at the conclusion of the 1995 strikes.

It is clear that protests in France often bring about change, and they are considered to be a respectable and even necessary part of the culture. The strength of numbers has a legitimacy of its own, almost regardless of the underlying rights and wrongs of an issue. When the strikes of November and December 1995 brought public transport to a halt and triggered huge traffic jams, millions of commuters were forced to get up before dawn and spend hours getting to and from work each day, and tens of thousands of companies were disrupted. Yet opinion polls suggested that there was a strong sentiment of support for the strikers among the French population at large. There were many people who would not have protested themselves, but saw the actions of the strikers as part of a justifiable snub to authority, a way of sending a message to the administration about both the broken electoral promises of earlier that same year, and the continued economic gloom that weighed heavily on the country.

French intellectuals and other public figures have long played a leading role to add legitimacy to public protests. The historian Eric Hobsbawm cites the Communist historian Albert Soboul, who detested the counter-cultural elements of 1968 but felt morally compelled to march '*quand le peuple descend dans la rue*'. If the philosopher Jean-Paul Sartre, who lent his name to the newborn *Libération*, was on the barricades in 1968, cinema directors and actors played high-profile roles in criticising the government's policy towards immigrants without working papers in 1996. In the 1995 strikes, the sociologist Pierre Bourdieu – already present in 1968 – lent his considerable weight. Ironically, a series of small, low-priced books launched by him in 1998 to provide radical analyses of contemporary affairs sold far better than the 80 different books reminiscing about 1968 that were published to coincide with the 30th anniversary. That suggested that while nostalgia for the period lived on, the real legacy of '68 was in a persistent radical strain of intellectual thought.

The ritual of protest

A foreign tourist in Paris stumbling into a typical French protest march could easily mistake it for a popular fete. Well-fed, smiling marchers in imaginative costumes and bright-coloured stickers chant to the rhythms of live music, while chewing on grilled spicy *merguez* sausages distributed along the route. For the typical demonstration is not a stony-faced affair with crowds of the impoverished and the unemployed spontaneously occupying the streets. It usually takes the form of public-sector employees bussed in to the city centre for a highly organized and orchestrated show of strength. But there are protests for every taste and occasion in France. In 1968, the revolutionaries of mid-May were counterbalanced at the end of the month by even larger numbers who marched in support of de Gaulle. In 1995, the movement by public-sector workers contrasted with (rather more modest) demonstrations by aggrieved commuters and others suffering as a result of the transport strike. Catholics gathering to see the Pope, virulent defenders of the secular state, the allegedly clandestine immigrants with working papers occupying the St Bernard church, the retired seeking pension rises: every interest group that wants attention knows the procedure. There is even a service on the Minitel telephone information system, 3615 Engrève, which provides the rundown on the latest industrial disputes and the disruption that is anticipated.

Strikes, reflecting the French 'anarcho-syndicalist' tradition, often take unusual, populist and colourful forms: farmers hand out produce to passers-by in front of hypermarkets that undercut their prices; or conductors refuse to check tickets on trains so that passengers travel for free. The Eiffel tower has been the setting for pork producers to let their piglets run wild; and for the owners of ski resorts to dump large piles of snow. When Moulinex, the household appliance company, decided to close its factory in Mamers in Normandy in June 1996, hundreds of the inhabitants – employees, shopkeepers and other residents alike – participated in a 'dead town' operation, stopping all activity for a day to march. But strikes can also often be extremely disruptive. Frustrated at being driven off the sites where they previously operated, fairground operators used the tactic of 'snail operations' to draw attention to themselves by driving very slowly around the Paris ring road to bring traffic to a near halt. Protests can also be violent: from farmers who set fire to railway equipment, to repeated instances of truck drivers who form roadblocks. 'The British show unrest on the streets in their cinema, but the French do their cinema on the streets,' says one French lobbyist, referring to such recent celluloid successes (in France as elsewhere) as *The Full Monty* and *Brassed Off.* 'At least the British approach makes money,' he adds.

The International Labour Organisation (ILO) ranks France very high up the list of industrialized nations for the number of days lost each year to lockouts and strikes. But if its analysis includes action taken by the relatively passive, lowly-unionized private sector, it does not quantify at all the disputes which take place within the agricultural sector or in the public administration. The French ministry for the public sector, which is responsible for collecting this information, does not provide it to the ILO, and its own data exclude such strike-ridden entities as the Post Office and France Telecom. Adding all these other elements together, almost 6 million days were lost during the recent peak year of 1995. Such displays of plumage – which are often effective in stopping or delaying proposed reforms – are largely concentrated among state employees: notably in education, health and transport. In March 2000, for example, demonstrations by teachers and tax inspectors triggered the reversal of two important government policy reforms, the resignation of two ministers and a cabinet reshuffle by Jospin.

When demonstrations do take place, there are nevertheless strict rules to be respected. When the CGT organized its May Day march in 1968 in the streets of Paris, for example, it was only after asking permission. In his analysis of the troubles of that year, Roger Martelli, the Communist party historian, mischievously breaks with the party line by suggesting that there may have been 'several tens of thousands' of people attending rather than the 100,000 claimed by the CGT itself. But there is no irony when he stresses that it was the first march that the authorities had allowed to take place since 1954. Hardly a spontaneous, revolutionary or anarchic action. Strikes do not require secret ballots in France to ensure that they are democratically approved, but they do require prior notice to be given to a company's management. In the same way, marches demand approval from the police.

There is often a sense of complicity between the authorities and protesters. Take the case of Crédit Foncier de France, a specialist bank that administered a state-backed low-interest loan programme to help those on modest incomes buy their own homes. A disastrous diversification into property development in the late 1980s triggered a severe financial crisis that wiped out the company's reserves, forcing the government to launch a takeover in 1996. When the finance minister proposed merging it with a competitor, staff carried out another 'first': they occupied the luxurious Parisian headquarters and took the state-appointed chairman 'hostage'. For six days at the start of 1997, Jérôme Meyssonnier remained inside the bank, periodically addressing his radicalised white-collar warders. But it was clear that he had anticipated the events ahead of time, and could have escaped if he wanted to during his 'captivity'. Given that he had some sympathies with the complaints of the staff and was himself opposed to the merger, he preferred not to antagonize them. Ultimately, after his 'release', the government withdrew its plan. The action had 'saved' Crédit Foncier, but at the cost of a huge blow to its reputation and attractiveness to potential saviours of the bank who turned their backs. Not to mention the additional costs for the taxpayer.

In the same way, while there was certainly brutal violence and injury during the conflicts between demonstrators and police in May 1968, many of those who lived through the events recall with astonishment that there was just a single death on the barricades. At a time when many lives were claimed in other cities around the world in similar protests, the students' own '*service d'ordre*' in France limited the excesses among their own numbers. Maurice Grimaud, the prefect of police in Paris at the time, sent a letter to every police officer in the city to hold his men in check. The lack of bloodshed reflected a willingness on both sides to refrain from excessive confrontation. It no doubt partly reflected the fact that so many of the students on the streets were the children of civil servants, politicians and other high-profile public figures on the other side of the protest. But there was also a degree to which the state was willing to tolerate a certain excess, or was fearful of pushing things too far.

It may also have learnt from the troubles a few years earlier. Things might well have been much worse in 1968 had one of Grimaud's predecessors, Maurice Papon, still been prefect of police. In 1961, at the height of tensions over the war for the liberation of Algeria from French colonial rule, up to 200 demonstrators marching through Paris were killed by the police. But then, the Algerians were in a sense outsiders to this orchestrated game of protests where everyone knows and obeys the rules. Take the case of the youthful Daniel Cohn-Bendit, by contrast. In spite of his fiery words, he swiftly wrote a pre-emptive letter of apology to Missoffe after the conflict at the swimming pool of Nanterre, to halt efforts to expel him from the university. Revolutionary action had clearly defined limits – even if he was later temporarily banned from re-entering France, under pretext of having insulted the *tricolore* during a speech in Berlin.

The timid state

When Breton farmers found themselves under severe financial pressure from falling cauliflower prices in spring 1998, they decided to lash out. They cited the usual scapegoats: middlemen with excessive margins, Spanish producers with lower prices, supermarkets which stripped out all profits for the farmers, even the weather. They were facing problems typical in many parts of Europe, with fluctuations in agricultural output, the difficulties of survival for small farms, and changes in consumption patterns which no longer gave the cauliflower the place in shopping baskets that it once had. They responded in a characteristic way, with a range of disruptive tactics to attract attention to their complaints. They dumped 400 tonnes of cauliflowers on an important regional bridge at Morlaix, rendering it impassable for nearly a week. Small groups went on the rampage, vandalizing and setting on fire railway signal equipment, bringing services on the high-speed TGV line to a halt and causing an estimated Ffr5 million of damage. Yet there was no immediate clampdown by the authorities, and instead Louis Le Pensec, the agriculture minister, opened talks that led to the release of emergency aid. While he may have joined others in condemning the farmers' actions, his rather more concrete financial offer brought home the effectiveness of their protests.

It was the latest in a number of high-profile disputes over the past few years that have shocked many because of the reluctance or the inability of the authorities to intervene. In a country in which power is supposedly very tightly controlled and centralized, in practice the state has too often proved to be extremely weak. It has shown itself far more willing to interfere in negotiations than to deal with the disruptive result of protests. The explanation is partly related to fear of the consequences of conflict. This sentiment was revealingly described by Edouard Balladur, the former prime minister who was asked in May 1998 by the newspaper *Libération* to reflect on his experiences 30 years before, when he was a 38-year-old adviser to Georges Pompidou, the prime minister at the time of the troubles in 1968. He described a period during which 'anything was possible' and 'the state was nothing more than an empty shell'. Prefects refused to return phone calls and carry out orders, and he argued that there was a risk of 'complete anarchy'. He defended Pompidou's decision – in contrast to that of de Gaulle's – to allow the movement to exhaust itself rather than to adopt a conflictual approach to bring it to an end, because 'I am not sure we had the means' to control a confrontation.

It was a memory that would haunt Balladur ever after. As prime minister in 1993–95, he would cede to the pressure of the street on more than one occasion. In early 1994, he proposed the CIP programme, designed to persuade companies to hire school-leavers and train them by allowing them to pay just 80 per cent of the minimum wage, on the assumption that the recruits spent the remaining 20 per cent of their time in job-related training. The scheme, portrayed as creating a new class of low-paid workers, triggered a wave of student protests in Paris and the provinces. In his memoirs, Balladur described the actions as 'more preoccupying than worrying' initially, but increasingly 'alarming' as they were repeated week after week, 'orchestrated and used by violent groups without any concern about the future of the young'. The protests nonetheless forced him to back down, blaming what he called 'an alliance of all the forces of conservatism'. It had happened before, when in January 1994 thousands took to the streets to protest against a change in the Falloux law, designed to provide additional help to private religious schools. And it also happened in late 1993, when violent industrial action at Air France ultimately led Balladur to approve the replacement of Bernard Bosson as chairman of the state-owned airline. The prime minister himself conceded that he should have let the talks take place directly between unions and management, but he could not resist intervening because 'there was an urgency, and the risk that the fire would take hold across the entire public sector'.

Other factors also play a role in explaining the weakness of the state. One is the 'republican' tradition, that resists the idea of the government turning against its own people. It mirrors the reasoning behind the curious fact that the French Communist party was among the most vehement critics of President Jacques Chirac's decision in 1995 to abolish compulsory military service for young men. The Communists opposed the creation of a professional army, arguing that the armed forces should be democratic, composed of individuals who would never turn their arms on their fellow citizens. If the state has never used a similar system for recruits to the police force, it has nonetheless frequently shown itself reluctant to intervene too directly in strikes. It reflects a fragile relationship between the state and its individualistic citizens that frequently threatens to turn sour. The mass of public opinion is vitally important, regardless of the logic behind reforms. Politically courageous decisions are rare because of a huge fear of the rule of the mob. It is no doubt one reason why there is a national obsession with opinion polls, as politicians seek desperately to keep in tune with voters. The Balladur government went as far as commissioning a poll of all 8 million people aged 15–25 in 1993, to assess their views and wishes, and which resulted in 1.35 million responses – not that it did his administration's reputation among the young much good.

The same pattern has been repeated again and again in contemporary France. The country naturally enough respects the right to strike. But discussions over the provision of a compulsory 'minimum service' in the transport sector have never progressed very far; nor have the authorities done much to ensure that those who want to go to work during a strike can do so. In the transport dispute of 1995, for example, the proportion of metro, bus and train drivers officially not working was often very small. But that did not stop the entire system from coming to a halt. For there was no effort by the police to protect 'scabs' who wanted to continue to work, any more than there were secret ballots to counteract the heavy peer pressure and fear of intimidation by those who were not in favour of the strikes.

But it is quite another issue when protesters can hold hostage other sections of the population with actions entirely unrelated to their work, and the authorities do nothing to respond. In November 1997, truck drivers demanding salary increases installed road blocks at 150 carefully chosen strategic motorway junctions across France in just a few hours. Over the next few days, it was they who dictated who would have the right to move around the country. They set up 'filter' barrages with their vehicles, and decided who they would permit to drive through. A single truck blocked all traffic through the Channel tunnel. With just a handful of exceptions, the police did nothing to intervene. The country ground to a halt. It was a similar pattern in November 1996, as it had been in February 1984 and in June 1992 (when, after a delay, the Socialist prime minister Pierre Bérégevoy did eventually send in tanks to clear the road-blocks). The state repeatedly showed its willingness to interfere in negotiations between truckers and their employers. But – as the truckers' unions argued in 1997 – it had shown itself incapable of enforcing with its labour inspectors the commitments made by employers at the conclusion of the previous strikes in 1996. Above all, as many ordinary French citizens complained, the state was distinctly unwilling to unblock the barrages and restore order to the roads. It persistently opted for the least conflictual solution, and one that cost it money, not only in economic disruption, but in the payment of compensation to foreign companies caught in the haulage dispute.

The state is never more timid than when faced with the agricultural lobby. In a ground-breaking case in December 1997, the European Court of Justice condemned successive French governments – of left and right alike – for failing to prevent its farmers destroying crops imported from other countries. In evidence examined over a decade, it highlighted numerous examples of shipments of Spanish strawberries, Belgian tomatoes and other produce which had been intercepted and destroyed, while wholesalers and retailers had been threatened. It said the police were often not present to prevent illegal actions taking place, or did nothing to intervene when they were. Demonstrations had been filmed and the perpetrators could be identified, but just a handful of prosecutions had taken place as a result. It is as though a collective guilt about the high levels of unemployment or other social problems creates a pressure to legitimize violence. Some citizens tacitly endorse it, and the state fears it or tolerates it as a way to let off steam and ease the risk of a broader explosion of public outrage.

The same culture of intimidation of the state in the face of violence recurred again just a few days after the court ruling, as the authorities stood by while groups of the unemployed occupied and damaged benefits offices around the country at Christmas 1997 seeking additional financial assistance. Not all their demands were granted, but over Ffr1 billion was soon released for 'urgent cases'. There is the handiwork of AC!, the radical unemployment militants who periodically hold up traffic on the country's motorways to seek 'contributions' from drivers – while the police stand by. Or of other unemployed protesters who in spring 1998 'crashed' four different restaurants in Lyon demanding to be served. Not to mention the bank employees who bricked up the entrance to the French Banking Association in a sign of their frustration with its negotiating stance.

What applies to the state as enforcer of authority and paymaster also applies to it as shareholder. When the management of the Caisse Nationale de Prévoyance (CNP), a then stateowned life insurance company, broke a taboo at the start of 1998 and asked the police to evict strikers from its offices, it found it necessary to publicly justify its action. It stressed that it had waited 'as long as possible' before acting: 20 days after employees had first occupied its building in Angers, and caused disruption in Arcueil and in its headquarters in Paris. Nearly 1,000 of its employees were technically civil servants employed by, but on *détachement* or secondment from, the Caisse des Dépôts et Consignations, a state-controlled financial institution. In 1988, discussions began on a partial privatization of CNP. These employees were offered the chance to reintegrate over the next decade into the Caisse des Dépôts – accepting a readjustment back to their previous, lower, salary scale and life-long job guarantee – or to remain with CNP and accept a change in status to something resembling that of private-sector workers. Ten years later, as the deadline approached, the unions resisted being forced to make the choice. They need not have worried. In the wake of their protests, the government took the easy option, discreetly adding a clause into a general purpose piece of financial legislation to allow employees to maintain both their status and their pay, without having to make a decision until 2008.

Timidity by the state is not always the pattern, but the exceptions come with important nuances. The government supported the tough line by taken by Air France's management when the national carrier's pilots grounded its planes in late May 1998, for example. But it had proved hard to win public support for individuals earning such high salaries, especially when the effect of their strike was to threaten to disrupt the world cup football championship taking place in France at the time. The left-wing newspaper *Libération* set the critical tone, portraying the strike as an archaic form of corporatist dispute in which it wanted no part. It carried a front page drawing of a Frenchman transformed into a red, white and blue aeroplane, beret on his head and baguette in his mouth. The reaction may well have been different had those on strike been lower-paid employees with the airline. As a French businessman put it, 'Let's wait to see if the state takes such a tough attitude when Air France stewardesses go on strike'.

Even outside the domain of social disputes, fear of intervention by the authorities has led to some extraordinary situations, and none more so than in the ultimate shrine to 1968, the university. Since the *évènements*, for example, academic administrators have scarcely dared to interfere in the lives of their students. Some campuses have become 'no-go' zones for the police, not because the law cannot be enforced but simply because they are not welcome. One teacher at the university of Bordeaux complains that cars are regularly vandalized and stolen on the site as a result. And *bizutage*, the initiation rites of students by their peers – especially in engineering and medical colleges – go ahead with little attempt by the authorities to step in. The result is unchecked practices that take place on campus, and which have in a few extreme cases led to new students being humiliated, psychologically tortured and even raped. Only in 1998 did the Jospin government promise measures to clamp down on such excesses.

The limits of corporatism

It is not easy to get hold of the little blue book that lays down the working conditions for employees of Electricité de France, the state electricity monopoly. Officials suggest that the document is too technical, of no interest or even confidential. But the contents are well worth examining. They detail a labyrinthine system of special entitlements and benefits for staff, that run from a bonus of two months' salary for an employee who marries, to compensation to a spouse who may periodically have to take phone calls at home on behalf of the employee. In total, there are some 50 payments on offer to top up the normal wage, and all of them are exempt from France's high social security taxes. There is even an allowance for staff who change jobs and lose existing allowances in the process. That is in addition to a 95 per cent reduction from the market price on their electricity bills for all staff. They represent benefits that could otherwise be passed on to the consumer in the form of lower tariffs. And they serve to highlight the generous conditions available to a 'labour elite', generally favouring public- over private-sector employees, and the employed at the expense of the unemployed – not to mention consumers and taxpayers.

Such privileges extend well beyond Electricité de France to companies and to public administrations alike. Take the austere Bank of France, one of the country's foremost preachers of greater competition and tighter controls on the level of government spending. In an era in which cheques and electronic payments are increasingly replacing the use of cash (more rapidly in France than in many other countries), it has managed to maintain 8,000 employees in 211 small, inefficient branch offices around the country, making it the most unwieldy central bank in Europe after that of Greece. It offers them relatively generous salaries and low-interest mortgages. It controls a large number of apartments which are available to staff at attractively low rents. And even into the mid-1990s, employees had the right to take *le quart d'heure chaleur* or a 15-minute pause every hour if the outside temperature exceeded a certain limit.

Apart from salaries, allowances and other fringe benefits, French employees have the substantial advantages offered through works councils or *comités d'entreprise*, which all companies employing more than 50 people are required to operate. The councils receive an annual payment from the employer which on average amounts to 1 per cent of the total payroll, regardless of whether there are profits to distribute or not. But for some enterprises, notably in the public sector, the cut is rather more generous, and the payroll is so large that the sums involved are enormous and *comités d'entreprise* have become businesses in their own right. For example, at the RATP, the heavily subsidized Paris metropolitan transport authority, it represents over 3 per cent of the payroll. That gives the *comité d'entreprise* an annual budget of some Ffr200 million, and nearly 500 full-time employees simply to manage the money, used on everything from cheap holidays to music lessons for the family. At Marseillaise de Crédit, a regional bank nationalized in 1982, the *comité d'entreprise* owns a vineyard near Montpellier, two vacation centres and a motorbike circuit, not to mention benefiting from an extremely generous pension scheme. 'Work anywhere you like during your career, but spend the last year before you retire with Marseillaise de Crédit,' a saying among bankers used to run. Employees had all these advantages, even though the French state was required to inject more than Ffr3 billion in taxpayers' money during the mid-1990s to cover the company's heavy losses, and rival banks were required to bail out its deficit-ridden pension fund.

Such *acquis* or benefits won over the years are often defended as being a way to supplement the relatively low salaries of public-sector employees. But the picture is far from clear-cut. Aside from the advantages of a guaranteed job and often shorter working hours, civil servants benefit from a range of bonuses which are exempt from social security contributions, which they pay at a lower rate than in the private sector. They work for fewer years to earn full retirement rights. They can take unpaid leave for training for up to three years, with the right to return to their previous job at the same salary. Some studies suggest that while senior civil servants undoubtedly earn less than their counterparts in the private sector, the reverse is true for those low down in the hierarchy. The privileges reflect sharp divisions between the public and the private sectors, the unionized and the non-unionized workforce, but above all between the employed and the large proportion of the French labour force that is unemployed. As in the factory towns of post-Soviet Russia where the employer once provided everything, lose your job as a public-sector employee in France and you also risk losing a range of benefits such as an apartment and complementary health assistance, becoming an outcast. Resign voluntarily from a job, and you do not even have the right to claim the reimbursement of social security expenses.

Much of the French labour relations system revolves around a series of 'virtual' structures and negotiations that give a disproportionate authority to the unions. While union membership was historically always lower than in many other countries, just 9 per cent of the workforce is unionized today. Yet the unions jointly manage the organizations that run the country's medical, retirement and other social security organizations, and they receive jobs and direct funding from the state in exchange. They dominate the seats on *comités d'entreprises*, which are a focal point for discussions with company managements, and on *prud'hommes* or labour tribunals. And yet all employees vote in these elections for whoever they want, whether they are themselves union members or not. Union delegates in companies are – rightly – protected by legislation that makes them difficult to fire. But many are also full-time militants who no longer carry out any work at all for their employer. That was the case of Arlette Laguiller, the official head and long-standing candidate in presidential elections on behalf of the hard-left political party Lutte Ouvrière, who was originally employed as a secretary with the bank Crédit Lyonnais. She is far from alone. There are armies of over 1,000 full-time union employees at each of Electricité de France and France Telecom, for example. They represent part of a self-perpetuating system that leaves union 'representatives' often far removed from the daily concerns of their fellow employees, many of whom in turn eye them with suspicion.

The unions' power is further diluted by their own internal divisions. In a mirror of the French political system, there is strong fragmentation, with a range of different and often feuding unions: the Communist-leaning CGT, the more moderate CFDT and CFTC, the traditionally anti-Communist but increasingly hardline FO and the recently created SUD. Each has its own ideological stance, and each has divisions for the different industrial sectors in which it operates. Each largely serves its own interests while being given power over institutions such as the social security organizations supposedly set up for the general interest. Analysing the twentyfold postwar decline in membership of the CGT since the second world war, the French academics Dominique Andolfatto and Dominique Labbé highlight trends that are taking place in other parts of the world, such as the growth in the unemployed, and the decline in manual labour in favour of service-sector jobs. But they also stress the increasing centralization and hierarchy of the union, its increasing remoteness from its rank-and-file members, and a nomination process for its own top executives based largely on their loyalty to the Communist party. It rejected economic proposals from two of its innovative and original thinkers with the telling phrase: 'Trade unionism is about demands and protests, not about producing a project for society'.

While some negotiations take place in the workplace between company and union representatives, many aspects of French labour relations are governed by collective agreements and even administrative decrees which cover entire industry sectors, and are equally far removed from daily realities. Until 1997, for example, France's self-employed insurance agents operated under legislation that dated from the late 1940s. The regulations offered little possibility for the agents to merge or raise capital so they could invest and become more professional. And they severely restricted the scope for the insurers whose policies they sold to pay them on the basis of their results. Until it was unilaterally renounced in 1998 by employers, French banks were still governed by a similar agreement, which set down a rigid, civil service-style pay-scale with automatic pay increases each year, offered archaic allowances for coal-carrying, working in the basement, or shoe-leather wear, and enshrined the principle of 'last-in, first-out' among employees: impossible to sack long-standing and unproductive staff before all the more recently hired young and well-qualified recruits have been fired.

A few months earlier, the banks finally gained government approval to overturn a decree dating from 1937 that severely regulated working hours. It stressed, for example, that all staff should have two consecutive days of rest each week, making Saturday opening all but impossible. Today, many French banks that open on Saturday are still closed on Monday to compensate. Companies find ways around such regulations, of course. Some banks on street corners even use two separate addresses and entrances to circumvent the law. But it is a tortuous and costly response to a situation that should long ago have been modified. In the same way, banks – like other French enterprises – seem to believe that a year is longer than 12 months, for they operate the bizarre practice of paying a 13th month (or more) of salary each year to their employees. It is a device which allows them to offer an end-of-year bonus, without integrating the amount into a pay rise which could never be withdrawn in the future.

In the same way as many of France's strikes are as much about ritual as reality, so its negotiations are often as much about appearance as content. While the unions – and until recently employers' organizations – were jointly responsible for managing the country's social security organizations on paper, the state plays a strong and growing role behind the scenes. While unions and employers were both brought together at the prime minister's office in December 1997 for a day to 'discuss' Lionel Jospin's proposals to cut the legal working week to 35 hours, it was clear that the decisions had been taken in advance. And while employee representatives sit on the boards of state-owned companies, and *comités d'entreprise* must by law be consulted on redundancy plans, all the real decisions are made beforehand with little prospect of modification. It is an increasingly surreal charade in which everyone shares responsibility. Successive governments have been too keen to legislate and involve themselves in attempting to micro-manage the economy. Employers have been too reluctant to hold a regular dialogue with employees' representatives. Unions have been too obsessed with their own internal power struggles to worry about recruiting or being close to ordinary workers. And employees have shunned rather than attempt to improve their unions. Paradoxically, France's problems could probably be resolved by stronger, not weaker, trade unions, but ones which acted differently, acting on behalf of the general interest and applying pressure for more continual co-operation and less explosive sporadic conflict.

The hangover of '95

When Juppé unveiled the details of his social security reform package to the French National Assembly in November 1995, he had little idea of the consequences it would unleash. He had been the darling of the political centre-right parties, and the clear front-runner to be prime minister whether Chirac or his rival Balladur won the presidential race that summer. And he was cautious. He had already sacked his outspoken economics minister Alain Madelin after less than three months in office for suggesting too publicly, frankly and prematurely the need for restructuring the civil service pension scheme. When he made his own policy speech on the subject, the risks seemed carefully calculated. 'Corporatism and selfishness will not be able to stop us,' he said in conclusion, to widespread cross-party applause.

The phrase would come back to haunt him, for his words would soon bring his political honeymoon to an end. He unveiled a series of measures including more rational management and curbs on excessive expenditure designed to attack the spiralling cost of the social security system, which had an accumulated deficit of Ffr230 billion. But within a few days, the initial praise was quickly forgotten. A series of transport stoppages, supported by marches around the country, brought France to its knees for weeks in probably the most disruptive strike since 1968. As the winter drew on, hundreds of thousands of Parisians were forced to abandon the trains and metro in favour of walking, cycling or driving. And those who used the roads often rose before dawn to get to work and returned home late into the night, after spending many hours in traffic jams. Others stayed in hotels or with friends to avoid commuting every day. Companies went bust, the economy suffered a new setback, and the principal beneficiaries were a handful of manufacturers and retailers of roller-blades and bicycles who suddenly found themselves with an unexpected demand from individuals other than their usual variety of customers. To a triumphalist commentator for the left-wing monthly newspaper *Le Monde Diplomatique*, the 1995 strikes were the first to take place around the world in reaction to the 'globalization' of the economy. To others, in place of the radical calls for a new society in 1968, they had rather more to do with the reactionary protection of existing 'acquired rights' or *acquis sociaux*, since the centrepiece of Juppé's reforms was a modification to the retirement regime for civil servants, and notably to a series of 'special regimes'.

Travel to a remote hill-top temple in Burma, a fortified town in Yemen, or a safari park in South Africa and there will always be one thing in common. The more exotic, remote and expensive it is to reach, the more chance that there will be a coach-load of French pensioners already on the scene. It is testimony to the generous benefits many now receive, thanks to a state retirement system by *répartition* – or pay-as-you-go – in which the working population funds the pensions of those who have retired. At least since the start of the decade, there has been a consensus in France that the present system is unsustainable. A combination of longer life expectancy and an ageing population means that for every 4.4 workers funding each pensioner in the early 1960s, there are just 1.6 today and will be an estimated 1.2 in 2025. Balladur, Juppé's predecessor as prime minister, took a first step to address the problem in 1993 by tackling the private sector. He capped pension increases, raised social security contributions and extended the number of years in work necessary to earn the entitlement to a full pension.

His successor had the more difficult task of attempting the same in the highly unionized public sector. Among the Juppé reforms was the proposal to increase the legal age of retirement for train drivers from 50, a legacy from the much more physically demanding era of the steam locomotive. With similar modifications to the pension conditions for metro drivers, he had in a single blow attacked two of the most sensitive pressure points of French trade unionism. The strikes that followed – and the widespread support they generated – reflected widespread frustration over persistently high unemployment and continued economic gloom, stoked by President Chirac's demagogic election promises just six months earlier to heal the 'social fracture' within France. But at root, they were triggered by the attempt to reform the drivers' retirement regimes. Juppé the heroic prodigy was swiftly transformed into Juppé the arrogant technocrat. His error was probably to attempt to do too much, too quickly, at a time when the French economy was sluggish. He became a scapegoat for long pent-up anger, and the strike became a convenient outlet for frustrations that went well beyond the interests of those threatened by his reforms.

The strikes would severely mark the remainder of Juppé's term in office, contributing in large measure to the defeat of his centre-right administration in the general elections of 1997. The resurgence of the conflictual spirit of 1968 overshadowed many of his subsequent policy decisions. Not only did he backpedal on a number of his social security reforms, but those who worked with him say that his willingness to undertake other policy changes was severely stunted. Resistance to any form of pension reform hardened. In late 1996, the government supported proposals for the creation of complementary top-up pensions for private-sector employees, supported by tax incentives and funded by investing the money in the financial markets. The trade unions denounced the proposals, arguing that the scheme threatened to weaken the state pension scheme, and in the process, their own power in helping to manage it. There was a strong element of hypocrisy in the criticisms, given that public-sector workers – not to mention politicians – had long had their own equivalent top-up pension schemes invested in shares.

The unexpectedly strong mood of 1995 clearly also marked the subsequent left-wing administration of Jospin. In spite of pledges within a month of his election to create a top-up pension scheme for private-sector employees, by spring 2000 he had only got as far as launching a new round of procrastinating consultations, while pledging that the basic *répartition* system would stay. And there was no mention of attacking the public-sector special regimes. The marches against education and tax reform which had first taken place were a painful reminder of 1995, and warned him of the risks of pushing his reforms too far. With his focus already shifting towards the Presidential elections of 2002, he was soon suggesting that any fundamental restructuring would have to wait until after that date. Pensions had in many ways become the final, logical but selfish, battle of the ageing generation of *soixante-huitards* as they began themselves to contemplate retirement.

7

The inability to say 'no'

It was not easy to spot the impending disaster facing Crédit Lyonnais in spring 1993. The French state-owned bank had just issued its latest glossy annual report, which contained dozens of graphics to show its performance in a positive light. Only buried away at the bottom of page 53 was the smallest reference to the losses of Ffr1.9 billion it had made in 1992. A grinning photograph of Jean-Yves Haberer, the chairman, sits above a reassuring introductory message that the underlying business is strong and that profits should soon return. But long before that would happen, his smile – and his job as head of the bank – would be gone.

In the coming months, Haberer was prematurely 'thanked' in the euphemistic language of French business, ejected from his post before his contract came to an end. As the extent of the problems emerged, it would take four state-backed rescue packages over five years to make good the bank's catastrophic policies, as well as the misguided attempts to shore them up. Ministers and civil servants stalled and struggled to conceal from the European Commission in Brussels the full cost of their salvage efforts. As the protracted talks dragged on into early 1998, Karel Van Miert, the EU competition commissioner who needed to approve the plans, exploded during a television interview in frustration at the intransigence of the French government. He blurted out just how much money might ultimately be required to save the bank: up to Ffr190 billion.

The figure highlights the cost of the most extreme example of France's most expensive exception: the state's approach to managing and restructuring public enterprises. It was a sum unprecedented around the world. The overall cost of bailing out the US savings and loans industry or the banking sector in Japan and Scandinavia may have been greater, but the collapse of no other single institution had cost so much, not even the highly fraudulent Bank of Credit and Commerce International. During the late 1980s and early 1990s, Crédit Lyonnais had embarked on a hugely ambitious expansion plan. It indulged in a frenzy of acquisitions, investments and lending characterized by the marketing slogan 'the power to say yes'. As the consequences of the strategy emerged, many began to wish that it had said 'no' rather more often. The state which appointed the bank's chairman proved incapable of removing him or even holding him in check. When it did finally react in an attempt to redress the problems, it was in a way that was both poorly conceived and ultimately very costly.

Crédit Lyonnais was only the most expensive of a number of rescues of state-owned companies that successive French governments were forced to undertake in the mid-1990s. There were other banks, such as Crédit Foncier de France, Comptoir des Entrepreneurs and Marseillaise de Crédit; there was GAN, the insurance group; and a range of non-financial groups including the Société Française de Production, a television production company that made losses in all but two of the 20 years up to 1998. The way the deficits were incurred and dealt with says much about the limitations of the management of public enterprises in the 1980s and 1990s. There are also lessons for the way in which French business works more generally, with a tight-knit elite which is secretive, hierarchical and often acting with scant regard for the rights of or returns to its shareholders.

As 1993 progressed, regulators concluded that the problems at Crédit Lyonnais began at the top, with Jean-Yves Haberer, the former head of the Treasury who had been appointed chairman in 1988. He was not directly implicated in or even aware of the reasons behind all of the losses. Some were the result of fraud. Others were linked to dubious business deals that were undertaken under pressure from politicians on the left and right alike. The deep and prolonged economic crisis affecting France in the early 1990s also played a role. But Haberer had been in charge, and he had undertaken a series of strategic misjudgements with very costly repercussions. A French parliamentary commission set up in 1994 to ponder the lessons to be learnt also concluded that Haberer was most to blame. It was a verdict that suited in equal measure civil servants, politicians and those appointed in his wake to clear up the mess.

In his role as chairman of Crédit Lyonnais, Haberer undoubtedly carried much of the responsibility. But he also personified many of the wider underlying problems with the French system. The losses at the bank generated by the time he was evicted – let alone the much larger amounts subsequently incurred – cannot simply be reduced to the fault of one individual or to a series of isolated incidents. They were the result of broader structural failures that reflected problems across much of the state-controlled corporate sector, and involved connivance and incompetence among many of the country's elites. To simply blame Haberer is to ignore the far more complex nature of the relations between business, government and administration in France, which have had a powerful impact well beyond the losses at a single bank.

The irresistible rise of the
inspecteurs des finances

The *Canard Enchaîné*, the satirical newspaper, dubbed them the 'Titanic promotion'. A small group of men within the country's most prestigious civil service administrative corps, the *inspecteurs des finances*, had presided over state-owned banks, insurers and other companies that had lost more than Ffr100 billion by the mid-1990s. Highly intelligent and politically connected public servants trained in the art of implementing ministerial orders, they were 'parachuted' into a business world for which they were often ill-equipped. They formed a network of connivance, mutual protection and support which at times impeded swift and necessary action to redress the problems in their respective companies.

Unemployment is not part of the vocabulary of the *inspecteurs des finances*. Two of their own run a large modern office to manage the careers of their colleagues, which is based in the gargantuan ministry of finance Bercy building. Those who have left the safety of its walls to take up a position in a state-owned enterprise or even a company in the private sector know that they can always return. They will be allocated a job or given a special project to undertake. Failing that, they will still receive a salary and pension rights. The *inspecteurs* share a strong mutual support network, a belief in their own supremacy and confidence in their ability to fulfill a sacrosanct mission. They get to know each other while training at the Ecole Nationale d'Administration (ENA), build their relations on assignments when they work together shortly afterwards, and cement them in assorted senior state jobs. They dominate the top echelons of the Treasury and the ministry of finance, and at a certain age most expect to move into the commercial sector, with the prospect of higher remuneration and greater autonomy. Their own often less than glorious record in the management of such enterprises has not stood in their way. The nationalizations of the early 1980s added a range of new outlets for their careers.

Jean-Yves Hippolyte Haberer was the archetype of the system. Born in 1932, he attended Science Po in Paris before entering ENA in 1957 as part of the 'Vauban promotion' which boasted such other personalities as France's future president, Jacques Chirac. As the best-scoring graduate in the class, Haberer chose the top-ranked *inspection des finances* corps, and rose through a series of senior positions at the French finance ministry before becoming director of the Treasury in 1978. In addition to penning two technical books over the decade, he found time to write *La fièvre atlantique*, an impenetrable, intensely intellectual novel full of abstract mathematical allegories, plays on syntax, word patterns and rhythm.

Haberer worked under the centre-right government of the late 1970s, as a special adviser to René Monory, the economics minister, and was appointed head of the Treasury while Raymond Barre was prime minister. Yet as the archetypal disinterested civil servant of his generation, he made an overnight switch in political allegiance in 1981 with the election of the Socialist François Mitterrand as president. He swiftly drew up guidelines for controls to prevent capital flight and drafted plans for the nationalization of a large number of financial groups. Even as Margaret Thatcher was launching pioneering steps to privatize the British economy in a move that would be copied around the world, the French administration was going in the opposite direction.

The expansion in state ownership soon gave Haberer his opportunity for a move. He may have had no experience of the commercial sector, but aged 50 in 1982, he was appointed by the state as chairman of the newly nationalized Paribas investment bank. With the election of the centre-right administration of Chirac in 1986, he was removed from his job 'without a word of explanation' as he later indignantly wrote. But in a sign of the protection offered to top civil servants, the 'punishment' he received was modest. He was kept on as honorary president of the bank, and chairman of one of its subsidiaries.

He would not have long to wait in the wilderness. When the Socialists returned to power in 1988, he became chairman of Crédit Lyonnais. But Haberer was far from alone in the list of *inspecteurs des finances* given such appointments. He was the seventh of ten chairmen of the bank since its nationalization in 1946 who had been picked from the same administrative corps. If members of the rival *corps des Ponts* and *Mines* dominated the top appointments into industry that were controlled by the state, the *inspecteurs des finances* had at least as strong a grasp on the financial sector. In banking, there were René Thomas and Michel Pébereau at Banque Nationale de Paris, Marc Viénot and Daniel Bouton at Société Générale, Philippe Jaffré at Crédit Agricole and Patrick Careil at Banque Hervet. In insurance, there was François Heilbronner at GAN, Jacques Friedmann at UAP and Michel Albert and Antoine Jeancourt-Galignani at AGF.

But if the financial system was one of the most important targets for the socialists' nationalizations, banking was at the core of their strategy. Crédit Lyonnais would be the most important tool in a set of interventionist economic policies, and Haberer was the perfect man to implement them. Over the decades, the bank had in many ways come to resemble the civil service with its bureaucratic structure and with much of its interest rate, lending and other commercial decisions determined by government. Haberer would adopt and adapt a structure that mirrored the operations of many French companies in the public sector, and reflected the ambiguities in the relationship between the state, political power and the economy. A pure product of the system that nurtured him, he would use it and extend it to its furthest extremes.

He supervised an extraordinary explosion in Crédit Lyonnais' lending, its investments, its subsidiaries and its activities. In the five years of his tenure between 1988 and 1993 the balance sheet doubled to Ffr2,000 billion, allowing it to boast that it was the biggest bank in the world outside Japan. It grew into a sprawling giant with 550 subsidiaries and investments in 1,500 companies. As Haberer proudly told the 1994 French parliamentary inquiry, in 1991–92 it alone accounted for 40 per cent of all of the capital injected into French businesses through rights issues and share options. 'If the other big banks had reacted in the same way, the problem of the lack of capital of French companies would have rapidly changed in a few years,' he said.

The quote reveals one of Haberer's main motivations. At a time when the French state was beginning to pull back from its tight control over the economy, he was exploiting the vacuum. Crédit Lyonnais was no longer simply a bank. It was so large that it was becoming a lever in macro-economic policy in its own right. The former head of the Treasury was reasserting his authority and his desires with the best instrument available to him, confusing his previous and current jobs in the process. In 1990, for example, he still considered it his role to contribute an article to the academic journal *Pouvoirs* on the conduct of monetary policy. Elsewhere, he talked about how banks had the 'right' to make losses. 'With Crédit Lyonnais, I was trying to build the big French and European bank that would strengthen our national identity,' he told the parliamentary inquiry. He did not see his purpose as narrowly serving the commercial interests of the bank, but rather to influence the shape of the entire French economy. His timing – both politically and economically – was severely misjudged, as recession gripped the country and the government changed.

The power of the prince

Talk to a French company about how it operates, and one of the first things staff produce is the *organigramme*. It is an organizational chart which lays out clearly the internal hierarchy of jobs. Firmly at the top – or at the centre with lines radiating out from it in all directions – is a single individual. There is no clearer indication of the concentration of power in most French companies than the title of that person. While their counterparts in the US, the UK and elsewhere usually split responsibilities between a chief executive and an often non-executive chairman, a single monarchical 'PDG' or *Président-Directeur Général* dominates in France. In the rare cases where the two roles have been given to different people, the division may be justified as a move towards Anglo-Saxon style 'corporate governance', with its emphasis on checks and balances. But the reality more often than not is that the title of *président* is little more than a gesture, an honorific title awarded to a senior individual who has lost out in an internal corporate battle – and may well be on the way out entirely.

More typically, the French PDG has all the formal power. Under French law, he or she is the individual solely accountable for the company's actions. If the appointments made to the board of many state-owned French companies were frequently limited to a small group of top civil servants, those nominated to lead companies in the private sector have sometimes owed their promotion to the personal whim of the chairman rather than factors such as proven commercial experience or a fair selection process based on the widest range of potential candidates. At the secretive Bic group, manufacturer of disposable pens, shavers and razors, for example, the founder Baron Bich was replaced as chairman after his death by his son Bruno. At least he represented the family shareholders, who between them controlled the company. Yet the same monarchic succession took place

during the 1990s at Club Méditerranée, the pioneering pur-
veyor of 'sea, sex and sun' holidays, between Gilbert Trigano and
his son Serge; and at the agro-food group Danone between
Antoine and Franck Riboud. In neither case did the son hold
more than an infinitesimal number of shares. The dominance of
one individual may prove highly successful in small companies,
and even in larger ones when the chairman is also the founder
and has a strong vision of the business and its future, or when
someone is brought in to bring about radical and painful
restructuring. But when it goes unchecked, it can also risk leading the company into self-destruction. If that is true in the private sector, it is even more the case in state-owned companies,
where the chairman is directly appointed by the government of
the day rather than being even formally accountable to the
board.

In a system bearing a remarkable similarity to the structure of
the civil service from which so many of the top appointees are
drawn, most PDGs have a *directeur du cabinet* and advisers, just like
a government minister. Beneath them is a rigid hierarchy. Each
executive has a precisely defined position in the corporate 'pyra-
mid', with a wealth of titles to match. Significantly, many of these
roles have no easy English translation: *directeurs généraux, directeurs
centraux, directeurs, directeurs adjoints, sous directeurs, directeurs auprès
du president*. At Crédit Lyonnais under Haberer, there were some
40 executives in such positions, all with a wealth of privileges to
match and to keep them sweet: a car, free telephone calls, an
allowance for their apartments, all paid for by the bank. François
Gille, successively secretary general, financial director and managing director at the bank, argues that there was an absence of
open debate that might have helped – or when necessary held
back – their chairman. 'Freedom of expression between us was
limited, not by some presidential ukaze but by a form of
censorship that we imposed on each other. Crédit Lyonnais
[was] sick of its army of bosses, small and large, each jealous of

their authority, touchy, quick to place blame on to others.'

In a mirror of the operations of the French state more generally, the appearance of a highly centralized group paradoxically belied an extremely chaotic exercise of power beneath the surface. As in feudal societies, the monarch ruled thanks in part to authority delegated to his barons. In many French companies, authority that should have been delegated was kept centralized, but more importantly, functions that should have been controlled by headquarters were often excessively dispersed. At Crédit Lyonnais, individual 'barons' camped on their own turf, refusing to co-operate with their 'rivals' and indulging instead in what Gille calls 'intestinal wars'. Very large loans were approved without being examined by any central credit committee. The lack of communication meant that the bank was not even aware of the full extent of its commitments and provisions. The situation was made worse by the *folie de grandeur* of rapid expansion into new areas of business.

In the absence of an extremely effective manager, such an organization was a recipe for anarchy. And Haberer's background was not essentially managerial. He was used to working less on operational than on political issues, with the support of some of the best civil servants that France had to offer. Displaced into a different organizational environment, and one in which he did not necessarily have much interest in implicating himself too deeply, he faced a very different challenge. 'Haberer didn't know what a company was,' says Gille. 'He had a macroeconomic vision. He didn't want to know about the balance sheet of Crédit Lyonnais. It never interested him. He was above it. He said his role was to define the strategy, and the shareholder would follow. He didn't accept the limitation of limited means – of people or of capital.'

Haberer led his 'barons' by example in their management-without-delegation approach. No better illustration exists than Altus, formerly Thomson CSF Finance, a specialist finance house in which Crédit Lyonnais acquired a 50 per cent stake in 1990, rising to 99.9 per cent over the following three years. It was run by Jean-François Hénin, the self-styled 'Mozart of finance' whom Haberer preferred to call the 'Verdi of finance, because Mozart died young'. Unfortunately for the bank, Hénin's masterpieces turned out to be both discordant and short-lived. Altus's aim, according to Haberer's own revealing phrase, was to do what Crédit Lyonnais 'didn't want to, didn't know how to or could not do'. He met Hénin every week, and attempted to ensure that he was kept free of any 'bureaucratic straitjacket' that would impede his 'creativity'. Altus's projects were often supported by scant documentation or none at all. As one of those brought in to clean up the mess discovered, the company did not even know how many investments it had. While its activities swelled, its staff numbers remained all but constant. Haberer even forbade Crédit Lyonnais' own team of internal auditors from inspecting the subsidiary's accounts for possible problems. That seemed safe enough while it was apparently providing its parent with substantial profits. Yet a more sober analysis later carried out by the Cour des Comptes concluded that inadequate provisions and tortuous legal mechanisms had concealed the true state of Altus, which lost Ffr5 billion between 1990 and 1993.

Similar anarchic structures existed in other state-owned companies too. At GAN, the insurance group, the chairman François Heilbronner oversaw the purchase of a controlling stake in CIC, a network of 12 regional French banks. It was part of his strategy of *bancassurance*, designed to create a powerful combined financial group that would use the banks' branches around the country and their lists of clients to sell insurance products. But it was also an over-ambitious attempt at empire-building in a business which the insurer did not understand and was ill-equipped to manage. The 12 chairmen of the different CIC banks were fiercely proud of their autonomy. When GAN arrived, they resisted attempts to come under the influence of their new owner. Each remained appointed directly by the government without even the say of the head of GAN. It was a recipe for disaster. One subsidiary of the group in particular indulged in a reckless expansion in lending to property developers just as the market was turning sour. GAN was ultimately forced to assume the huge losses, which make up a large part of the state rescue plan the government was forced to broker in 1997 and which is likely to cost taxpayers up to Ffr23 billion.

The silence of the boardroom

Compagnie de Suez could not have adopted a more suitable corporate logo after its privatization in 1987. The mighty financial and industrial conglomerate that had once built and operated the Suez canal chose to represent itself as an archway held together by a bright red keystone. It symbolized perfectly the immense stresses and mutual dependence between the new owners of the group and the companies which had bought their stakes from the state. Suez was the epitome of the French system of 'core' and 'cross' shareholdings that tightly bound its biggest investors together. It was a system that seemed to offer protection and support, but which was riddled with conflicts of interest and would ultimately prove highly destructive. It originally responded to the problem dubbed by the *inspecteur des finances* Michel Albert 'capitalism without capital'. It fell victim to what might be more accurately called 'capitalism without capitalists'.

When the centre-right government of Chirac launched a programme of privatizations after its election in 1986, ministers were faced with a challenge. While they approved of the free market, there were limits to their liberalism. With an under-developed French stock market, a lack of pension funds and little domestic money available for investment, they were afraid that the nationalized groups they put up for sale would be swallowed up by foreign corporate predators. Jacques Friedmann, a classmate of Chirac at ENA, and his assistant and fellow *inspecteur des finances* Jean-Marie Messier, came up with the idea of core, stable shareholdings or *noyaux durs*. The concept was nothing new. Indeed, it drew on an approach dating at least from the 1960s which had already been used by both Suez and its long-standing rival Paribas until they were nationalized in 1982.

A small group of 'friendly' corporate investors would acquire a significant proportion of the shares in the newly privatized groups, and take boardroom seats. In doing so, they would form an alliance powerful enough to scare off hostile buyers and even block potential take-overs. The friendly investors often included UAP, to which Friedmann would later be parachuted in as chairman, and Crédit Lyonnais. The proportion of shares bought in each company by the state-owned insurance groups – often 5 per cent or more – exceeded the conservative guidelines laid down by fund managers designed to spread risk as widely as possible. But the objective was more political than to earn the best return for the policyholders whose money had been entrusted to them. In more extreme cases, cross-shareholdings developed in which two companies would buy a proportion of each others' shares and their chairmen would sit on each others' boards. Suez was linked in this way to UAP, the petroleum giant Elf and the building materials group Saint-Gobain.

The original idea was that such arrangements would only last for two or three years until the newly privatized groups had become strong enough to fend for themselves. But once in place, the mechanisms stuck. The result was a system characterized by the influential businessman Marc Viénot in a critical report on French corporate governance in terms of the children's song *'je te tiens, tu me tiens, par la barbichette'* or 'we've got each other by the short and curlies'. It certainly protected the companies concerned from hostile takeovers. But it also generated corporate

sclerosis, as a cosy group of directors protected their own interests rather than acting on behalf of the company and its shareholders, or as a check on the excesses of the chairman. At Suez,
there was a complete deadlock. 'It was the example *par excellence*
of what bad French capitalism could be,' says one insider. 'If the
minutes were complete, they would show that nobody ever
asked about Suez's interests in reaching any decision.' Businesses
were bought and sold because the transaction suited one or
more of the other companies with a seat on the board, such as
the purchase by UAP from Suez of the German divisions of the
insurer Victoire. Other deals were halted because they posed a
threat to the activities of the group's shareholders. France's two
leading rivals in the utilities field, Lyonnaise des Eaux and
Générale des Eaux, both had investments in Suez, which they
had no interest in seeing emerge as a competitor.

At Crédit Lyonnais, the board showed little ability to hold
the whims of its chairman in check. François d'Aubert, secretary
of the French parliamentary inquiry, concluded that the bank's
directors demonstrated a 'passivity and a strange absence of
curiosity'. Non-attendance was frequent, information was limited and rarely circulated in advance, and decisions were often
taken ahead of the board meetings. Personalities such as Jean
Pierson, chairman of Aérospatiale, Raymond Lévy, the former
head of Renault, and Marc Ladreit de Lacharrière, managing
director of l'Oréal at the time, rarely posed embarrassing questions. They were to subsequently argue that the board's power
was limited, given that the state owned the bank and directly
appointed its chairman, and that they did not therefore have the
same role, responsibility or power as in a private company. It was
true that, as in other state-controlled companies, the French
cabinet made the decision on who would be chairman – even if
it went through the rigmarole of formally naming someone to
the board which then subsequently 'elected' them. But the
limitations on the bank's directors did not prevent them from

pocketing their fees, rubbing shoulders, or basking in the prestige that membership of the board gave them at the time.

The state's own representatives on the board were equally restrained in meetings. The explosion of nationalizations in the early 1980s meant that there were many demands for representatives of the Treasury to be directors of state-owned businesses. And there was a hierarchical insistence that these representatives should be head of a department. So Crédit Lyonnais was allocated the head of international affairs rather than the more suitably qualified but over-occupied head of financial and monetary affairs. Pierre Gisserot, one of the state's other nominees on the board, told the parliamentary inquiry that sensitive information was not always divulged. 'The board [wasn't] mute. It was informed too late and it was really considered as a recording studio,' he said. The decisions were being made elsewhere.

If conflicts or a sense of powerlessness have limited the effectiveness of the directors of some French companies, fear of the consequences has done so in others. Viénot recalls that when he first joined the board of Société Générale, while it was still controlled by the state, the directors 'hid behind their papers, and did not speak unless they were spoken to'. But more generally, it has been lack of interest or a reluctance or inability to invest much time in each directorship that has been responsible for the weakness of French corporate boards. The tight links between members of the country's business elite mean that a handful of individuals dominate in many of the most influential companies, cropping up again and again on each others' boards.

The marginalization of minorities

They may not have realized it at the time, but generations of investors forged a Faustian bargain when they bought shares in the specialist property bank Crédit Foncier de France. In

exchange for the promise of healthy financial returns, they sacrificed even what nominal future rights they would normally
have had to determine the way in which the company was managed. Like so many similar entities, an ill-judged diversification
in the early 1990s led to heavy losses – and ultimately the
replacement by the government of the chairman. But the difference was that while the state dictated who ran Crédit Foncier,
it had not nationalized the bank. In fact, it did not own even a
single share. It was only in 1996, under a centre-right rather than
a left-wing government, that the state acquired the bank in an
effort to staunch its losses.

Founded in the nineteenth century to help fund Baron
Haussmann's ambitious reconstruction of Paris, Crédit Foncier
became the principal vehicle after the second world war for a
programme of government-backed mortgages for those on low
incomes. With its lending underwritten by the state, which paid
a steady commission on its activities, the company was comfortably profitable. Quoted on the stock market, it built a reputation
as a sure investment, something that could be safely recommended to the 'widow of Carpentras'. But unlike most companies, in which the shareholders have at least some say in who
runs the company, the state unilaterally appointed the bank's
chairman or 'governor' as well as other top executives and board
members. The nominations provided a comfortable sinecure for
top civil servants nearing the end of their careers with nowhere
else to go – until things started to go wrong.

Similar arrangements to limit the powers of shareholders
applied to other companies. During the era of nationalization in
the early 1980s, as well as the '*ni-ni*' period of neither privatization
nor nationalization during Mitterrand's second presidential
term, there was no question of diluting the state's control while
the socialists were in government. But nor was the state able to
sufficiently finance the desired expansion of those enterprises it
owned. So it introduced a form of capital without representation,

of shares without voting rights, called *certificats d'investissement*, notably at GAN and Crédit Lyonnais. Investors had the right to inject money into nationalized groups in the hope of healthy returns, but they had no way to intervene in how they were run.

The practice is not restricted to the public sector. Corporate France has long employed a range of devices to limit the voice of minority shareholders, whether individual investors or even large financial institutions that are not represented on the board. When the US Disney Corporation decided to open its Eurodisney theme park outside Paris in the late 1980s, it allowed local investors to take a 51 per cent stake in the company. But when financial difficulties hit in the mid-1990s, investors discovered that the real power lay not in the quoted business in which they owned the majority of the shares, but in a separate holding company governed by an obscure piece of legislation: the *société en commandite par actions*. Disney had exploited a special legal form which allowed it to offer equity to others but to keep all the control for itself. It had used a device already employed by a number of well-known and long-established French groups, from the tyre manufacturer Michelin to the venture-capital group Siparex.

A range of other techniques also help restrict shareholder power. Many companies award double voting rights to the shares held by certain investors, ensuring that they have more power than others. The drinks group Pernod Ricard and the advertising agency Publicis are among many with shareholder pacts by which family members or other influential investors consult with each other before changing the size of their holdings, and sell to each other rather than to outsiders. Some companies have even imposed limits on the total number of votes that a single shareholder can cast. Danone introduced a maximum of 6 per cent in 1993, for example. All are systems which can reward long-term shareholder loyalty and prevent destructive hostile bids. But they also limit the threats to remove inefficient or incompetent incumbent managements.

If rights to vote are restricted, so is access to information. In most French companies, it is very difficult to discover even who holds shares. While in the UK, for example, a full list of investors with their names and addresses can be publicly consulted, allowing them to group together, the majority of French shares are held anonymously via banks. Communicating with them all is laborious if not impossible, preventing the 'proxy solicitations' that are common in the US, whereby groups of minority shareholders club together to vote for or against resolutions at a company's annual general meeting. There is also considerable opacity surrounding the larger shareholders, who under French law are not obliged to disclose how much of a company they own but only when they increase or decrease their ownership beyond a few significant thresholds such as 10 per cent and 33.3 per cent.

French executives also hate to reveal their own remuneration, and the details they are obliged to disclose by law are minimal. Marc Viénot in 1999 dismissed demands for greater transparency as *voyeurisme*, and recommendations for greater openness from the employers' federation in January 2000 did little to modify the status quo. It suggested that all salaries and stock options of the top executives could be lumped together into a single anonymous sum, buried in the financial notes to the accounts. Jacques Calvet, the former chairman of the car manufacturer Peugeot, even famously took the *Canard Enchaîné* to court for publishing his tax bill, which showed that he had paid himself a handsome salary increase even as he was demanding austerity from his employees.

There are similar weaknesses in more general accounting information, restricting the ability of shareholders, regulators and analysts alike to understand the true health of French companies. In the 1992 accounts of Crédit Lyonnais, for instance, note 24 mentions in a single phrase the creation of Ffr1.3 billion in 'general provisions' against loans and investments that might never be paid back. It was a sum calculated in a manner which

Kevin Pilgrem, an auditor at Coopers & Lybrand who worked on the accounts, described in more explicit terms in internal documents as 'minimalist'. Yet the figure had been endorsed by the Treasury, the Bank of France and the Banking Commission, not to mention by Haberer himself, who was ultimately responsible for hiring the auditors and paying their Ffr7 million annual fee. Everyone hoped that the property sector would recover in the following year, allowing the losses to be gently staggered or offset by other profits and never even publicly revealed. 'Once the highest French authorities had taken this position, we considered that we could simply certify the accounts with this mention,' Albert Pavie, one of the auditors, told the parliamentary inquiry.

In other words, there was a form of heavy collective persuasion by management, regulators and the state to avoid any public statement by the auditors that would weaken the bank. It was a form of pressure renewed, incidentally, for the 1993 accounts under the new chairman, Jean Peyrelevade. Pavie says that he had not planned to approve the accounts, and finally did so only after a series of meetings with regulators – 'in the interests of Crédit Lyonnais and of Paris as a financial centre' – who were keen to avoid anything that might weaken the bank. It was a softly-softly approach, common among banking auditors around the world, which may arguably have been necessary to avoid a market panic and a run on deposits. But it was one which certainly did not serve the cause of transparency for the bank's outside investors. And it was one that did not please Jean Arthuis, the centre-right finance minister who was left to renegotiate the rescue plan for the bank and who himself trained as an auditor. He considering suing the firms which had approved the bank's accounts, only to be advised against by his civil servants, who effectively warned him that to do so would risk making auditors more reluctant to give in to the government's views in the future.

Political scape-goating

When Chirac launched a fierce battle in 1998 to nominate the governor of the Bank of France as head of the new European Central Bank in Frankfurt, it provoked irritation among many of his European partners who thought the decision had been resolved months before. But it also seemed a peculiar act for a president who had two years earlier hinted in a television broadcast that he believed Jean-Claude Trichet bore personal responsibility for failing to do more to highlight the problems at Crédit Lyonnais. When it had served his interests to discredit Trichet when he was fighting for an interest-rate rise to boost economic growth, he showed no hesitation in doing so. But his attack on a senior civil servant, who had little scope to defend himself, was the latest in a long-running tradition of creating smokescreens to divert responsibility from politicians.

It may well be that Trichet should have acted sooner in his respective roles as director of the Treasury and governor of the Bank of France. He was head of the Banking Commission, which failed in the words of one insider to go 'far enough, fast enough and hard enough' in its examination of Crédit Lyonnais. But even if there had been connivance with his fellow caste-member Haberer, it would have been weaker than that between the bank's chairman and senior French politicians. None more so than with Pierre Bérégevoy, the Socialist economics minister and then prime minister whose humble background was as far removed as it was possible to be from the *inspection des finances*, and whose tragic suicide in 1993 prevented him from explaining his position and placed a taboo over any serious questioning of his role. Bérégevoy was fascinated by Haberer's personality, and gave him a very free rein. It seems clear that the highest levels of the French civil service were aware of the problems at the bank, and communicated their concerns to their minister. But they were brushed off.

Trichet wrote to Bérégevoy in 1989 warning him against CLBN's lending to buy Metro Goldwyn Mayer, for example. He wrote in 1991 expressing concerns about Altus. He advised against the bank taking large stakes in the state-owned companies Aérospatiale and Usinor-Sacilor. Yet his advice was systematically ignored. Bérégevoy once said, 'There's only one real banker in France, and that's Haberer'. And Haberer's defence today is that everything he did was approved by the government, which was his majority shareholder. If it was true, it would represent a serious failure of the autonomy of judgement that he should have been exercising as chairman of a bank. But his decisions appear to have been frequently endorsed by his political masters.

It would be too easy to suggest that the problems of Crédit Lyonnais were the fault of the Socialist administrations of the 1980s, any more than that they were the result of poor judgement over the years by civil servants. After all, the bank had been supervised by many different governments over nearly half a century. More than 60 criminal investigations have been launched into its affairs, and French magistrates are probing questionable deals linked to the centre-right RPR party as well as to the Socialists. Aside from any illegal activities, the way in which the successive centre-right governments after 1993 handled the rescue of Crédit Lyonnais may have proved as costly as the original mistakes they inherited from their predecessors. Speaking to a packed press conference in 1995, Edmond Alphandéry proudly announced that the Ffr45 billion rescue package he had just agreed was a once-and-for-all measure that would 'not cost the taxpayer a penny'. Yet he approved a bail-out mechanism that is likely to end up costing three or more times that amount. He ordered that some Ffr200 billion of rotten loans and poor investments should be stripped out of the bank for sale, and set objectives that two-thirds should be sold off in three years. The result was to create a 'fire-sale' – at a time when the economic sluggishness of France was already depressing prices – which further reduced the amount that could be made good from the crisis.

His successors Alain Madelin, who appointed the commercial court judge Michel Rouger to coordinate these asset sales, and Arthuis, who was in power once the restructuring got under way – came under criticism for political interference in the way some of the more sensitive investments were sold. These included hasty moves to sell the stake held by Crédit Lyonnais in the family-holding company of François Pinault, the businessman and long-standing client of the bank who is a close friend of Chirac. Dominique Strauss-Kahn, Arthuis's Socialist replacement in 1997, did not hesitate to suggest that there had been 'implicit or explicit interference' in the way assets were sold. Yet to replace Rouger, Strauss-Kahn nominated Raymond Lévy, a man whose integrity may not be in doubt, but who sat mutely on the board of the bank during its most disastrous period of expansion. If the 1994 French parliamentary inquiry set up to seek the causes of the losses at Crédit Lyonnais had deliberately set out to throw critics off the track of their own fellow politicians' responsibilities by focusing its criticisms on Haberer, it could not have done a better job.

Complicity and impunity

Soon after his appointment to Crédit Lyonnais, Haberer received a call from René Thomas, chairman of Banque Nationale de Paris and a fellow *inspecteur des finances*. Using the familiar *tu* form, his counterpart said: 'As they must have told you, we agree on the balance sheets between us, I'm top, you're second and we arrange it between ourselves before finalizing the accounts.' Only to find that Thomas gave him a falsely low figure so that he could be sure to outstrip Crédit Lyonnais. It was an example of the regular contact and complicity that took place between members of the managerial elite of state-owned enterprises.

Haberer was often willing to defend his own kind. In the preface to a book on the history of the bank published in 1989, he criticized the author for insufficiently praising the legacy of one of his predecessors, François Bloch-Lainé, the chairman in 1967–74 who 'finally brought Crédit Lyonnais out of the nineteenth century'. Others took a different view. After all, it was Bloch-Lainé who had dismantled accounting systems that provided detailed information on the profits of the bank's different divisions, and removed a system linking employees' pay to their performance. He was in charge at the time of a crippling and costly strike in 1974, which led to an extraordinary agreement with unions that would last for a decade: the bank stopped recruiting anyone with higher education qualifications. The idea was that bankers could be hired as unqualified teenagers and trained internally. The consequence was that, at a time when banking was becoming more and more complex, Crédit Lyonnais was left with a huge skills vacuum among its managers. And Jean Saint-Geours, whom Bloch-Lainé appointed as his managing director, pushed the bank to offer fixed-interest loans to customers in the early 1970s, just ahead of the oil shock that triggered a substantial rise in rates. The result was to push Crédit Lyonnais into the red for just the third time in its 110-year history. It reported losses of Ffr177 million in 1974, which wiped out more than 10 per cent of its capital, triggered a discreet intervention by the Bank of France and forced a recapitalization including a loan of Ffr500 million from the government.

But Haberer knew Bloch-Lainé well, and had every reason to defend the period. After all, from 1973 he sat on the board of Crédit Lyonnais as a representative of the state. Both men were *inspecteurs des finances*, as was Bloch-Lainé's son, who was working at the time in the ministry of finance. So was Saint-Geours.

More recently, so were the successive governors of the Bank of France formally charged with supervising Crédit Lyonnais in the 1980s and 1990s, Jacques de Larosière and Trichet, who had also previously been directors of the Treasury like Haberer. So too were other senior civil servants responsible for regulating the bank or acting as the state's representatives on its board: Pierre Gisserot, for example, a director of Crédit Lyonnais who would later head the bureau that manages the careers of *inspecteurs*; or Denis Samuel-Lajeunesse, a director on behalf of the Treasury.

If Haberer leapt to the defence of his own kind, he was equally scathing about those outside his caste. He dismissively said of his successor Jean Peyrelevade, a graduate of the rival Ecole Polytechnique, at the parliamentary inquiry: 'He lacks, in his culture, to have gone to ENA.' Conversely Peyrelevade, who had every reason as the new chairman of the bank to point a finger at his predecessor, had no qualms in suggesting that Haberer's decision to buy control of International Bankers, the troubled bank run by his predecessor Jean-Maxime Lévêque, may have been the result of 'friendly and Parisian connivance between *inspecteurs des finances*'.

It would be too easy to draw out conspiracies based simply on *consanguinité* or the intimate relations between *inspecteurs*. But the fact that so many of these individuals had worked together in the past in a range of different roles bound them together when for the purposes of their jobs they should formally have had a confrontational role towards each other. Yet it is difficult to criticize former colleagues – let alone superiors. Ariane Obolensky, former head of monetary and financial affairs at the Treasury, told the parliamentary inquiry that 'we have respect for our bosses' and 'Mr Haberer is my former boss. He is someone for whom I have the greatest respect'. Intriguingly, Haberer himself wrote in 1992 that while chairman of Paribas, he was subject to criticism that he may have been treated more respectfully and received more consideration from former colleagues because he was ex-head of the Treasury. In reply, he writes cryptically: 'I have no means of confirming or refuting this assertion'. The tensions are all the more exaggerated when the system of *parachutage* means that those under scrutiny by a civil servant may be a future boss or 'gate-keeper' with the power to recruit them.

What can be said with certainty is that it had little effect on their later careers. De Larosière went on to manage the European Bank for Reconstruction and Development. Trichet was named to replace Wim Duisenberg as the second head of the European Central Bank. Bloch-Lainé had his mandate at Crédit Lyonnais terminated in 1974 but went on a decade later to head Banque Worms, a subsidiary of the state-owned insurance group UAP. The company lost more than Ffr14 billion in property lending in the late 1980s and early 1990s under his tenure. Saint-Geours resigned in 1975 from the bank, but would pursue a distinguished career, ending up as chairman of the Commission des Opérations de Bourse, the stock market watchdog. In between, he occupied posts as chairman of the state-owned banks CIC and Crédit National. It was a seat he would keep conveniently warm. For when Haberer was ousted from Crédit Lyonnais, he was not sacked but instead transferred for the next six months to the chairmanship of Crédit National. He subsequently moved into retirement, but was allowed to keep his generous pension, chauffeur-driven car, secretary and an office.

There were worse abuses elsewhere. Several senior executives passed into accelerated early retirement at Crédit Foncier de France once the state took the matter in hand. Yet one left with a Ffr2.15 million redundancy package, only to assert his rights to be re-integrated on a comfortable salary to a position with his previous employer: the Treasury. Arthuis attempted to annul the decision, but he was overruled by the courts.

The end of the beginning

When Jacques Friedmann grabbed the microphone at the 1995 annual general meeting of Suez shareholders, he was setting off a new phase in the evolution of French capitalism. In an all but unprecedented public upbraiding, he lambasted the chairman, Gérard Worms, for the way in which he had been holding secret talks with potential partners and for the apparent lack of strategy of the group which had dragged it into huge losses of nearly Ffr5 billion. There were personal reasons for the attack, not least Worms's opposition to Friedmann's proposed merger plans with UAP, the group of which he was now chairman. But it marked a phase of more aggressive pressure by shareholders that would push Worms to resign, and set in train a wide-ranging restructuring of the group. Within two years under its new head, Gérard Mestrallet, its activities had been streamlined, businesses sold off and most of its cross-shareholdings unwound, and it had merged with the utilities group Lyonnaise des Eaux.

In the second half of the 1990s, many aspects of old-style French capitalism were being called into question. Pressure from domestic and international competitors, top management changes, the demands from more aggressive – and often foreign – investors and from customers all conspired to bring about change. The transformations taking place in the public sector played an essential role. A mixture of ideological evolutions and a simple desire to be rid of loss-making companies motivated governments of left and right alike to continue to sell off the rump of state-owned businesses. The property and economic crises of the early 1990s dragged many financial companies heavily and abruptly into the red. The sell-offs that followed opened the way for considerable corporate restructuring. By the end of the decade, just a handful of companies remained in state hands. Successively GAN, UAP and AGF in the insurance sector, and CIC and Société Marseillaise de Crédit among the banks, had been sold. By 1999, even Crédit Lyonnais itself, one of the most problematic of all, was ready for privatization. The same was gradually happening in other state-controlled sectors, as minority stakes in France Telecom and Air France were put up for sale.

The state's inability or unwillingness during the 1980s and early 1990s to provide sufficient investment capital for many nationalized industries had left them fragile. Its attempts to force them to absorb other loss-making state enterprises, such as both Crédit Foncier and Comptoir des Entrepreneurs for AGF, added further to their weakness. The lack of tough management decisions to reduce the size of the workforce, at a time when the economic growth of the period would have made the transition relatively painless, left them with a high cost base, creating a far greater challenge in trying to cut the number of employees at a time of high unemployment and low growth. When such vulnerable companies were introduced on the stock market, it was only a matter of time before they were swallowed up by aggressive predators more able to take such tough decisions.

In banking, Crédit National was soon acquired. In the insurance sector, only some last-minute face-saving gave the appearance that the giant Axa had 'merged' with rather than swallowing up UAP. Generali of Italy broke multiple taboos by not only launching the almost unprecedented spectacle of a hostile bid on the French group AGF within months of its privatization, but also by being a foreign company. The government may have attempted to stall Generali's bid on administrative grounds, but no alternative domestic bidder came forward with sufficient funds. The price of finding an alternative 'white knight' saviour was to let AGF fall into foreign hands. It was bought by Allianz of Germany. The cosy world of *entente* between competitors in many business sectors was breaking down.

It would be too much to say that such events represented the beginning of the end for French-style capitalism. At Suez, for example, Friedmann may have helped bring about reform, but he was criticizing the management and structure of a company that he had helped create and run. He was part of a generation that was being forced to adapt. The centre-right administrations of the mid-1990s still preferred 'Franco-French' solutions when they sold off companies. The approach was taken up with even fewer complexes by the socialists. As Crédit Lyonnais was geared up for privatization on the stock market, the preferred solution that emerged was for a core group of friendly shareholders to take a significant proportion of the equity, protecting the bank from too swift a takeover. Crédit Agricole, the mutualist bank, was ultimately allocated more than 10 per cent of the shares in the sale in summer 1999. And Peyrelevade, its chairman, was no outsider but a Polytechnicien who had almost been nominated by the Socialists instead of Haberer to run the bank a first time in 1988. But by the late 1990s, the era during which the state could dictate events, control companies and use them as instruments of its own policies was finished.

Haberer's real misfortune was to be among the last of the previous generation, a servant of the old regime at a time when the state was losing or relinquishing its powers in financial institutions. He was a victim of political *alternance* and economic transformations which meant he no longer had the job that he believed he had, nor the skills to cope with the challenges he faced. While placed under formal investigation by magistrates in late 1998, he is unlikely to receive any criminal sanction. But in a sense, he has already paid dearly. For a man of his personality, the criticism he has received has destroyed his reputation. And perhaps worst of all, since the 1994–95 edition, his name has been removed from *Who's Who*. For the extremely proud bearer of a *légion d'honneur*, that is probably the worst punishment that anyone could have inflicted.

The extremes of power

They were four hateful, insensitive and inaccurate words that few public figures anywhere in the world would have dared say – and fewer still would have risked repeating. But for Jean-Marie Le Pen, leader of France's extreme right-wing National Front party, they formed a phrase that he would apparently relish. For him, uttered first in a radio interview in 1987 and numerous times since, the extermination of the Jews in the Holocaust was merely 'a point of detail' in the history of the second world war.

For a politician who has repeatedly taken legal action against journalists who call him racist, Le Pen has accumulated more than his fair share of fines and other punishments in the French courts: in 1987 for provoking hatred, discrimination and racial violence when he talked about 'a real invasion' of immigrants; in 1993 for a rhyming 'play on words' between the surname of the minister Michel Durafour and a crematorium; in 1997 for calling Fodé Sylla, head of the anti-racist group SOS-Racisme, a 'big, mad zebu'; and in both 1991 and 1997 for his 'point of detail' remarks.

Yet – in one of the ugliest of France's exceptions – the National Front and other kindred extreme right-wing parties have become a significant political force. After a decade of obscurity following its creation by Le Pen in 1972, its influence exploded in the 1980s and 1990s. In perhaps the high point of his career, Le Pen himself won 15 per cent of the vote in the first round of the presidential elections in 1995, and in the same year his party scored a first by gaining control of three significant-sized towns in the south of France. In the general elections of 1997, it repeated its 15 per cent score and in 1998, it gained decisive power as a member of ruling right-wing coalitions in five regional councils elected across the country.

One reason behind the party's support is undoubtedly a vein of racist sentiment among the French. Jews remain a periodic target for Le Pen's tongue, but he has chosen above all to turn the newer immigrant groups living and working in the country into scapegoats: notably those with ethnic origins in France's former colonial territories in West Africa and in the Maghreb – in Tunisia, Morocco and Algeria. In doing so, he has tapped into contemporary concerns not just about immigration, but over the very nature of the distinctly French concept of national identity.

But the extreme right has succeeded in winning the support of voters far beyond this group. It has acted as a barometer for the underlying frustrations which successive political parties in government have failed to successfully resolve or often to even meaningfully discuss: unemployment, urban juvenile delinquency, changing social values and growing global competition that have seriously destabilized the French as they are forced into a painful adjustment after the relative comfort of their post-war economic boom. The party of the extreme right has also formed a channel for the feeling of frustration at the corruption scandals that have gripped its political rivals.

Le Pen's personal capacities as an exceptional orator and a potent *provocateur* have certainly helped his party win support. And he has shown considerable political savvy in exploiting every opportunity thrown his way. But the National Front has also benefited from the cynical manipulation of its political opponents. It has served the Socialist party under both François Mitterrand and Lionel Jospin as a way to split the vote of their right-wing rivals in successive elections. And it has even provided many of the leaders of intensely divided centre-right parties with a rare common target that they can attack, in order to better define themselves.

The electoral support for the extreme right reflects the accumulation of the failures of France's mainstream political elites to come to terms with the problems and sentiments of a large section of popular opinion in the country, on whom they have traditionally turned their backs. Its relative success is a depressing testament to the problems that challenge the country today.

The ugliest meets the most shameful

There are not many languages in the world that have a special word for 'unemployment', distinct from the word for 'employment'. But over the last few years, *chômage* has taken on that role in French, symbolizing the persistence of the phenomenon. If strong electoral support for the National Front is one of the ugliest of the country's exceptions, substantial unemployment is one of its most shameful. It would be hard to argue that the two were not connected. At nearly 10 per cent of the workforce or more than 2.2 million people, France has one of the highest rates of joblessness within the EU. It is true that such stark figures can be nuanced, that they may conceal a significant black economy and that they include some who receive a comfortable level of social security benefits. Equally, there is no doubt that other countries such as the UK have indulged in numerous statistical manipulations to reduce their reported levels of unemployment over the years, which make international comparisons fraught with difficulty and inaccuracy. But by the same token, a

1997 study by the Commissariat du Plan suggested that the 'true' rate of French unemployment is also much higher than the official figures, standing at nearer to 7 million people. Few families are not touched in one form or another by its effects.

Yet the paradox is that unlike the more cyclical pattern it has followed in other countries, rising during recession and falling during periods of stronger economic growth, unemployment in France has behaved more obtusely. During the 1980s and 1990s, it has acted like a ratchet, increasing during slumps but reducing far more modestly if at all during booms. Much unemployment has not been associated with the financial difficulties of employers, but has come instead at a time when they have been reporting high and growing productivity. Businesses have generated greater wealth without a corresponding increase in job creation. Many explanations have been put forward, but there is a broad consensus – from the Paris-based Organisation of Economic Cooperation and Development, to Michel Camdessus, the Frenchman who until February 2000 ran the Washington-based International Monetary Fund – that it relates at least in part to the rigidities of the French labour market.

The heavy and rising social security and other taxes levied on employers mean that the total costs of employing a worker are close to double the wage they receive. Until reforms proposed in 1998, the multiple layers of 'professional tax' levied on companies by local authorities were calculated on the basis of staff numbers and investment levels: the most effective possible incentives to dissuade companies from hiring. And successive regulations with good intentions have had the opposite effect: a law to make it difficult to fire anyone aged over 50 has meant that few employers are willing to hire people over that age. Another making compulsory the creation of works councils in companies of more than 50 people has created a boom in businesses which are just below the threshold. Legislation restricting how to fire employees with long-term contracts means that more and more are being hired on short-term ones with far less security. And the imposition of a relatively high minimum wage has acted as a strong discouragement for employers to recruit entry-level staff. There is a clear correlation between increases in the minimum wage over the past decade and the rise in unemployment among inexperienced, young and unskilled workers.

Successive French governments of left and right have done little to tackle such underlying problems. The most significant – and controversial – labour market proposal put forward by Jospin's left-wing government in 1997 was to introduce a 35-hour maximum legal working week. Yet the Socialists' election manifesto on the subject barely mentioned its effect on job creation as a justification, stressing instead the need to create greater leisure time. Although the idea that reduced working hours will create the need for new jobs sounds attractive, the experience has proved far more ambiguous. Many companies have reasoned simply that their labour costs will rise as a result of the measures and that they need to cut costs in order to boost productivity in response, often by reducing staff numbers in anticipation. The Jospin government's other significant labour market proposal has been a programme of state-funded job creation. It is a humane and arguably necessary measure to provide the young unemployed with a first job and initiation into the culture of work. But it requires substantial public money that will demand extra taxation. And it risks competing with some equivalent jobs already provided by the private sector, while creating short-term jobs with few prospects for promotion or training.

If incumbent French governments have done little to reduce unemployment or even to propose concrete solutions, it should be no surprise that the simplistic solution of repatriation touted by the National Front have found a sympathetic ear among those who feel most threatened. The growth in support for the party over the last few years has come above all from the relatively unskilled and manual workers, as well as from shopkeepers and small business owners, who feel the pressures of the state most directly. No surprise too that the National Front's equally demagogic promises for tougher law-and-order policies should have been well received by those living in inner city areas where crime and delinquency have grown hand-in-hand with high unemployment. The party's proposed solutions may not be realistic, but they show a concern for the daily worries of voters that are often neglected by France's leading parties. As the proportion of blank and spoilt ballots has illustrated in recent elections, there is a significant and growing protest vote that finds no response to its preoccupations in the solutions of the traditional left and right.

Political scleroses and policy vacuums

You might have thought that being prime minister of France was a full-time job. But it was clearly not enough to keep Alain Juppé busy. Until his general election defeat in 1997, he not only led the centre-right government, but also managed to be head of the RPR, the ruling party founded and led by Jacques Chirac, who had at least relinquished the role once elected as president of the republic in 1995. But Juppé also found time to be mayor of Bordeaux, one of France's largest cities. His multiple jobs illustrated the intense centralization of the domestic political system, with the accompanying and thoroughly ingrained system that goes with it of 'cumulation of mandates': national politicians frequently also hold local, regional or European parliamentary seats – not to mention a range of positions with quasi-governmental bodies. In a country so centred on decision-making in Paris, that might make some sense: those whose power is entirely removed from the capital have little chance to have their voice heard or their vote counted. But it also creates a system of co-option, and limits the scope for any counterweight to bring about change in the interests of the regions. And it allows a small number of politicians to amass considerable power, accumulating a range of different positions for themselves while denying a larger number of citizens the possibility of attaining meaningful elected office.

The cumulation of mandates makes any fundamental administrative reform all but impossible. In a recent example, when Jospin proposed cutting down the number of mandates that a politician could hold, the Senate quickly voiced its opposition. The result is a country with an extraordinary number of different elected positions, with 550,000 politicians running the country's 36,700 different local communes alone. Others control cantons, municipalities, urban regions, departments and regions, right up to national posts as senators, deputies, president and the seats in the European parliament. It is a system that is not only wasteful of resources, but which also creates an enormous brake on reform. With one or another set of elections nearly always on the horizon (and very often one of their own mandates among those at stake), French politicians have a vision that is even more short-term than most of their counterparts in other countries. They are nearly always thinking about the next campaign, in a way that limits their freedom to take decisive action. In 1994–99 alone, there were more than eight elections at these different levels.

French politics also reflects the national trait of fierce individualism, with multiple parties competing and periodically splitting under the influences of different headstrong leaders who are incapable of working together. It is evident on the political left, where the Socialists in the ruling left-wing coalition formed in 1997 compete with the Mouvement des Citoyens, the Parti Radical, the Communist party and the Greens (just one of three different environmental parties). Not to mention the more extreme hard-left Lutte Ouvrière, which won seats in regional assemblies in the 1998 elections, and its

even more obscure rivals which won seats in the European Parliament in the 1999 elections, such as the Ligue Communiste
Révolutionnaire. The only compensation is that the extreme
right also does not escape the trend, and has recently severely
divided its own vote. Bruno Mégret, Le Pen's *dauphin*, was
expelled from the National Front in late 1998 and formed the
rival National Republic Movement. And Philippe de Villiers
briefly joined forces with the former Gaullist Charles Pasqua to
create the anti-European Rassemblement Pour la France (RPF),
drawing off voters in a less extreme direction before splitting off.

But nowhere is the situation worse than on the mainstream
political right. After all, France is an inherently conservative
country in which the majority of citizens vote for parties on the
right. Yet the Socialists have won control of the National Assembly three times in the last two decades, and the presidency twice.
One reason is the enormous divisions between rival right-wing
parties which split the vote. The centre-right coalition that governed between 1993 and 1997 embraced the Gaullist RPR, but
also the UDF, itself an umbrella organization containing a range
of different parties. That did not stop rival RPR and UDF candidates competing against one another in elections – not to mention periodically 'independent' RPR candidates to boot, diluting
the vote of any one contender still further. After their electoral
defeat in 1997, the RPR and UDF refused a merger, choosing
instead to create yet another umbrella organization, the Alliance.
Spurned by the UDF for forming an alliance with the extreme
right in Rhône-Alpes in 1998, the local president Charles Millon created yet another party, La Droite. Within a year, the RPR
would change its head three times – from Philippe Séguin to
Nicolas Sarkozy and Michèle Alliot-Marie – in response to
internal feuds and the humiliation of scoring just 13 per cent in
the 1999 European elections.

The consequence of such divisions has been to fundamentally weaken the support of any one political movement. But

paradoxically, the large number of parties has not necessarily led to a broad diversity of ideologies. Many movements have chosen a strategy of attempting to win votes by making all-encompassing promises which offer little by way of a clear or distinctive vision. With the exception of the paper promises of the newly-emerged Démocratie Libérale under Alain Madelin, no party dares claim to be very economically liberal, for example. Listening to the speeches of Chirac or Séguin, it is often difficult to draw a distinction in their interpretation of latter-day Gaullism from much that is offered by the new 'leftist realism' of Jospin. In his 1997 speech to RPR militants, Séguin was as quick as his left-wing rivals to condemn 'ultra-liberalism' and the 'casino' economy of the market, for example. On immigration, law and order, protectionism, the European Community and many other topics, the principal parties have created a policy vacuum. 'Mainstream' UK Conservatives or US Republicans support hard-line views on such themes. But in France, they have been adopted by the National Front alone. France's parties have adopted a form of 'political correctness', eschewing serious debate on such topics and abandoning them in the process to extremists.

Professionalisation and petty privilege

When Jacques Toubon, the former Gaullist justice minister, launched an ill-fated bid to dethrone Jean Tiberi as mayor of Paris in 1998, the incumbent lashed back decisively. The countermeasures were reported light-heartedly by the national media, but they proved highly effective. They were also very telling. Allies of Toubon in the city hall were deprived by Tiberi of the privileges to which they had long been entitled: offices, newspaper subscriptions, and – most painfully – their chauffeur-driven cars. It would be one thing if such perks were available simply to government ministers and other top officials. But in

France they are distributed far more widely: to former ministers, to municipal councillors around the country and to some civil servants even in relatively modest positions. When legislation on decentralization in the early 1980s gave more power to regional government, one of the first decisions the local politicians often made was to approve spending on sumptuous new marble-clad headquarters. They formed part of a set of luxuries which firmly separate France's ruling class from those to whom they are supposed to be accountable.

If political incumbents often benefit from a comfortable situation, there are generous mechanisms in place that comfort them even when they lose power. One of the defining factors of France's Fifth Republic has been the high proportion of elected officials who are drawn from the civil service: a heavily over-represented 22 of the 29 initial members of Jospin's cabinet and 295 of the 577 deputies in the National Assembly elected in 1997. Many have the right to take unpaid leave from their jobs, but then to return several years later to a guaranteed position on their previous salary if things do not work out or if they fail to win re-election. Some are even paid by the state while they are neither office-holding politicians nor civil servants. Take the case of Jospin. While head of the Socialist party when it was in opposition in the mid-1990s, his salary was paid by the state, via the government department for which he had previously worked, the ministry of foreign affairs. When he came under attack for this 'fictitious job', he argued in his defence that it was not illegal but a common practice used by many other politicians. That much was true. Under the existing system, politicians who are former civil servants can request to be 're-integrated' into the administrative corps in which they used to work.

After leaving political office in 1993, Jospin had formally applied to return to a job in the ministry at what he judged to be an appropriate level, such as an important ambassadorship. But Juppé, who had been named foreign minister in the new centre-right government, vetoed the appointment of a political rival to such a position. Jospin could therefore claim his salary in 'compensation' for having requested a job which was refused to him. The result is a self-perpetuating and mutually beneficial system for civil servants-turned-politicians from all parties. It is a mechanism that allows them to be paid by the state not only while elected but also while out of office and working for their party – or for their own interests. The loser is the taxpayer and the public administration, which has been deprived of some of its more experienced employees by a deeply embedded network of political conflicts of interest and by a set of rules that perpet-uates a system of sinecures.

Other mechanisms also exist to cushion the fall of the coun-try's politicians. In an attempt to separate the executive from the legislature, new ministers must resign their seats in the National Assembly. That might seem risky in France, with its frequent cabinet reshuffles and changes in regime. In fact, each minister has a *suppléant* or substitute of their choice who takes their place in parliament and keeps it warm for them. Once they are ousted, they recover the position, shielded at least until the next national election. Certain categories of career politician are pro-tected even more directly. Seniority by age, regardless of merit, is given legal status, because election to the Senate is forbidden by law for those aged under 35, and in regional elections when two candidates score exactly the same number of votes, it is the older who is judged the winner. The degree of French political gerontocracy was highlighted in the battle for the succession of the leader of the Senate in 1998, between the 75-year-old incumbent René Monory and his ultimately victorious rival, the sprightly 70-year-old Christian Poncelet.

The result of such safety nets has been to create a profession-alized political class, shielded from the economic and employ-ment uncertainties faced by most of its voters. The large number of politicians who are civil servants, including many teachers, is well out of proportion to their weight in the total population. By contrast, there are few businessmen or others with a background in the private sector. And if French politicians are unrepresentative of their electorate, they are also relatively unaccountable to them. The system of cumulation of mandates means that few national politicians spend more than the weekend with their local constituents, while their other political jobs and financial security mean they have little to fear even if they are voted out of office.

Corruption and collusion

When Eric Halphen, a French magistrate, decided to search the private apartment of Jean Tiberi in June 1996, he got more than he bargained for. He had chosen to target a dangerously prominent individual: the mayor of Paris, guardian of the secrets of a sprawling political system built up by Chirac, his Gaullist patron, ally and predecessor for 14 years at the city hall. Halphen was investigating influence-peddling in the allocation of building contracts for public housing in Hauts-de-Seine, in the western suburbs of Paris. A growing number of witnesses he had interviewed alleged connections with the mayor. In the apartment, he unearthed other material that would lead both Tiberi and his wife Xavière to be placed under formal investigation. His finds included a gun, a quantity of cash, and a poorly written, illiterate 36-page typewritten report on the subject of links with the third world. Accompanying documents showed that Xavière had been paid Ffr200,000 by the Essonne district council for this 'consultancy work', a sum that the Gaullist head of the council later said was negotiated directly between him and Tiberi. The case was one of a growing number of high-profile political corruption cases over the last few years that have helped boost the disillusion of the French electorate with the main parties.

As shocking as the pitiful report were the extraordinary efforts made to block the investigations into it. On the day that Halphen decided he had sufficient grounds to raid the Tiberis' apartment, he followed usual procedure and took with him representatives of the judicial police force. But when the commander learnt where they were going, he withdrew his support. As details of the report leaked out over the summer, political pressure from the centre-right grew to remove Halphen from the case. Based on the argument that an inquiry into the report did not fall within his jurisdiction, it was transferred to Laurent Davenas, the public prosecutor for Essonne. When Davenas went trekking in the Himalayas on holiday in late October 1996, his zealous deputy Hubert Dujardin took charge and made it clear that he would move swiftly to open a formal inquiry. Such a decision would make it far more difficult for politicians to interfere and cancel judicial proceedings. In a last-ditch effort, the ministry of the interior sent a message to the French embassy in Kathmandu to find Davenas so that he could intervene. Senior politicians in Paris went as far as authorizing the charter of a helicopter to search for the prosecutor. Its efforts would prove fruitless. By the time the judge descended from the mountains a week later, the case was already under way. But it would not get far. The Tiberis' lawyer managed to have it struck out, arguing that Halphen had had no right to use information or launch an investigation into a case different from his original inquiry. The lack of independence of the public prosecutor from the country's politicians was shown in full.

Many examples of political corruption, often financed by contract-seeking companies, have emerged in France over the last few years, touching a wide range of businesses and the entire spectrum of political parties. The fact is that scandal unites rather than divides the country's politicians, making the choice all the more difficult for electors. It is perhaps not by chance that the very word *affaires* means both business and scandal in French.

The Gaullist RPR is under investigation in relation to payments by companies made to militants within the party in exchange for the award of business. The Parti Républicain is under inquiry for exorbitant billing to advertisers for its in-house magazines, and for questionable loans via Luxembourg and cash transactions via Switzerland. Nor does the political right have any monopoly on such dubious goings-on. The current head of the Communist party, Robert Hue, and his long-running and now deceased predecessor, Georges Marchais, were both placed under formal investigation in 1996 in connection with substantial payments made by contractors to Gifco, a consultancy arm linked to the party. In the first case of party political financing to come to trial, Henri Emmanuelli, a senior Socialist politician and former treasurer of the party, was stripped of his civic rights and given an 18-month suspended sentence in 1996. The party's Urba-Gracco 'consultancy' operation had levied 3–5 per cent of the value of contracts in exchange for its services in assuring that companies won tenders.

An important distinction needs to be made between different types of political corruption. Illegal party financing by companies is bad enough, given the distortions it creates to fair competition. But it at least mirrors an international problem with which politicians in many countries are being forced to grapple. While somewhat less frequent, however, there have also been numerous examples of personal favours to French politicians in recent years. Among those cases made public because they came to trial, there was the luxurious Parisian apartment made available to Alain Carignon, the centre-right mayor of Grenoble, as part of a package of Ffr20 million in favours granted to him by a water company that is now a subsidiary of the utilities giant Lyonnaise des Eaux, in exchange for being awarded the contract for his town in 1989. And there were payments of over Ffr30 million to Michel Noir, the centre-right mayor of Lyon, during the 1980s and early 1990s by his son-in-law businessman Pierre Botton, for a variety of campaign and personal expenses. There was the Ffr13 million paid by Jacques Médecin, the centre-right mayor of Nice, into Switzerland and the US via the association Nice Opéra that he had created. He fled to Uruguay when the facts emerged. And there was the Socialist mayor of Angoulême, Jean-Jacques Boucheron, who escaped to Argentina after running his town into bankruptcy with public money channelled through a range of screen companies and into his own accounts.

The sentiment of frustration with mainstream parties and politicians as a result of such affairs has been reinforced by a perception of immunity for and complicity among those who have been implicated. As Elisabeth Guigou, the Socialist justice minister, told *Le Monde* shortly after her nomination in 1997, describing political interference in the judicial process: 'In principle, there is no intervention, but in reality one interferes by telephone, in total opacity. I don't want any more of that.' Other members of her party were clearly less convinced. When in the same year the appeals court confirmed the conviction of Henri Emmanuelli in the Urba scandal, Jospin cancelled meetings at short notice to show his 'solidarity', and François Hollande, the new head of the Socialist party, briefly hinted that he would seek a presidential amnesty. In an event which is likely to play a critical role in the 2002 Presidential election, the French were astounded to watch a posthumous videotaped confession of the property developer Jean-Claude Méry released in autumn 2000. He claimed to have creamed off cash from a series of public construction projects, much of which was handed to the RPR in the presence of the party's founder and then mayor of Paris, Jacques Chirac. That Chirac's response was muted – dubbing the claims 'abracadrabadesque' – was perhaps not surprising in the circumstances. But Jospin was just as silent. His party had also been a beneficiary, and Dominique Strauss-Kahn had intriguingly long held a copy of the videotape, which he claimed never to have watched.

The reaction of other leading political parties, themselves more or less compromised by covert financial support, was limited, further fuelling the impression of a conspiracy by the country's political elite. Just as contemptuous was the eight-month suspended prison sentence given to the former minister of justice Pierre Méhaignerie in 2000 for illegal funding of the centre-right Centre des Démocrates Sociaux (CDS) of which he was treasurer. He was conveniently let off because of an amnesty for party funding scandals carrying sentences of less than nine months.

The ugly underbelly of racism

On the night of 8 May 1990, five young men broke into the Jewish cemetery of Carpentras, a historic town in south-east France with a synagogue that dates from 1367. The group, members of a skinhead gang with professed sympathies for the extreme right, set to work vandalizing 34 graves. But they went further still. They smashed open one tomb, disinterred the corpse of Félix Germon and impaled it on a parasol. When the case was finally brought to trial in April 1997, their acts were condemned by the court not only as 'odious' in their own right, but also the result of 'the most primal and violent anti-semitism'. But it was only the most extreme and high-profile of a series of attacks on Jewish burial grounds that have taken place before and since, many not even reported in the press. It was also evidence of a far broader underlying sentiment of racism and racial conflict in France into which the National Front has been able to tap.

During the presidential election campaign in February 1995, three National Front militants set off one evening armed with two guns into a northern district of Marseille to stick up posters in support of the candidature of the party's leader, bearing the slogan, 'With Le Pen, three million immigrants repatriated'.

Bumping into a group of teenagers returning from a music rehearsal, they shot out, killing Ibrahim Ali, a 17-year-old from the Comores Islands. Three months later, at the annual May Day 'red, white and blue' rally organized by the National Front in Paris, a young marcher descended to the banks of the Seine and pushed Brahim Bouraam into the river. Three other militants who were close by looked on passively as he drowned. Writing in *Le Monde* just after the Carpentras verdict, Henri Hajden-berg, head of CRIF, the French council of Jewish associations, expressed concern that while tens of thousands had demon-strated on the streets of Paris in indignation following the dese-cration at Carpentras, far fewer showed up for a march in support of Bouraam, a living person 'whose only crime was to be Moroccan, and on the path taken by those who pushed him into the river.'

With his 'point of detail' and his sporadic comments that there are too many 'foreign' players in the French football team or that there are 'inequalities' between different races of people, Le Pen does not expect or even necessarily hope to win support from the majority of the country's voters. But he knows – and such racially-motivated attacks help prove – that there is a significant and even violent minority to whom his words appeal. A larger proportion still are at the very least not put off by his remarks. An alarming opinion poll conducted in late 1997 for the French Human Rights Commission showed that 38 per cent of the French declared themselves to be racist, compared with 23 per cent of the Germans, 22 per cent of the British, 21 per cent of the Italians and 13 per cent of the Spanish. Le Pen's objective, unlike that of Bruno Mégret, appears to be less to create a party that will ever win sufficient votes to govern France, than to raise his per-sonal profile as a 'champion' of popular sentiment.

Some analysts suggested that the French are simply more open and honest in expressing their opinions than the citizens of other nations. That may explain why they are so numerous in voting for the National Front, let alone in discriminating – albeit more discreetly – in everyday life. Certainly, outside the realms of sports and entertainment, there are very few French men or women of Arab or African origins in high-profile positions who could influence decisions or act as role models, as politicians, newscasters, or senior figures in leading businesses or government administrations, for example. There is often a degree of geographical segregation of immigrants that surpasses those in other countries, creating pockets of social deprivation that defy easy integration. In the 1960s and 1970s, like their counterparts elsewhere, the French constructed ugly concrete towers to help ease the housing crisis triggered by immigration and urbanization during the post-war economic boom years. But where other nations have inner cities with districts of crumbling concrete blocks close to the centre, France has remote *banlieues* or suburbs. It served the mutual interests of planners, businessmen and politicians – notably the Communist party in search of a new electorate – to create such districts, building 'mushroom towns' on greenfield sites around its larger cities. But with the closure of many of the local factories that provided employment, the residents have been left isolated and firmly separated from the more prosperous inhabitants in the mixed use zones of city centres.

Ambivalence towards anti-semitism and other forms of racism is reflected in France's institutions and in policy-makers' reaction to problems of discrimination. It was only in 1995, for example, that Chirac had the considerable political courage to admit the responsibility of the French state for the deportation of Jews during the Vichy regime of the second world war. In the following months, Juppé finally launched an inquiry into the appropriation of Jewish assets during the war and the question of compensation. And Maurice Papon, for years protected by Mitterrand, whose own connection with Vichy and its officials is now well established, was finally put on trial for his role in deporting Jews while deputy prefect in Bordeaux. As the European Commission Against Racism and Intolerance of the Council of Europe argued in its 1998 report, the frequent changes in immigration regulations in France over the last few years have created 'a climate of mistrust and resentment'. It called for improvements in the implementation of laws against employment discrimination, and greater efforts to hire more ethnic minorities to the police force, where it highlighted a number of cases of the ill-treatment of detainees of non-European ethnic origin.

The limits of integration

The mountainous border region of Alsace might seem to be a curious location for extreme right-wing sentiment. Annexed and press-ganged into service in the German army to be sent to the Russian front during the second world war, many Alsatians bear no particular sympathies for the extreme right. Boosted by plentiful local activity and foreign investment, incomes are high and unemployment is substantially below the national average. Urban tensions and delinquency are minimal. Yet Alsace has provided record support for the National Front, voting at up to 25 per cent for Le Pen in the 1995 presidential elections, and in some towns at over 40 per cent for the party in the 1998 regional elections.

One reason is the large number of immigrants in the region, a mirror of the situation in many parts of France that support the National Front. The French demographer Hervé Le Bras has gone as far as to identify a (much contested) correlation, arguing that the vote of the National Front in any region can be expressed in the form of an equation: 6 per cent + (1.7 x the percentage of foreigners). For while there may be considerable anti-foreign sentiment in the country, France has historically maintained very open borders, and has proved capable of absorbing a large number of immigrants. One-quarter of the population today claims at least one parent or grandparent of foreign origin, almost twice as many as in Britain, and far higher still than in Germany or Italy. Bolstered by its proud history as the cradle of the 'rights of man', France has always welcomed political asylum-seekers. In 1881, it introduced one of the most liberal nationality laws of any country, based on the *droit du sol* or the right of anyone born on French soil to acquire citizenship. Its low birth rate, coupled with a heavy death toll in the first world war, pushed it to actively recruit immigrants in the early decades of the century. In the economic boom of the 1950s and 1960s, both the government and private-sector agencies actively recruited foreign labour. The first Turkish labourers to arrive in 1964 at Strasbourg railway station were greeted by a fanfare and a bus to take them to work.

It was only following the oil shock of the early 1970s, and the realization that many immigrants had settled down and established or sent for their families in spite of the economic downturn, that the mood began to sour and the National Front gained a foothold. Much of the hostility towards and fear of immigrants with strange customs 'overwhelming' the country is based more on perceptions than reality. After all, the proportion of those born in North Africa is far lower than those from Portugal and Italy, for instance. Given that immigrants tend to be less well qualified, disproportionately employed in lower-skilled blue-collar jobs, more prone to unemployment and more exposed to social disruption, it is not surprising that they weigh heavily in the statistics for delinquency and related offences. A relatively small number of anecdotal incidents, such as the periodic high-profile police round-ups of suspected Islamic fundamentalists, risks exaggerating the problems that exist.

Nonetheless, the wave of riots and hunger strikes in the mid-1990s which involved *harkis*, the Algerians who supported France against the war of independence and had to be resettled after decolonization, was only one of the most recent illustrations of the difficulties of integration. A study published in 1997 by Insee, the official statistical institute, suggested that on some criteria such as mixed marriages, France was able to absorb immigrants very effectively. Of the 1.7 million couples in 1990 in which at least one of the partners was an immigrant, for example, the other was born in France in 51 per cent of cases. But it also revealed that immigrants had less 'professional mobility' (the shift during their lives towards more skilled jobs) than workers born in France, and less social mobility (a change towards more skilled jobs than the previous generation).

The historical precedents, illustrated by leading politicians bearing names such as Sarkozy and Poniatowski, suggest that France has been at least as capable as any other nation of integrating successive waves of immigrants over time. The difference today is the effect of a prolonged economic recession, which has not just put people out of work but created a culture of unemployment passed between generations. It is partly for this reason that respected academics as much as National Front militants have begun discussing the idea of formal immigration quotas, arguing that France has at least temporarily reached the limits of its capacity to absorb those from other cultures. There is also the question of the darker skin colour of more recent immigrants, and its role in discrimination – even if the state refuses to acknowledge the possibility. Official statistics do not even have categories showing the ethnic origins of the French. Once immigrants have obtained French nationality, they are considered under the constitution to be equal to all others. The principal is laudable. The problem is that the reality of integration is far more difficult to verify, and virtually a taboo to research. As part of the same logic, politicians have systematically refused to sign the Council of Europe's charter for regional or minority languages, pleading 'problems regarding certain constitutional provisions, practical and financial implications and the political philosophy of the Republic'. France even lodged a reservation to Article 27 of the International Convention on Civil and Political Rights, arguing that it does not recognize the existence of ethnic and linguistic minorities.

The attitude reflects a particularly French model of integration. While the US, the UK and other countries have encouraged the idea of multiculturalism, there is little support for such an approach in France. It is a country bound together as much by an intellectual concept of nationhood as by anything based on geography, blood or ancient history. For the historian René Rémond, 'French identity is based on unity, and even unicity.' Embrace the values of the republic, master the language, work within the system and France offers a life that is far more meritocratic than many others. But stand out as someone different, defy the dominant trend, and you risk becoming an outcast. The Human Rights Commission survey suggested that up to 50 per cent of the French considered themselves 'ethnocentric'. That may partly reflect the fact that so many have foreign origins themselves. In their fervour to adapt to their host culture, they show little tolerance for those who refuse to do the same, just like the Americans who, while making play of their ethnic roots, defiantly spout American values and proudly sport the stars-and-stripes flag outside their homes.

Alsace, with its high immigrant population and its history of successive forced integrations into Germany and France, is a case in point. Those with distinctive identities that they have been forced to abandon have no desire to allow more recent immigrants to do otherwise. The Turkish immigrants in the region, with a language and culture which makes them far more 'foreign' than those drawn from the Maghreb, are more visible precisely because they have found it more difficult to integrate. It is perhaps no coincidence that the Strasbourg school district has proved to be one of the most zealous proponents of a policy which began in the late 1980s: to discipline the growing number of young girls (often of Turkish origin) who attended school wearing the Muslim headscarf. It expelled 53 in the period 1994–96 alone. The disciplinary actions – even though frequently overturned by the country's highest constitutional court on appeal – won support not only from the National Front, but from the mainstream parties of the left and right alike, the ministry of education and public opinion in general. They reflected a widespread belief in the French approach to integration, with its secular republican tradition in schooling. It is nonetheless ironic that the expulsions took place in a region which – thanks to the nineteenth-century Concordat agreed between the two countries when it was re-annexed by France from Germany – itself breaks with this model. In contrast to every other part of France, there is religious education in schools, crucifixes on courtroom walls, and both priests and rabbis who are paid by the state.

The failure of damnation

In March 1998, the appeal court of Aix-en-Provence imposed a three-month suspended prison sentence and a Ffr50,000 fine on Catherine Mégret, wife of Bruno and the National Front mayor of Vitrolles near Marseille. She was found guilty of 'complicity to provoke racial hatred' for her comments in an interview in the *Berliner Zeitung* newspaper in the previous year, when she approvingly cited Le Pen's phrase that 'there are differences between races, differences between the genes'. *Le Monde* responded shortly afterwards with a weighty double-page article highlighting policies cited in National Front documents and comments made by its leaders. Some, such as Le Pen's 'detail of history', shocked. But a number of the other quotes would have caused far less outrage if they had been uttered by anyone out-

side the party, let alone by politicians or voters in other countries around the world. The newspaper's approach highlighted
the frequent outrage and indignation in response to the party's
rising influence – a strategy of *diabolization* or demonization
which has manifestly failed to work.

Le Monde cited Le Pen saying that he had a 'limited, elitist'
conception of culture and that he considered rap to be a fad and
a 'pathogenic excrescence', for example. It is a view that might
be rather reactionary, but would be at least as likely to appeal to
the typical reader of *Le Figaro* or the *Daily Telegraph* as to the
average National Front supporter. So might Le Pen's critical
views on the Maastricht Treaty, which he said would 'destroy
our national identity' and 'transfer sovereignty to a European
federal super-state', a view that is shared by the French Communist party and a large proportion of the British population. *Le
Monde* flagged in bold type Bruno Mégret saying: 'Official trade
unionism as it exists today is no longer legitimate. The supposedly representative unions no longer fulfil their duties to serve
employees', an opinion which is not entirely false.

Mégret's views on journalism were perhaps more unsettling.
He called for 'a high media authority' to re-establish the balance
between all the families of [political] thought', and to promote
the 'fundamental values of the country'. But how strange that
there were no similar condemnations when Jack Lang, the
newly appointed Socialist minister of culture, argued in an
interview in 1982 that the parliament and government should
'impose on the radio and television controllers precise requirements and remind them that they are not simply at the service
of their personal ideas, but the cultural and intellectual development of the entire country'. And – as Mégret himself has
pointed out – the insensitive remarks of Raymond Barre, the
former centre-right prime minister who said that not only Jews
but also 'innocent French' were killed in the bombing of a synagogue in Paris in 1980, would have no doubt been exploited far

more had they been uttered instead by Le Pen or one of his progenies.

As for Catherine Mégret's judicial punishment itself, like that of Le Pen and other members of the party over the years, it would have raised eyebrows in the US, where the remarks might have been widely criticized but would no doubt have triggered innumerable offers from lawyers willing to defend her right to free expression. The condemnation largely served to generate ample free publicity for some highly disagreeable and contestable opinions. It is far from clear that the judgement had the effect of alienating anyone from the National Front, or even acting as a deterrent to others from uttering the same sentiments, at least in private.

Time and again, attempts to politically exploit the National Front by trying to isolate it have backfired. Catherine Trautmann, the Socialist minister of culture, for example, won few supporters when she announced that she would ban a magazine associated with the extreme right from the French national library, as though the action would do anything more than limit the material available to serious researchers. And time and again, a vacuum that could justifiably have been filled by others is left open to be seized by the National Front. When Juppé was placed under formal investigation in August 1998 in relation to the financing of the RPR while he was a deputy mayor of Paris, the mainstream parties closed ranks around him, offering only the mildest criticisms. The result was that it was left to Mégret to capitalise on the event and express surprise at the obvious but explosive fact that if Juppé was under investigation, why not Chirac, 'the mayor, who could not have been unaware' of what was happening, no doubt winning him extra votes in the process that could have gone to others with less extreme views had they not been so clannish.

When the National Front decided to hold its 1997 annual conference in Strasbourg, the mainstream parties held a huge demonstration in the city. Yet Alsace went on to report the highest levels of support for the party in the elections of 1998. Throughout the 1980s, organizations such as SOS-Racisme with its slogan '*Touche pas à mon pote*' (Leave my mate alone) – often manipulated by the left for its own political aims – arranged huge anti-racist marches. They may have perhaps helped deter some who would otherwise have voted for the National Front, but they have done little to slow down the party's progressively rising support.

But destroying the National Front is manifestly not the principal objective of its opponents. The relationship between the party and those of the mainstream is ambiguous and symbiotic. If they have not exactly created it, they have certainly found it to be useful on occasions. Rather than attempting to ban the party as undemocratic, they content themselves with periodically lambasting individuals within it. Jean-Marie Le Pen proved a handy whipping boy for politicians such as the Socialist Bernard Tapie, for example, who built his popularity around colourful television confrontations with the leader of the extreme right. Tapie's patron, Mitterrand, went further. By introducing proportional representation in the 1985 regional elections, he was well aware that he was handing seats in the local assemblies to the extreme right. In doing so, he helped divide the mainstream right, reducing its power. The Socialists exploited the same situation in the 1998 regional elections, only rarely offering to withdraw their own candidatures and support the right in order to block the National Front.

The political right has proved equally enthusiastic in demonizing the National Front. From Chirac to Séguin, François Bayrou to Philippe Douste-Blazy, innumerable politicians have all but defined themselves in opposition to Le Pen's party, rather than coming up with more original positive policy stances. It was one of their own, Valéry Giscard d'Estaing, who as president of France in the mid-1970s gave credibility to anti-immigrant feeling when he (unsuccessfully) attempted to launch a series of repatriation programmes. And it was the Gaullists who first dabbled with ideas of national preference, and who gave initial political patronage to the National Front militants Bruno Mégret and Yvan Blot before they split off in a more extreme direction.

The limits to extremism

When Chirac used one of his rare extended television interviews at the start of 1997 to call for a justice system freer from the risk of political interference, it was not by chance. But for his party, it was already too late. Just 18 months into his presidential term, his RPR grouping had come under severe criticism. There were allegations of vote-rigging and corruption against Tiberi, his successor at the Paris city hall. Juppé, the prime minister who had had a solid reputation for integrity, had been tarnished by suggestions that he was taking advantage of below-market rents in city-owned property for himself and his family. The justice minister, Toubon, had played a role in attempting to deflect judicial investigations into the cases against both men.

While high unemployment, the strikes of 1995 and the arrogance of the administration all played a role, there is little doubt that scandals also affected the views of the voters when Chirac called an election in 1997. The electorate chose to castigate corruption, just as it had done in 1993 by ousting the Socialists after a second presidential term for Mitterrand that had been mired by *affaires*. Jospin was able to exploit his own puritan image, backed up by a Protestant upbringing. He was careful to ensure that none of those he appointed to his new cabinet risked being placed under investigation. Hence Robert Hue, the leader of the Communist party and a member of the left-wing coalition, was passed over for a ministerial position in favour of three of his more junior colleagues. Similarly, the taint of the scandal around Jean Tiveri – combined with the right-wing parties' usual hopeless division – propelled the left to power in Paris city hall in 2001.

In other words, the French electorate had shown that it was willing to castigate corruption, and the country's parties had begun to realize the necessity of reform in order to win back support. Opinion by political leaders has started to shift on other topics too. The system of cumulation of mandates has come under increasing attack as part of a broader debate concerning the operation of the Fifth Republic. More superficially, there has been a round of self-indulgent 'born-again' baptisms. The CDS has become Force Démocrate, for example, and the Parti Républicain has been transformed into Démocratie Libérale. Séguin, who took over from Juppé as head of the Rassemble-ment pour la République (RPR) after the 1997 electoral defeat, admitted as much in the magazine *Paris Match* during his cam-paign to amputate the last two letters of the name and call the party simply R, 'so that our movement is not embarrassed or called into question by events from the past'. But he could not even get that far, with his proposal failing to win sufficient sup-port from his militants.

If the blunt instrument of elections has increasingly repri-manded parties for their failures, other counterbalances have also started to come into play to redress shortcomings in the political arena. French magistrates may have been slower and less bold to act than their mafia-fighting Italian counterparts, but they too have begun to take bigger steps and to attack more sen-sitive targets in recent years. None has been more courageous than the Paris-based magistrate Eva Joly, who in 1998 launched a case for corruption against Roland Dumas, Mitterrand's con-fidant and former minister, in relation to influence-peddling linked to the oil group Elf Aquitaine. Dumas denies the charges, but it was an unprecedented act against a man whose position as head of the Constitutional Court – until he finally grudgingly resigned in February 2000 – made him the fifth most senior official in the French Republic. Details of other cases – of Boucheron and Médecin, Noir and Carignon – are known because they too came to trial as a result of judicial inquiries. The regional Cour des Comptes auditing bodies set up to accompany decentralization have begun to catch up with corrupt local politicians.

But the problems are far from resolved. Political manipulation has no doubt played a role in determining which of the many recent corruption cases have got under way, with those on trial often deliberately 'sacrificed'. After all, it was under a centre-right government that the opposition Socialist Tapie was convicted. And while the same regime was in power when the pioneering judgements against the centre-right politicians Michel Noir and Alain Carignon were handed out, both had become outcasts, making many enemies by splitting away from their colleagues in the RPR to create their own reformist movement.

The higher profile given to the fight against corruption has also had an unfortunate corollary. It has given the impression that the mainstream parties are all rotten, or *tous pourris*, in the phrase of the National Front. The extreme right, excluded until recently from power, has been able to use its distance in its favour, giving it the appearance of being 'clean' of scandal. In the same way, it has been able to act as an outlet for voters frustrated with its rivals' limited solutions to social problems, unemployment and other challenges facing France today. Aided by the undeniable distance between France's political class and its electorate, the National Front has proved adept at cultivating the idea that it is a 'grassroots' party in touch with voters – without ever being forced to implement any of its demagoguery.

Now that it has achieved some executive power in municipal elections, the limitations of its own policies and personnel are more visible. Its own record in office begins to look equally unimpressive. There have been cases of corruption and incompetence. It has demonstrated monarchical, undemocratic tendencies stronger than its rivals, with the nomination of the wives in place of those among its leading figures who faced being debarred from office: Le Pen, Mégret, Jean-Marie Chevallier and Jacques Bompard alike.

There will always be an underlying sentiment of racism in France, but not necessarily more than in many other societies nor influential enough to present a serious challenge to power. Sympathy for the National Front appears to be levelling off, with the divorce between Le Pen and Mégret splitting its vote, and the recent reduction in unemployment temporarily releasing the social pressures that help the extreme right to flourish. Election results also seem to show a slow-down in interest. In the 1999 European elections, the extreme right found that one-plus-one equalled less than two, with Le Pen's and Mégret's voters between them accounting for 9 per cent of the vote, compared with 10.5 per cent in the previous 1994 Euro elections. Nevertheless, with a score of 13 per cent going to Pasqua's and de Villiers' RPF, there were still questions about the failure of the mainstream parties to respond to voters' expectations. And a 2000 poll for *Le Monde* suggested that while 80 per cent of the French rejected Le Pen's ideas, only 62 per cent considered his party a danger for democracy, down from 73 per cent in 1999.

Probably the only really effective way to deal with the National Front is for France's mainstream parties to tackle the structural factors that have allowed it to flourish: social problems and unemployment. They also need to reduce their own cronyism and develop a firmer foothold among constituents. That might help address the concerns of the significant minority within the electorate which feels abandoned by its political leaders.

The furthest shore

Sitting in his office in Ajaccio in June 1996, Claude Erignac, the prefect, had painted a bleak picture of Corsica. Just four months after his appointment, the French state's most senior representative on the Mediterranean island summed up the situation bluntly: 'All the indicators are preoccupying. I don't see any sectors which are not worrying.'

Erignac's mission to bring about the government's programme of reform, encapsulated in the phrase 'firmness and dialogue', would be short-lived. It was brutally cut short just 18 months later, in a way that no one had imagined. On the evening of 6 February 1998, he dropped off his wife at the Centre Kalliste cultural complex in the Corsican capital, and parked his car nearby. As he walked back towards the building, two gunmen approached and shot him dead.

His murder triggered widespread revulsion among Corsicans, whose respect he had quickly earned, and outrage across France. It sparked a huge and aggressive investigation headed by Jean-Louis Bruguière, the anti-terrorist judge who brought Carlos 'the Jackal' to trial, and it set in train a series of other high-profile inquiries and hard-line nominations to senior jobs on the island.

Yet in many ways, Erignac's assassination was only the most extreme manifestation – and even the logical extension – of a spiral of violence in Corsica linked to nationalism and criminality, an escalation of events that had been festering for more than 20 years, with historical roots dating back over many centuries.

For while many hundreds of thousands of tourists enjoy the sun, beaches and mountains on 'the island of beauty' each year entirely oblivious to the underlying tensions, the lives of those who live and work in Corsica are touched daily by conflict. What Northern Ireland has been for the British, or the Basque country to Spain, Corsica is to France – with its own characteristic twists.

Violence, corruption, poverty, idleness: there is a cocktail of Corsican stereotypes that drives most of the French to conclude that the island is a nation apart, with rules and traditions that owe nothing to its continental 'master', that there is even a distinctive 'Corsican chromosome'. Responding to the mischievous jibe of certain foreign tourists that 'France would be wonderful without the French', a top Parisian businessman replies: 'That's exactly what we say about Corsica.'

The divide with the mainland is emphasized even more by the significant fringe of outspoken Corsican nationalists, who frequently talk about their 'colonisation', grieve for the suffering and exploitation of their ancestors and vaunt their historical achievements, including universal suffrage enshrined in a constitution during a brief period of independence which pre-dated the French Revolution.

But, in the same way as the Corsicans swallow the ends of their words, leaving the final vowel unspoken, so their view of a tyrannical Paris-dominated state imposing its will does not spell out the full extent of the complex relations between the rocky island and its mainland neighbour to the north-west.

There is certainly a sense of separation that extends far beyond the mere physical barrier of 200 km of sea between the two land masses. But while there are many distinctive aspects to

Corsica, as there are to other parts of France, there are also elements which suggest on the contrary that it is the very epitome
of French society and the way it operates – even if stretched to
the furthest extremes.

In short, Corsica provides a useful way to highlight the functioning of the French state and French society. It is arguably the
exception that proves the rule. But in many ways, it is the perfect
example of the concentration of all the characteristics that are at
work across the country and comprise the French exception.

The dominant state

One word comes up again and again in the conversation of Max
Simeoni. An intense man who helped found the Union du Peuple Corse, an 'autonomist' political party, he talks frequently
about all things 'Jacobin': the centralization of the French state,
its constitution, its manner of operating. 'The Corsican economy has always been weak since France managed it,' he says.

For him, the island has suffered ever since 1768, when France
acquired Corsica from its Genoese rulers, who were happy to be
rid of the troublesome nation that had declared itself independent in 1755. That brought abruptly to an end a brief but golden
period for the nationalists under Pasquale Paoli, who introduced
universal suffrage and a written constitution ahead of the
French Revolution.

Simeoni cites customs regulations imposed by France in
1818 which remained in place until 1913, which had the effect
of de-taxing all imports to Corsica to keep their prices attractively low, but heavily taxing exports from the island to the
mainland, making them prohibitively expensive and undermining the economy of the island.

He also has many more contemporary examples of exploitation or simple neglect. In the economic sphere, he cites the

negotiations with the European Union in the build-up to the Maastricht Treaty in 1992. 'France did not fight for special treatment for Corsica in the way that other countries did for their peripheral zones: the Channel Islands, the Canaries, Rhodes, Madeira and so on.'

There is no doubt about the poverty of Corsica. There may be abuses and frauds, and official statistics are not always easy to assemble, but the island had an unemployment rate in 1999 of 11.9 per cent, more than 1 per cent above the national average. It has an ageing and poorly qualified population that is thinly spread, with the lowest gross domestic product of any of France's 22 regions apart from Languedoc-Roussillon and Limousin, standing at just Ffr106,000 in 1996.

The domination of the French administration has been manifested in many other ways. Simeoni argues that Corsicans were used as cannon fodder, suffering disproportionately high casualties in war. He cites a number of important planning decisions taken in the 1960s and 1970s which he considers were made in a high-handed manner with scant regard for the concerns of the local population and with little effort to consult them. There was a project to install a nuclear power research centre near Calvi; the 'red mud' scandal of mercury discharges off the northern cape that the French state failed to resolve; and a report by the US-based Hudson Institute which recommended the development of mass tourism on the island without seeking the views of the residents.

There were also strong efforts by the French state and its representatives over the decades to suppress the local language, which has its roots in the Genoese dialect of Italian. 'I was in the last generation that was forbidden to speak Corsican at school,' says Simeoni. 'They used to hit children who used it, or who made faults when speaking French.' His anecdote is not isolated. The experiences of his generation helped spark the creation of the island's hard-line nationalists in the 1960s.

'Angèle', a former militant nationalist, says: 'I am not French by language, culture or geography, and certainly not by history.' She recalls a fierce battle in the 1960s in the townhall of Bastia with a French official who refused to allow her to give her new-born daughter the same name as her grandmother. The civil servant considered that her choice was too Corsican. The French state still retains this power of veto for names it judges inappropriate.

Concerned about the potential risk of encouraging nation-alist sentiment, the French state went as far as issuing municipal decrees in the 1970s to ban the music group Cantu U Populu Corsu, with its distinctive Corsican 'polyphonic chants', from singing in the island village of Cargèse. I Muvrini, another group which has won international acclaim and now plays to full houses in the most prestigious venues of Paris, was as recently as the early 1980s forbidden from playing in its own regional capital, Ajaccio.

While such music is now broadcast nationwide, and Corsi-can is today taught in local schools – albeit only as an option which often takes place at lunchtimes or the end of the day – many locals lament the refusal of successive French governments to sign the Council of Europe's charter on minority languages. And they continue to demand implementation of a promise first made by Mitterrand in 1981 and finally voted in 1991: 'the recognition of the Corsican people' as an entity apart in the French constitution. The decision has never been enacted: it was judged unconstitutional by the Conseil Constitutionnel, the highest legal body to rule on such matters.

The spiral of violence

In July 1996, the calm of the attractive seaside port in Bastia in northern Corsica was shattered by a huge explosion. A car bomb went off, killing one man and seriously wounding another. Two years before the death of Claude Erignac, it symbolized a significant step in the development of Corsican violence: an increasingly desperate escalation that risked harming passers-by with no connection to the 'oppressive' French state; and the growing internecine warfare between different nationalist factions.

Drive around the winding mountain roads of the island, and multi-coloured graffiti on buildings and road signs bear witness like geological layers to the names of different nationalist movements that have come and gone over the years. Like French political parties which have often proved incapable of remaining united and coherent over more than a few years, the Corsican factions have endlessly subdivided over the past quarter of a century in splits linked as much to personalities as to policies.

Yet graffiti are the least of the problems in Corsica. Since the mid-1970s, individuals, houses, businesses and government offices alike have suffered far more directly. There have been dozens of deaths more or less closely connected with the nationalist struggle over the period, more than 9,000 bombings – with an average in the late 1990s of more than one a day – and many thousands of threats.

The acts have become so commonplace that Michel Goudard, head of the Banque Populaire for Provence and Corsica, told a French parliamentary inquiry in 1997: 'Bombings are now totally banal. It's become a "normal" form of expression: up to 200 grammes, we consider not very serious; we replace the door and undertake the necessary repairs. By the kilogramme, it becomes much more serious.' He told politicians of the continual psychological pressure in relation to lending decisions on his bankers, one of whom had suffered a sudden nervous breakdown; of the regular armed robberies and a number of instances in which the families of bankers had been taken hostage.

Such events seem a long way from the ideals of the young

radicals who launched the Corsican nationalist movements in the 1960s. Frustrated by both the perceived dominance of the French state and the corruption of the traditional political clans that governed then and now, local militants began to assemble. The Corsican 'struggle' was hardly on the scale of the liberation movements taking place at the time in Africa, south-east Asia and Central America. But it was the nearest equivalent available for the politicized students of the late 1960s, who were receiving their education – courtesy of the French state – in the hot-blooded atmosphere of the universities of Marseille, Aix en Provence and Paris. 'It was the romanticism of youth,' says Max Simeoni. 'We wanted to live a great adventure in the service of the world. There was a sentiment of frustration, that France was treating us like a colony and that we had to cut the umbilical cord.'

Mathieu Filidori, a student in Marseille in the early 1970s who abandoned his studies to become an agricultural union organizer in Ghisonaccia on the eastern seaboard of Corsica, says: 'At the end of the eighteenth century, Corsica was a modern state. But by the 1960s, the eastern coast was abandoned, there was no electricity, the railway had been closed and we still had malaria.' He helped organize the Front Paysan in 1973, which carried out bombings on buildings of the French administration as well as the preferred target: the *pieds noirs* or Algerians of French origin who were forced to resettle after decolonization. The nationalists resented the fact that some had been offered land and financial help by the French government to move to Corsica, assistance never given to the locals, where they took over farmland and established vineyards using sometimes fraudulent methods.

Jean-Pierre Santini, a schoolteacher on the northern cape of Corsica, acknowledges taking part in bombings in the 1970s, while stressing that he always tried to discourage excessive violence. He had been a member of the Front Regionaliste Corse in 1968, and from its creation in 1976 helped co-ordinate the FLNC, the National Front for the Liberation of Corsica, heavily inspired by the FLN movement in colonial Algeria. He recalls the secret codes – with militants identifying each other by passing cigarettes held between the little and ring finger – the clandestine operations and the night-time press conferences with the militants hooded by balaclavas. Since he could not go to a commercial printer to produce official stationery for a terrorist group, he had a rubber stamp made up in the name of a fake company, F.LINAC, from which he scratched out every other letter. It became the way of authenticating FLNC communiqués.

But the thrill of such cloak-and-dagger militantism would be stained red from early on. While Max Simeoni has always stressed a more moderate political line, it was his own brother Edmond, a doctor, who contributed to the start of the bloodletting. Armed with a shotgun, he occupied a *pied noir* wine cellar in Aléria, close to Ghisonaccia, with fellow 'autonomists' in his ARC movement in August 1975. The French government reacted strongly, sending in large numbers of heavily armed police. In the battle that followed, two gendarmes were killed. Another died a week later during a riot in Bastia. The following May, in the weeks building up to Simeoni's trial, the FLNC was born during a 'blue night' of bombings. A period of intense repression began.

It was not long before the militants started seeking money to finance their operations. They created the 'revolutionary tax': initially asking sympathetic businesses for financial support, and then raising the stakes towards extortion, picking on targets such as Club Méditerranée, which operated three holiday villages in Corsica, and the package tour company Nouvelles Frontières. 'It's expensive to be clandestine,' says Yves Stella, another ex-member of the FLNC, who like Filidori and Santini spent time in prison for his activities until Mitterrand granted an amnesty after his election in 1981. 'There are trips to be paid for, support for prisoners and their families. At one point we had 100 prisoners. The revolutionary tax was the least perverse and dishonest system.' For those that were initially reluctant to pay, threats and bombs often helped persuade them.

There would also be companies founded or fronted by known nationalists. The most blatant was Bastia Security, an armed transport company carrying money to the island's banks and shops, which quickly established a near-monopoly with tariffs to match: double those elsewhere in France. It provided the militants with both funding and a source of employment for its members, not to mention the legitimate excuse to carry guns.

With such operations came conflict, as the clandestine movement transformed itself into a form of clan of its own. A first generation of often more intellectual militants began to pull out, to be replaced with more hard-line members often without any real ideology. The original activists had created a multi-headed beast that they could no longer control. Small groups carried out acts linked more to criminality than to political gestures. 'Guns replaced grey matter,' in the phrase of Dominique Bucchini, the Communist mayor of the Corsican town of Sartène. 'Now it's pure and simple racketeering,' says Stella, who like Santini has long since left the movement.

A full-scale split in the movement came in 1989, when Pierre Poggioli and his supporters left the A Cuncolta Naziunalista, the public political face of the FLNC, to found the Accolta Naziunale Corsa after denouncing the organization's mafia-like drift. A year later, Alain Orsoni branched off with his Mouvement pour l'Autodetermination. Each of the three resulting political groups was more or less explicitly linked to armed, clandestine factions, which carried out assassinations of each others' members and turf struggles over businesses linked to one or another group. The divisions were the genesis of a cycle of tit-for-tat killings that would dominate and destabilize the nationalists during the 1990s.

The failure to govern

Robert Sozzi, a militant in the FLNC, had just left his apartment one morning in June 1993. Within minutes he was dead, shot at close range on the way to his car. Still living in the same flat, Letizia Sozzi, his wife, says that other members of the movement killed him in response to what she argues was his stand against corruption. 'They needed an example and he was chosen,' she says. 'It worked. Others are afraid and have kept quiet.' But his death also symbolized the apparent intransigence of the French state. FLNC activists, including a Corsican lawyer, have even boasted that their organization was responsible. Yet it was only in autumn 1998, after a long period without much evidence of any inquiry, that a suspect was finally placed under formal investigation as a result of a link to the high-profile Erignac case.

For all the nationalists' complaints about the dominance of the French state, the escalating cycle of violence that gripped Corsica in the 1980s and 1990s suggested that the authorities in Paris were far from omnipotent. Between murders, bombings, threats, fraud and other forms of crime, most of which have never been resolved, the island seemed no longer to obey the 'state of law' which applied elsewhere in the republic, and which the vast majority of its residents have long demanded. Where the state was not needed, it was over-present. Where it was most needed, it was apparently absent.

There is clearly some hypocrisy in the nationalists' criticisms of the French legal system. All too happy to be immune from prosecution – or subject to amnesties – when their militants were implicated in violence against the state, they became far more vocal when their own came under attack. Their ambivalence and their implication in all aspects of local society in spite of their small numbers have contributed to the contradictions of a system of justice under which all Corsicans have suffered. The question is whether the state has proved incompetent and incapable in its efforts to control the island, or more cynically if it has instead been unwilling to intervene.

There is no doubt that violence in Corsica has deep historical roots. In the same vein as adjacent southern Italy, Corsicans have a long tradition of carrying and using weapons. As Seneca put it: 'The first rule for the Corsicans is to take revenge, the second to live by robbery, the third to lie, the fourth to deny the gods.' Well into the twentieth century, families preserved their honour and resolved conflicts between themselves without recourse to the authorities. Vendettas were widespread, as were acts of banditry, with those responsible going into hiding in the maquis or rural undergrowth. There were 5,000 murders or attempted murders in the period 1820–58 alone. Even now, village weddings and other festivities are celebrated by discharging guns into the air.

The legacy of crime remains strong on the island today, matched only by a very widespread perception of immunity. Dominique Bucchini, the highly respected Communist local mayor whose outspoken attacks on nationalists have made him and his town a preferred target for threats and bombings over the years, is a case in point. No attack was worse than that of 20 June 1996 in which a bomb exploded in his garage, propelling his son out of the adjacent bedroom window and just leaving time for him and his wife to escape the engulfing flames that followed. He says that he knows his attacker and has placed his faith in the law to bring him to justice – but so far without effect.

There are, of course, crimes that go unsolved in Corsica for the same reasons that they do in other parts of France and around the world: lack of leads or of sufficient evidence. There are also particular handicaps that make the job of the police and investigators particularly hard on the island: the difficulty of recruiting and retaining experienced staff; the kinship pressures and aggressive threats that they come under; the considerable workload; the fear of witnesses to come forward and provide testimony; and the culture of silence, *omèrta*, or *acqua in bocca* (water in the mouth) as the Corsicans put it.

Judicial decisions naturally have to be based on reasonable proof, not on rumour. Yet in an island of just 260,000 people, predominantly living in small rural communities, it is difficult to believe that the identities of the authors of many of these unresolved crimes are not known. Particularly given that Corsica has a density of one policeman for every 223 inhabitants, compared with a national average of 435. That gives the department of Haute Corse the greatest concentration of police anywhere in the country, and Corse du Sud the third highest.

There have long been suggestions that the state has been directly involved in infiltrating the leading nationalist groups, and even accusations that its *barbouzes* or secret service agents have themselves perpetrated acts in the name of one or other of the clandestine organizations. In May 1999, Bernard Bonnet, the prefect appointed to replace Erignac and restore order to Corsica, was dismissed and placed under investigation after three policemen said he had ordered them to destroy a beach-front restaurant long operating in defiance of planning permits. Their bungled effort had been designed to appear as an attack by nationalists. The incident appears to indicate highly dubious practices within France's law enforcement apparatus, if not a covert action implicating those at the very top of the government.

Successive French governments have at the very least played a dangerous double game by holding discussions and by bargaining with violent nationalist leaders. Cross-examined by the 1997 French parliamentary inquiry on Corsica, Jean-Paul Albert, general secretary of the association of examining magistrates, confirmed that there were periodic 'interventions' by politicians in judicial inquiries and 'difficulties' linked to policing policies put in place by the authorities.

No incident is more notorious than that which took place at the golf course of Sperone in 1994, and which has become part of Corsican folklore. Tipped off in advance, specially trained police were sent down from Paris, and intercepted a group of FLNC militants red-handed in the process of sabotage. Arrested and brought to the French capital for judgement, they were subsequently released ahead of their trial as part of a negotiation tactic of Charles Pasqua, the then RPR interior minister and himself ethnically Corsican.

But the examples have continued since. When Jean-Louis Debré, his replacement in the government of Alain Juppé, made an official visit to Corsica in January 1996, his message was one of 'firmness' and a refusal to talk to terrorists. Yet he arrived the day after a now infamous night-time press conference arranged by the nationalists near the mountain village of Tralonca. Although it seems likely that the event happened with the approval of the government, the police claim to have been unaware in advance of the operation. Intriguing, given the presence of dozens of journalists who attended the gathering, at which 600 hooded and armed 'militants' declared a temporary 'truce' to allow the minister time to negotiate yet another attempt to bring an end to violence. Local gendarmes took down the details of dozens of car number plates of those in attendance, and images of scarcely concealed faces behind tight balaclavas were subsequently reproduced hundreds of times in newspapers and on television. Yet Debré refused even to answer a question at his own press conference the following day on whether he would open an investigation into the affair.

When a formal inquiry, which has never been concluded, was finally opened 11 months later, it came only after a new escalation in nationalist violence, when militants took the rare step of targeting a high-profile, theoretically well-protected building on the French mainland: the city hall of Bordeaux, controlled by the then prime minister Juppé. It was a precursor of what would happen with the investigation of the death of Claude Erignac, which triggered many arrests and brought an influx of extra policeman to the island. It was an understandable reaction to the death of such a high-ranking civil servant. But it also served to fuel the belief of many Corsicans that they live under the control of an imperious state which is able to devote substantial resources to investigate terrorist actions which touch the mainland, but is otherwise apparently willing to let the Corsicans simply get on with killing or disturbing each other.

The compromised state

A slim yellow tower that locals called the 'minaret' hovered over the luxurious modern headquarters of the Corsican regional assembly building in Ajaccio until recently. It was clearly visible from the road, where an official sign provided details of the construction permit necessary for changes to the building, including the phrase: 'maximum height from ground level: 21.50 metres'. The problem was that the tower was 33 metres high and had not received planning permission. Until its demolition was ordered by Bernard Bonnet, the newly appointed prefect, in summer 1998, it stood as the perfect symbol of the defiance of the law by individuals right to the highest levels of authority.

For if the apparent lack of willingness of the French state to resolve overtly nationalist-linked crime in Corsica is bad enough, it has often been compounded by a reluctance to attack a far broader range of activities which risk disturbing the delicate local social, economic and political balance of power. The litany of cases of abuse that has been identified, but which has not led to any significant penalties for those involved, highlights the dysfunctions that operate across France, but which find their most extreme manifestation in Corsica.

There are a few aberrations in Corsica which have been

institutionalized in legislation or legal decisions. The ancient Miot decrees, for example, exempt Corsicans from the usual French requirement for heirs to provide the state with information on their inheritance within six months of a death. The result has been to create huge uncertainties over the ownership of land, since title cannot be firmly established. The owners may be reluctant to undertake investment as a result, and the sale and transfer of property to others are difficult. Hence much land remains neglected and uncultivated.

The French state has often simply turned a blind eye to abuses. There is José Rossi, head of the Corsican Assembly even though he is under investigation for abuse of public funds and favouritism in the award of government contracts. There is Paul Natali, currently a senator, who was unchallenged head of the Chamber of Commerce for Haute Corse until 1999 and of the regional council until 1997 despite investigations since the start of the 1990s against him for tax evasion and favouritism. Or there is Gilbert Casanova, head of the Chamber of Commerce for Corse du Sud, who owes more than Ffr20 million to the tax and social security authorities as well as assorted banks and regional development agencies. Hardly the most shining examples to hold out of the business community. But they are nonetheless representative. Corsican companies have huge unpaid bills, with very low compliance for VAT, even though it is only levied at a specially low rate of half the normal French level.

Every enforcement agency in Corsica reports threats to its compliance staff and bombs which often handily destroy vital documentation and computers just as investigations are reaching their conclusion. There were two huge blasts at the Corsican Office of Hydraulic Equipment in 1995 alone, for example, and over 150 in the last decade at local tax offices. Yet little effort has been made to take an obvious step, by moving at least some of the administrative functions of these offices on to the mainland to safeguard them from destruction.

Then there is the case of Crédit Agricole, the most important bank in Corsica, which has been responsible for distributing successive programmes of state aid to farmers over the generations. A team of government financial inspectors sent in to examine its records in March 1997 – in spite of explicit threats – unearthed fundamental dysfunctions in the institution. Loans were made without even the most rudimentary analysis of risk; there were favourable conditions for those connected to the management of the bank; false declarations; and diversion of funds to projects entirely unrelated to their objectives. The bank's top management, having initially denied that there was anything wrong, swiftly replaced key members of its local team with a crisis group brought in from Paris.

The real scandal was not the extent of the problems, but rather the fact that the state – like the bank – had been aware of them for years and did nothing about them. It was common knowledge that there were gross abuses taking place in the allocation of farm aid, for example. In 1997 alone, the problems had been raised elliptically during the French parliamentary inquiry on Corsica, and very publicly in the annual report of the Cour des Comptes. A number of the abuses and those guilty of perpetrating them had been identified by a previous finance inspectors' report – in 1993. Yet it was only five years later, after the death of Claude Erignac, and another inspection mission, that legal investigations got under way. The new prefect ordered the destruction of the illegal makeshift beach-front restaurants at Ajaccio. But as one local put it: 'Every prime minister and interior minister in the last 15 years has eaten in them without anything happening.' More than that, many politicians have been directly implicated. 'In Corsica, the mayor is known as Mr 15 per cent,' says Father Mondolini, an outspoken Catholic priest closely linked to nationalist circles. That represents considerable inflation over the take in other parts of France. The situation has begun to improve, but many Corsican politicians still operate against a long-standing backdrop of impunity – while being far from impecunious.

The sometimes deliberate absence of law touches on business and money, but it stretches into every field of activity in Corsica. Take the case of Jean-Pierre Santini, the ex-FLNC organizer converted into upstanding and outspoken civic activist. He wrote to the prefect of Haute Corse in spring 1997 to challenge the legality of quarrying on his local beach near the village of Barrettali, that had been authorized by his mayor. An assistant to the prefect replied that he had requested an inquiry from the regional director of industry, whose responsibilities had not allowed him to provide the necessary information. Over a year later, he had heard no more.

However, the most telling examples of the problem of 'non-law' in Corsica are those that touch directly on political life. Electoral fraud on the island is a standing joke. Dominique Bucchini describes how his opponents in the National Assembly elections handed out voting slips made out in the name of their candidate, along with cash and tokens for the purchase of household equipment. Not all voters have to be present for their voice to count. Indeed, it should come as no surprise that *urne*, the French word for a funeral urn, is also the word for a ballot box. As one former Corsican mayor notably put it: 'I don't vote for the dead, I carry out their last wishes.'

And the presence of the state as regulator of fair elections? Taking advantage of the period of just ten days during which voting registers are open for inspection, Dominique Yvon, a Corsican civil servant in the village of Morosaglia, noticed in the 1989 municipal elections that some of the same individuals were registered to vote in two or three different constituencies. 'I filed an objection, but in 1992 the judge ruled that the case should not be examined,' he says. 'He said that he had recently been appointed, had inherited 1,000 cases and could not treat them all.'

France's system of cumulated mandates means that many

local politicians also have a significant power base outside their region, especially in Paris. Until his death in 1998, for example, Jean-Paul de Rocca Serra was mayor of Porto-Vecchio, a member of the National Assembly for Corsica and head of the Corsican regional assembly under the centre-right RPR party label, after previously being a senator. In 1994, Jean Baggioni, the head of the Corsican executive council and a member of the UDF-RPR centre-right alliance, was also simultaneously a member of the European parliament, mayor of his local village of Ville-di-Petrabugno, a member of the Haute-Corse departmental council, as well as principal inspector for the ministry of youth and sport.

This system of multiple hats has made it much more difficult for successive governments to bring about reform. It is no surprise that some of the more radical policy innovations in Corsica – from the decentralization of the early 1980s to the new authoritarianism of the Jospin government in the late 1990s – have come under left-wing administrations, given that Corsica is generally a power-base for the right. 'The combination of mandates means that local politicians can control decisions all the way up to the highest level,' says Yvon. 'There is no political counterbalance – everything is arranged between them. Even if today they are in opposition, tomorrow they will be in power, so they don't denounce things too loudly.'

Indeed, the 1997 French parliamentary inquiry into Corsica, dominated by the centre-right politicians who were then in government, heard testimony on numerous occasions about electoral fraud. But on the two instances when they interviewed Emile Zuccarelli, the socialist mayor of Bastia who was then in opposition in the National Assembly, for example, they did not ask him a single question on the subject. Mr Zuccarelli subsequently became a junior minister in Jospin's cabinet in 1998, and his own first deputy mayor, Ange Rovere, was suspended on charges of electoral fraud.

For many observers, the decentralization undertaken in Corsica as elsewhere in France since the 1980s has itself been a retrograde step. Instead of taking any courageous move to clean-up or rationalize the underlying institutions, it simply took the easy solution: to add supplementary levels of administration and greater financial autonomy. For an island of less than 260,000 people, Corsica has now has 360 communes, including 150 with less than 100 inhabitants each, two departments each with its own council and elected chamber of commerce, and a regional assembly in Ajaccio. 'Local politicians have became feudal seigneurs with absolute power,' says Yvon.

The limits of protectionism

The *Napoléon Bonaparte* dominates the port of Bastia. A magnificent, gleaming and enormous cruise ship which connects the island to France, it might serve as a proud symbol of Corsican modernity. Many see it instead as another stinging slap in the face delivered by Paris. It is the archetypal outcome of a confused and contradictory national economic development policy with consequences ranging from the ineffective to the disastrous.

The history of the *Napoléon Bonaparte* began with good intentions. In the 1970s, the French state decided to take action to reduce the higher costs of living in Corsica, which are partly a reflection of the extra transport costs. 'It was something very typically French,' says Yves Stella. 'The state decided to abolish the sea.' The idea was to build a 'virtual bridge' with a package of financial aid designed to compensate for the additional cost of the crossing. This *continuité territoriale* now amounts to over Ffr940 million a year.

But the money was swiftly 'captured' by certain interest groups. Looking to the past more than the future, and to existing entities rather than a more innovative way to distribute the money, the state decided to split the funding between the two principal modes of transport to Corsica – air and sea – as a function of the volume of existing traffic. The result is that the vast majority of the subsidy each year goes directly to the SNCM, the state-controlled Corsican-Mediterranean ferry company, which relies for 80 per cent of its business on the routes between the French Mediterranean coastal ports and those of Corsica. And yet it provides little local employment, since its headquarters is based in Marseille. The company makes considerable losses each year, linked to a long legacy of heavy over-staffing, and often has priorities very different from those that would benefit Corsica.

The *Napoléon Bonaparte* is exemplary. One of the world's largest and most expensive such ships, it has far too much capacity to be anywhere near full on most of its trips between Corsica and the mainland. That is partly because it was conceived with the idea that it could be used for other, longer voyages and pleasure cruises. In the meantime, it sits empty for most of the day on the quayside representing a huge waste of investment. As a way to squander money supposedly earmarked to help the Corsicans, that might seem bad enough. But the initial costs of the ship were also far higher than they should have been. The SNCM seemed to be taking a logical decision when it put the construction out to tender. It had a bid for Ffr943 million from a Finnish shipyard. But the contract was instead awarded to the state-run yards of Marseille, which demanded Ffr1.12 billion. The political and economic interests of other parts of France held sway over Corsica once more.

By distorting competition, and by encouraging a monopolistic carrier which needs to be heavily subsidized in order to survive, the French state has helped shield Marseille's dockers, shipbuilders and sailors from economic reality, and contributed in the process to further throttling of the Corsican economy. By often failing to intervene – or only doing so belatedly – in the frequent dockers' and SNCM strikes, not to mention those of fishermen periodically blocking the Corsican ports, it has contributed to the all too frequent isolation of the island. That unions have the right to strike, few would contest. But that they cynically always choose to do so in summer, when Corsican farm produce is ripe and ready to export, and tourists are eager to arrive, represents another severe blow to the island's economy.

In addition, instead of the *continuité territoriale* being used to help promote sensible cost reductions, it is largely distributed in response to two conditions: that there are preferential fares offered to Corsicans, and that all the island's ports are served. The consequence of the former is that there are no incentives to help encourage tourists come to the island and spend money locally, which would help the economy. And the consequence of the latter is to add huge costs, since Corsica has no less than six ports. Where most regions might develop their hinterland infrastructure – notably their roads – first and then worry about links to the sea, the insular politicians have turned things on their head.

Some alternative carriers do exist on the sea routes. There is the CMN, partly owned by CGM, which was itself until recently state-owned, and partly by the SNCM, its principal rival. The situation hardly encourages price battles. And there is Corsica Ferries, a private company run by a Corsican who – spurned by France – set up in Italy and is able to offer competitive tariffs for connections with the mainland without subsidies, suggesting that the money paid to the SNCM could be far better used for other purposes in Corsica.

What is true for sea travel is equally true for the air. The French state's attempts to block domestic competition meant that Air Inter, the state-owned carrier now taken over by Air France, had a near-monopoly over a number of years. Local politicians helped block landing rights for rival airlines – even seasonal charters – which might have helped reduce prices for

Corsicans and lure in additional tourists. CCM, the Corsican-Mediterranean airline, which serves some routes, is hardly a rival, given its shareholders include the SNCM and Air France. Thanks to the *continuité territoriale*, the airlines offer the same system of privileged tariffs for Corsicans – to the discrimination of tourists. And there is the same extraordinary infrastructure: where Paris has two commercial airports, and most isolated mountainous regions in continental France are lucky to have one, Corsica has no less than four – Bastia, Ajaccio, Calvi and Figari – all of them served by regular flights.

If the *continuité territoriale* has been misspent, it may also be fundamentally misguided in its conception. For while it is true that prices are high in Corsica, on average 4 per cent more than in Marseille and 11 per cent more for food, it is not clear that the gap is explained by additional transport costs. The fact that this differential has increased since 1989, when value-added tax was cut to half the level that applies in the rest of France, suggests that some of the balance may have been swallowed by local retailers. The regional competition directorate estimates that profit margins in Corsica are often greater than elsewhere in the country. Yet over a number of years it has brought just a single cartel to court and that only with limited success: a case of collusion among petrol stations on the island in 1989. So once more, the state has chosen an easy financial and highly interventionist form of support, in the form of aid to transporters, and avoided a conflictual and regulatory one that would arguably do far more to help reduce the cost of living for Corsicans and make the island more attractive to tourists.

If the French have practised protectionism on a grand scale, the minority of violent Corsican nationalists, backed up at least tacitly by a larger number of residents, have done so locally through a variety of means. François Ollandini, a successful Corsican tour operator, describes the three 'crimes' used to justify the bombing in 1989 of a modest coastal tourist development of 44 bungalows owned by his sister and her husband, a non-Corsican. They were *spéculation*, because some of the lodgings were to be sold; *spoliation*, because some buyers would not be Corsican; and *bétonisation* or concreting of the environment.

If such action has been taken against locals (although not against other tourist developments linked to certain nationalist sympathisers), it has also been used as a weapon to discourage French and foreign tourist investment. Club Méditerranée closed one of its three holiday villages on the island after a bombing. Just a handful of other large leisure groups and hotel chains are present, while the local hotels are suffering from a long-standing lack of investment. 'Tourism requires lots of capital,' says Ollandini. 'We need big investors. But the few who have come have been threatened.' The result is that Corsica has no more hotel rooms today than it did 20 years ago, and it has neglected more comfortable accommodation in favour of unsightly and often unauthorized camping sites which contribute only minimal benefits to the economy.

If insular hostility has discouraged investors, it has also spurned the fresh energy and ideas of new human talent. While the *pieds noirs* who settled in Corsica in the 1960s may have benefited from resettlement aid not available to the locals, there is little doubt that the motivation for bombings against their property was as much driven by jealousy and racist sentiment as more pure ideological motives. Nor did the local suspicion of non-Corsicans stop in the 1970s. Two hundred teachers from mainland France left in the wake of threats and bombings in 1986–87 alone. The French administration today has enormous difficulties finding civil servants from the mainland willing to serve even short stints on the island. 'We practised a form of regional preference here,' says Ollandini. 'We are a country that exported our children but did not accept others coming here.'

The symbiosis with Paris

For a museum which ought to be capable of attracting tourists and historians from across the world, the three-storey building in the old town of Ajaccio is as disappointing on the inside as it is nondescript on the outside. There are a few cheap facsimiles of historical documents, some uninspiring paintings, a little worn furniture and occasional notices in spartan rooms indicating that their original use is unknown. It seems a strange tribute to Corsica's most famous child: Napoleon Bonaparte himself.

It is true that France's former emperor does also have a slightly more impressive monument in Ajaccio. There is a statue on top of a stone-faced slope engraved in equal measure with Napoleon's military victories and his continuing contributions to contemporary society: the civil code, universities, the Bank of France, the *légion d'honneur*, the Cour des Comptes, the Concordat and the Conseil d'Etat. It was built in the 1920s, and funded by the Bonapartists of Argentina, and sits all but unvisited on the outskirts of the town.

The ambivalence towards the man, just as much as towards the cruise ship named after him, reflects not only the conflicts but also the symbiosis between Corsica and France. For while Buonaparte was born locally, he soon turned his back on the island, even dropping the 'u' from his name to frenchify it, and citing approvingly an aide who suggested that if Corsica could only be pushed under water with a shove from a trident, then it should be. It was also Napoleon who first proposed creating two departments on the island, deliberately launching a form of 'divide and rule', even if he also showed some favouritism to his family home by switching the regional capital from Bastia to Ajaccio.

Their Corsican connections did not prevent either him or his cousin Napoleon III from achieving the ultimate positions of power in Paris. It was hardly the typical outcome for colonial subjects, yet it was a perfect example of how the centralized French state has operated over the centuries: sacrifice your background, play the system and you can achieve great things. The nationalist Simeoni shares this view. 'France is the only European country which maintains an eighteenth-century vision of the nation state,' he says. 'Paris is the only capital that impoverishes all the other regional cities. It sucks in everything. That mentality has been internalized in Corsica. We have become self-colonized, and more French than the French.'

While there are few French of Arab origin or from other former colonies who have senior positions in the administration or in public life, there are innumerable Corsicans. Take Jean-Cyril Spinetta, the top civil servant who now chairs Air France. Or Jean-Marie Colombani, head of *Le Monde*. There is Jean-Charles Marchiani, the politician and ex-high-profile prefect allied to Charles Pasqua, the former hard-line Gaullist interior minister who is himself Corsican via his parents. Not to mention Jean Tiberi, the mayor of Paris, and the 'Corsican floor' of the city hall, where he is surrounded by members of the community such as Claude Comiti, his head of communication.

Like their counterparts from other regions in France, the Corsicans who have moved on to the mainland – and especially to Paris – firmly maintain their roots. The number of second homes on the island has risen from 24,000 in 1975 to 60,000 today, of which some two-thirds are owned by Corsicans. Add to that the numerous romantics who have claimed the place as their own over the years – a litany of top politicians, media figures, showbiz personalities and businessmen – and it is understandable that Corsica has often received a favourable ear and a disproportionate dose of compassion and assistance. The reality is that Corsica may not have benefited from exceptionally large amounts of financial aid, but it has survived far better within the French model than its Mediterranean island neighbours, slowing down a probably inevitable process of emigration and impoverishment.

While the weather may be hotter, the language different and the sense of identity more distinctive than on the mainland, there are intimate and reciprocal links between Corsica and France. The Corsicans have proved canny at exploiting their 'colonial masters' to the full, often succeeding in Paris while maintaining an insular base to which they can periodically return. In many ways, the problems facing Corsica are precisely those challenging the entire French model today: a large but ineffective state, which is capable of occasional strong-arm tactics but prefers to dispense favours among corporatist and political tribes; and a subsidized, distorted and manipulated economy managed in a way that has done little to help its development. The island is the epitome of the broader difficulties of France taken to explicable but inexcusable extremes.

Jospin made a distinct and courageous break with the past during 2000 when he developed the 'Matignon accords' with Corsican nationalist leaders, offering the prospect of an experimental period of greater autonomy to local politicians. It nevertheless cost him the resignation of his republican interior minister, Jean-Pierre Chevènement, and failed to prevent a wave of bombings on the island and the mainland since. The best hope, as many Corsicans say themselves in private, is that the death of Claude Erignac may have served at least one purpose: to wake up the national state and force it to implement the underlying intellectual values of the republic which it is supposed to represent, rather than to tolerate the very different practices which have become its characteristics over the last few decades. The subsequent actions of Bernard Bonnet show just how difficult that objective is proving to be.

Still so special?

When the global banking giant HSBC announced that it was paying $11bn to buy Crédit Commercial de France (CCF), on 1 April 2000, it was far from an April Fools' Day joke. Many had assumed that the protectionist instinct of French managers, supported by state intervention if necessary, would prevent such any such crossborder takeovers, particularly in a sector which politicians and regulators alike had long considered sacrosanct and keen to shield from outside influence. CCF had certainly seemed to be respecting the principle when it rejected a previous offer in late 1999 from the Dutch-based financial group ING, which had first raised the unprecedented spectre of a French bank falling into foreign hands.

In fact, Charles de Croisset, CCF's chairman, had simply taken a commercial decision by turning his back on ING and waiting for a better offer to come along. The saga showed just how open to global influences France had become. De Croisset himself was born in New York to an American mother. His bank had purchased a number of foreign institutions, including Charterhouse in the UK. And while CCF had a predominantly French executive management, the fact that it was quoted on the Paris stock exchange had long given foreigners the chance to buy its shares.

In fact, by the time of HSBC's bid, more than half of the bank was already owned by non-French investors. In 2001, HSBC went further, acquiring via CCF the previously state-owned Banque Hervet. It was a further example of France's increasing openness towards the international economy.

In cultural and gastronomic matters, just as in business, the image of anti-foreign sentiment in France belies reality. When Burger King pulled down the shutters for the last time on its flagship fast food outlet on the Champs-Elysées in July 1997, the news was reported with relish by the national and international media. But any impression that the closure was the result of Gallic hostility to hamburgers and chips was severely misplaced. In spite of its reputation as the home of *haute cuisine* and a hotbed of anti-American sentiment, France has become one of the world's more important markets for junk food.

Burger King's retreat was less the consequence of an unreceptive public than that it had simply come too late and too timidly into a fiercely competitive market. Its meagre 39 outlets were insufficient to bring it the necessary economies of scale to survive. The proof came in the fact that its shops were quickly gobbled up by its leading rivals: McDonald's and Quick. Indeed, McDonald's has firmly established itself as the leading restaurateur in the country, with 858 outlets by the end of 2000 and sales of Ffr11.5bn, making France its third largest market in Europe after Germany and the UK.

The same lessons can be drawn from the Disney theme park just to the east of Paris. By the time of its inauguration in 1992, it had become something of a Europe-wide joke. Many intellectuals sneered and criticized, attacking it for American imperialism. One even called it a "cultural Chernobyl". Poor weather, union conflicts, battles with contractors – on almost every count, it was condemned in advance to failure. The prognosis seemed borne out by its early losses and the need for a huge debt restructuring in 1994.

Yet most of the financial problems were less the consequence of local hostility towards the park than the result of how it had been financed, with a disproportionately large annual management fee creamed off by its US Disney parent. French investors suffered disproportionately as the company's shares plummeted because they had proved so enthusiastic in buying them in the first place. Jacques Chirac, the Gaullist mayor of Paris at the time, and Laurent Fabius, the Socialist prime minister, had actively fought off rival bids from the UK and Spain to lure the park to Paris. The statistics today appear to have justified their decision. The business hands over more than Ffr1 billion in taxes to the French state each year, and it has become the most popular paying tourist attraction in Europe. There were 12.5 million visitors in the 1999–2000 season, including over 40 per cent who were French and many of whom had come for repeat visits.

If anything, the principal error of the French state's negotiators and of Disney alike was to insist on too many European elements. In contrast to the US parks, wine is now on sale and the restaurant menus have been tweaked to meet local tastes. But in other ways its success over time has been matched by an increasing Americanization. It changed its name from Eurodisney to Disneyland Paris, and soon replaced its first chairman, a US citizen largely chosen for his perceived "fit" in Europe, with a French wife, a degree in medieval French and a background in arts administration. He was replaced successively by two others – Philippe Bourguignon and Gilles Pélisson – who, while French, were both trained in a more hard-headed US business style with considerable foreign corporate experience.

In spite of a reputation driven by its own rhetoric of insularity and a rejection of other cultures, France is continually adapting – and even adopting the products of its supposed cultural arch-enemy, the US. Beneath the conservative image, huge transformations have been taking place under the auspices of a new elite. The change has been driven by both domestic and foreign pressures, and is forcing many traditional exceptions to disappear. The country's continuing evolution will be determined by the fortunes of at least four underlying characteristics: the drive for equality, the strength of its elites, a penchant for intellectualism and a temptation to navel-gaze.

The new nomenklatura

His style is slick, his vocabulary *à la mode*, his actions match his words. At first sight, Jean-Marie Messier seems the perfect incarnation of the new face of French business. He stresses the importance of shareholder value, and has embarked on a whole-hearted restructuring to re-focus the group he runs into activities including the 'new economy'. He willingly speaks English, and has not hesitated to negotiate alliances and takeovers beyond the boundaries of France. In 1997 he inherited the sprawling utilities company Générale des Eaux from the long-ruling septuagenarian Guy Dejouany, renamed it Vivendi, moved its headquarters, sold off many of its peripheral subsidiaries, and disentangled its cosy and complex web of cross-shareholdings. Yet Messier's ascension also reflects a large degree of continuity with the past. He was parachuted into his position from the blue-blooded establishment investment bank Lazard Frères. He began his career as an *inspecteur des finances* working for the state. And in the late 1980s he worked as a top adviser to the finance minister Edouard Balladur, devising the very system of cross-shareholding for newly-privatized companies that he now denounces.

Messier is not alone. Take Henri de Castries, who replaced Claude Bébéar as chairman of the insurer Axa in May 2000. Unlike his corporate counterparts in other countries, he also began his career in that most elite of civil service roles as an *inspecteur des finances*, working at the French Treasury until 1989.

Both men are examples of what might be called France's new nomenklatura. Just as many of the most powerful members of the communist system in the Soviet Union have become the leaders of newly capitalist Russia, so many *enarques* and other high-flying civil servants have made the transition to the private sector in France over the last few years. They are proof of the state's past ability to attract and train the best of the nation's youth for its own purposes. But they are also testament to the transformations now taking place in French society which are luring many into business instead.

A generation and more ago, the best and the brightest were tempted by the Ecole Nationale d'Administration, followed by a long-standing career in the public service, perhaps capped in their 50s with a final highly remunerated post or two in a (probably state-owned) enterprise. Since the 1980s, they have left the state for the commercial world increasingly early – in their 40s and even 30s. Now many of the more recent and most talented school-leavers are turning directly to HEC, Essec, ESCP and other business-focused *grandes écoles*. ENA has lost much of its former glory, and the alumni of these other educational institutions are beginning to make their mark in middle and upper management in French companies without having spent the once obligatory qualifying period working for the state.

The transformations taking place in the business sector – and notably within its managerial elite – are an important sign of change more generally across France. Not only because companies are so powerful in their own right, but also because they have traditionally been so intimately linked to the state, and hence to both the administration and to political power. What happens to them is a litmus test for other aspects of society. The evolution in the career paths of the new generation of French managers are a response to the diminishing influence of the state as a result of the wave of privatizations since the late 1980s, and the declining role of the government as a client or participant in

corporate decision-making. The dominant criterion for recruiting top-level executives has correspondingly shifted from choosing people able to navigate the corridors of power to choosing
those who have proved their skills as managers and profit-
generators. But there has also been a cultural shift, as the prestige
of working for the state has declined. The apparently effortless
move of the nomenklatura from the public to the private sector
has highlighted the way in which some of the country's brightest individuals have anticipated or followed the evolution in
French society towards a more market-based economy.

That is not to say that French business has become purely
Anglo-Saxon in its style of operations. It retains some highly
distinctive characteristics. Claude Bébéar, the former chairman
of Axa, has turned his company from an obscure regional insurer
into one of the world's largest and best-regarded financial
groups. Although he graduated from the prestigious *Ecole Polytechnique* in the 1950s, he spurned the public sector by moving
immediately to work for the company where he built his entire
career. Instead of a "golden parachute", he had the more unusual
offer of a "golden balloon". He was recruited by the then chairman – the father of a class-mate – as the *dauphin*, with the
promise of succeeding him in the future. It was a powerful motivation to stay loyal, but it also gave him the unparalleled chance
to get to know the business thoroughly from the inside before
he gained control.

Axa owes its strength to a distinctly French corporate structure. It had never been in state hands, but it was formed by the
merger of a number of insurance "mutuals" or cooperatives
which are technically owned by their customers. By Bébéar's
own admission, the success of the acquisition spree of rival
insurers that he launched in the 1980s and 1990s to build the
group up to its current size was the result of this benevolent
ownership system. He was shielded from the pressure of short-
term profits that would have been demanded by stock-market

investors. It was only when he was forced to issue new shares to pay for the takeover of the French insurer UAP in 1996 that Axa's mutuals lost their dominant control over the group.

The same structure applies to one of France's most powerful banks, Crédit Agricole. Aided in the past by special government privileges including exclusive rights to provide state-backed loans to farmers, it is also a mutual. Without the need to pay out large dividends to shareholders, it has been able to amass huge reserves of accumulated profits over the years to use as a war-chest for acquisitions and investments. Some recent purchases have included the investment bank Indosuez, the consumer credit company Sofinco and a 10 per cent stake in the bank Crédit Lyonnais at the time of its privatization, putting it in a prime position to fully acquire the bank in the future. And while it can launch stock market raids to buy other companies, it is protected from any reciprocal hostile takeover because it is not itself quoted.

The strength of the country's mutual sector provided a wel-come salvation for the Jospin administration's desire to create 'Franco-French' national champions, rather than see its residual state-owned financial institutions pass into foreign hands. Crédit Mutuel bought the state-owned bank CIC. The mutual Groupama acquired the state-owned insurer GAN. The for-merly state-controlled Crédit National was initially introduced to the stock market, but then taken over by the cooperative Banque Populaire. Even among the commercial banks quoted on the Paris stock exchange, the unseemly hostile bid made in 1999 by BNP for Société Générale and Paribas ended with BNP buying Paribas, while for the moment Société Générale remained independent. The restructuring was accomplished among *confrères*, without any foreign banks becoming too directly involved.

Another group of successful French companies is those char-acterized by tight family control, often combined with a high

degree of openness to international ideas and talents. There are
the self-made men like François Pinault and Vincent Bolloré,
who did not emerge from the heart of the state, but who have
become increasingly powerful forces in the mainstream of
French business. Some of the country's best-known and successful international brands – the cosmetics producer l'Oréal,
the fashion designer Chanel, the tyre manufacturer Michelin, or
the biros and shavers company Bic – are characterized by a
dominant shareholding controlled by a few individuals. They
have tended to be secretive, avoided state ownership, and
spurned parachuted *enarques* in favour of home-grown talent.
L'Oréal might seem to be the most French of businesses, but it
is run by a Welshman, Lindsay Owen-Jones, who has spent his
entire professional career with the company. He started off, like
all new recruits, peddling the company's wares in order to get to
know its products. The financial director of Bic is a Scotsman.
And while Chanel may still be associated by most people with
its founder Coco, it is now run by the Wertheim brothers, who
live abroad and who rely on the design inspirations of the
colourful ponytail-wearing Karl Lagerfeld, a German-born resident of Monaco.

But if some of the country's most successful businesses owe
their prosperity to a distinctly French structure or history, there
is little doubt that the trend is increasingly towards a more
Anglo-Saxon system of shareholder capitalism. Successive governments have unwittingly strengthened such external forces by
neglecting to boost the role that domestic investors could play.
By refusing to create pension funds and requiring insurers to
place the majority of their funds into bonds, they have deprived
France's equity market of French money. The result has been to
leave foreign investors to acquire a substantial proportion of the
shares of quoted domestic companies, representing well over a
third of the value of the Paris stock exchange, and over half in
the case of some individual companies. These shareholders are

increasingly keen to ensure that they get value for money.

Take Club Méditerranée, the original and much imitated 'sea, sex and sun' holiday resort operator. It operated as a family-run company since the late 1950s, but in 1997 its leading investor, the Italian group Exor, flexed its muscles and ousted Serge Trigano as chairman as its fortunes waned. He was the son of the joint founder, but he had been handed the top job in spite of holding only a tiny fraction of the company's shares. Exor replaced him with Philippe Bourguignon, a professional manager who had proved himself with the turnaround at Euro Disney. At Group André, the fashion retailer, US and British investors clubbed together to force boardroom changes in April 2000, shifting to one side the 83-year-old Jean-Louis Descours, who had reigned as chairman for almost 30 years. And when Pierre Suard, the head of the engineering group Alcatel Alsthom, was placed under formal investigation by a French magistrate on corruption allegations in 1995, foreign investors played an important role in replacing him with Serge Tchuruk. Little by little, shareholders are taking on the vested interests of incumbent corporate management and imposing their own will.

Forces for change

The Parisian magistrate Eva Joly took an exceptionally risky step in 1998, when she placed under formal investigation Roland Dumas, François Mitterrand's confident and former foreign minister, on allegations of corruption in relation to the oil group Elf. The charges at the time were far from proven, and Dumas still denied them when his trial began in 2001, but it was an extraordinary act to even begin judicial proceedings against such a powerful man. At the time – and until he reluctantly and belatedly resigned in February 2000 – his position as head of the

Constitutional Court made him the fifth-ranking person in the French Republic.

Over the last few years, such counter-attacks on monolithic power have been growing fast. The media have acquired more teeth, public attitudes towards corruption have hardened as more has become known, and individual citizens are even beginning to seek redress through the courts when the state refuses to do so for them. But no evolution is perhaps more striking than that within the judiciary itself. France is not Italy, and it has not experienced anything like its Mediterranean neighbour's "clean hands" attack on the pervasive influence of the Mafia. But its judges have nevertheless shown a remarkable new boldness. Indignant victims of their inquiries have begun to complain about a 'republic of judges' exercising excessive power, a clear sign that they are beginning to have an effect.

One factor behind the change is the alternance of different parties in power, and the increasing period under *cohabitation* between a president and a government of different colours. There is an intriguing inverse correlation between the progress of investigations against politicians of a particular party or their allies, and whether they are in power at the time. Bernard Tapie, the colourful Socialist who mixed politics with football and business, got his comeuppance on match-rigging and corruption charges while the right was in charge. So did Michel Noir and Alain Carignon, the mayors of Lyon and Grenoble respectively. Both were on the right, but they had attempted to set themselves apart with a breakaway modernizing political movement. Inquiries against them swiftly followed. The centre-right Pierre Méhaignerie was judged in a party funding scandal once the left had come to power. Outside the strictly judicial domain, Pierre Joxe, the former Socialist justice minister and head of the Cour des comptes, broke with a sacrosanct tradition in 1997. He refused to accept the reintegration into his organization of Patrick Stefanini, an *enarque* who began his career at the Cour before moving into right-wing politics, and who was seeking a job after his role as political adviser to Alain Juppé came to an end with the 1997 election. Joxe questioned Stefanini's competence to resume his early career, and the circumstances by which he had been paid as an inspector for the city of Paris while in reality working for Juppé.

The arrival in positions of authority of outsiders to the system may also have a role to play. It is interesting to note that some of France's more aggressive judges in recent years bear names indicating their foreign origins – and implying a greater cultural distance from France's scandals and its pressures. Eva Joly is Norwegian, and her fellow judge on several high-profile cases, including Elf, is Laurence Vichnievsky, who is of Slavic origin. Their *confrère* Renaud van Ruymbeke has a Dutch background. In the same way, it is perhaps no mere coincidence that the scandal which brought down the European Commission in 1999 related largely to a French politician, and was instigated by a Dutch investigator. Paul van Buitenen, who was an internal auditor working at the Commission in Brussels, began an anti-corruption investigation which identified alleged excesses in the office of Edith Cresson, the former French prime minister. While at first hushed up by his bosses, his work ultimately triggered a vote of no-confidence and resulted in her immunity being lifted so that she could be prosecuted.

In many other aspects of French life, the European Union has proved an enormous force pushing for change from outside national borders. Ironically, the institutions built up in Brussels and Strasbourg in the postwar years owe much to the energies of such visionary Frenchmen as Robert Schuman and Jean Monnet. With the system of *cabinets* around the different commissioners, the continued widespread use of French in the corridors, and its citizens well represented at all levels of the hierarchy, the French continue to firmly impose their imprint. Yet the EU has broken free of the shackles of its parent in recent years and rebelled against it, creating a new and significant counterbalance to French policy-makers. Like the country's judges, its electorate and even its parliament, it has become a new counterweight to the excesses of power.

It only took a few weeks after the general election of May 1997 for the new left-wing government of Lionel Jospin to renege on one of its most high-profile manifesto pledges. In spite of a call to halt privatizations, the prime minister soon conceded that he would go ahead with the planned sell-off of GAN, the state-owned insurance company. The breach would swiftly grow. After 'consultations' for form's sake, he went ahead in the following months with a limited 'opening of the capital' of France Telecom. The bank CIC would soon be sold off, and plans were drawn up for employers and other private investors to acquire shares in Crédit Lyonnais, Air France and the life assurance group CNP. In a few months, he had masterminded a greater shift in assets away from the state than the centre-right administration of Alain Juppé had managed over the previous two years.

One of the more important factors behind these decisions was the weight of Brussels. Karel Van Miert, the Belgian competition commissioner at the time, had all but imposed privatization as a precondition for the French state to inject new cash to rescue such struggling groups as GAN and Crédit Lyonnais. The EU was equally instrumental in applying new commercial pressures on Air France and France Telecom by authorizing the liberalization of their respective markets, leading to the introduction of tougher competition. Similar challenges face such remaining monolithic state enterprises as Electricité de France and the Post Office. The pursuit of the single European currency is also having an effect in removing protectionist barriers. The so-called Maastricht criteria have limited France's margin for manoeuvre in areas such as increased public spending or debt. And the launch of the European Central Bank in Frank-

furt reduces still further the risk of national political interference
over interest-rate policy within the euro zone.

The EU's leverage can be exaggerated. Technically, for
instance, it cannot demand privatization as a condition for
approving state bail-outs. That remains a subject for member
states to decide. And when examining cases such as the troubled
banks Crédit Lyonnais and Marseillaise de Crédit, it was faced
into humiliating backdowns after approving once-and-for-all
rescue plans that were swiftly followed by second or even third
salvage plans – with scant respect for the conditions that the EU
had tried to impose. The growing influence of the EU on
France has certainly not gone unchallenged. National policy-
makers have defied Brussels on cases as varied as wild game
hunting regulations, environmental clean-up rules and even on
the withdrawal of subsidies for non-existent cows in Corsica. To
qualify for the Maastricht criteria, France indulged in some
cunning creative accounting by transferring directly to the state
the Ffr37-billion pension fund accumulated by France Telecom.
It was a move which reduced the national debt in the short
term, while obliging it to meet the far larger cost of paying the
retirement benefits of the company's employees in future years.
The juggling of the figures, incidentally, was judged acceptable
in Maastricht terms by the handily French-dominated Eurostat
statistical committee in Brussels.

In helping set up the EU, France has created a series of
mechanisms and a voice for other nations to exert their weight
in a way that has inevitably reduced its own national autonomy.
As with their counterparts in the UK and other member states,
French politicians have used Brussels as a convenient scapegoat
to justify their apparently reluctant implementation of unpopu-
lar policies. But the relationship between the EU and France
remains very close, and has if anything accelerated under the
Jospin administration. After all, the Socialist Jacques Delors was
the Commission's long-standing president. And other French

civil servants with left-leaning sympathies who have worked in Brussels have returned to Paris to play an ever increasing role in domestic policy-making. There is Pierre Sellal, the former deputy head of France's permanent EU delegation who became head of the cabinet office of Hubert Védrine, the foreign minister; François Villeroy de Galhau, former head of the office of Dominique Strauss-Kahn, the economics minister, who was then appointed head of the tax service; and Pascal Lamy, Delors' former *chef de cabinet*, and then a top executive at Crédit Lyonnais, before being appointed the EU's trade commissioner in 1999.

Under the most simple interpretation, France has created in the EU a hydra with far greater power and hostility towards its parent than it ever imagined. Under a more cynical analysis, the country's leaders have helped create a mechanism to force through change which they themselves see as desirable, but for which they are unwilling to take responsibility. Blaming Brussels has certainly proved a handy way for domestic politicians to deflect the burden of controversial reform in the short term. The danger is that in the longer term it risks unfairly under-mining the EU's credibility by creating a domestic political anti-European backlash.

Tighter European cooperation has also had the effect of reducing France's independent room for manoeuvre in other fields even beyond the remit of the EU. When the government announced a restructuring of its defence industry in 1998 with the partial privatization of both the electronics group Thomson CSF and of Aérospatiale, the aerospace company, it was under pressure from its European partners. Frustrated by the relatively slow pace of change by their common neighbour, the UK and Germany began pushing ahead independently with their own combined alliances. The same can be said for Airbus, the joint venture which has taken an increasingly commercial stance in its policies in recent years – partly because of the pressure of its foreign as much as its French state shareholders. External forces for change also came from crossborder corporate deals, such as the creation of the pharmaceutical company Aventis in 1999 by the merger of the French Rhône-Poulenc with the German Hoechst.

Equality before liberty

When Jospin made the announcement introducing means-testing for family allowances in his first major policy speech after the general election of 1997, it provoked a huge outcry. It might have seemed to be a progressive move, saving Fr4bn and concentrating resources where they were most needed: for those on lower incomes. Yet the political right, united with a number of conservative Catholic family associations, swiftly called for its repeal. One of its flag-wavers, the former minister Jacques Barrot, called for the principle of universality. The left was just as vocal in its criticism of the move, with the Communists rallying under a slogan saying that the benefits were 'a right for every child'. Within a few months the proposed reforms had been scrapped.

It was just one example of how even if 'liberty, equality, fraternity' are the theoretical guiding principles of the French Republic, they do not necessarily operate in that order. In political rhetoric, as well as in many aspects of daily life, equality often appears to dominate over liberty. An Englishman relates an example. Travelling one Friday evening on an Air France flight from Paris to London in economy class, he took the liberty of asking the stewardess if she would sneak him a mini-bottle of champagne, normally reserved only for business-class passengers. She agreed, but was not sufficiently discreet. As his French neighbours in economy class saw what was happening, each greedily demanded equal treatment.

The idea of equality and social justice is certainly laudable. There cannot be many equivalents in other countries to the Syndicat National Unifié des Impôts (SNUI), a tax employees' union which annually presents a critical assessment of the French government's fiscal reforms. It is hard not to sympathize with its views, especially when it identifies dozens of very high-income individuals who take advantage of the large number of loopholes that exist in order to avoid paying any tax at all. This same desire for redistribution and for a progressive tax system has led to the continued application in France of a wealth tax for the super-rich.

But an egalitarian philosophy also brings its drawbacks. The Napoleonic system of equal division of assets between all children has reduced inequality but led to the destruction of many family-owned businesses when the heirs could not agree on a common fate. The public outcry in 1999 when it emerged that Philippe Jaffré, the head of Elf, would receive stock options worth Ffr200m following the merger of his company with TotalFina, showed just how sensitive questions of money remain in France. It perhaps reflects a mixture of the long-standing Catholic guilt towards money with the Republican idea of equality. This ambivalence creates the risk of a trade-off between social justice and economic growth. Reforms to France's system of stock option have dragged on over several years as a result of political resistance, for example. Yet current legislation has acted as a brake compared with the more flexible approach that has proved so successful in the US in fostering entrepreneurial talent in high-tech and start-up companies which have little money and so attract people with the promise of future profits.

Equality and the related word 'solidarity', are often poorly defined, more demagogic slogans used across the political spectrum than realistic approaches to governing contemporary France. Alain Juppé's government had a junior minister in charge of 'solidarity between the generations', for example, and under Jospin the ministry of labour was called the ministry for labour and solidarity. Yet there was considerable puzzlement and debate in the French press after Jospin unveiled the title for a newly-appointed junior minister in March 2000 responsible for the 'economy of solidarity'. The man in question, Guy Hascoet, a Green party politician, could himself only rather tortuously define it as 'new activities which ... introduce solidarities through solvent economic activity, whether profitable or not'. As the newspaper *Les Echos* joked in a nod to the way wines are classified, the job was part of a growth of '*appellations (non) controlées*' in the cabinet.

In the higher-education sector, selection has long been a taboo. Any suggestion that entrance to university should be based on merit, rather than provided as a right, is enough to send students into the streets. The result is a hugely painful and wasteful system. Hopeful participants often queue for hours ahead of the start of registration, in order to fight their way on to the more popular courses which are allocated on a first-come, first-served basis. Ill-qualified and poorly prepared undergraduates then drop out in large numbers during their first year of studies as they lose interest or go beyond their depth. The opposition to selection in universities also ignores the double standard in higher education between the best qualified and the rest. France's large network of *grandes écoles* practise rigorous selection, creaming off the best students who have studied and performed well in the *prépas*, special state-funded schools which prepare them for the entrance exams of the *grandes écoles*.

The rhetoric of equality can also conceal a multitude of self-interests. Basic health-care is provided free by the French state. Yet innumerable top-ups to provide more reasonable, comfortable and comprehensive cover – such as for dental treatment, extended sick leave, a single room in a hospital and quicker access to non-urgent treatment – are provided through a network of so-called insurance 'mutuals'. These groups, already proof that medical services are not available equally to all, are funded by premiums, and hide some strong commercial savvy behind their banner of solidarity. They have benefited from special tax breaks which put them at an advantage over their commercial competitors, and have indulged in cross-subsidies and opaque accounting. They are essentially private health insurers in all but name, shielded by privileges that are not offered to their private-sector competitors.

The SNUI itself seemed to be fighting for another understandable – if unrealistic – social cause when it opposed efforts by the Jospin government to restructure the tax administration system in a way that would involve closing or reducing activity in some of its multitude of rural offices around the country. It was part of a broader project to merge two notoriously inefficient empires, one in charge of assessing tax, the other of collecting it, which often fail to communicate with each other. Yet for all the rhetoric of helping the poorest and maintaining equality between citizens, the SNUI largely exists to defend the rights of its own members. Its concern for a simplified administration, that would be less costly and more accountable to the taxpayer, was less important than its desire to defend its members' own jobs – at the taxpayers' expense.

Fraternities before equality

A curious blue or red plastic circle clings to the lapels of thousands of Frenchmen. It is a none too discreet reminder that they are proud holders of the *légion d'honneur*, the system developed by Napoleon which today has over 100,000 members. Most countries have some form of similar honours system to reward their deserving citizens. But how many recipients elsewhere go so far as to wear a badge that instantly establishes their status to all-comers? The playwright Feydeau was so struck by the obsessive search for such rewards by his fellow citizens that he even wrote *Le Ruban*, a farce on the subject.

Although France may overall be a more egalitarian society than many others, the divisions between its less and its more privileged members, and the rigid barriers that separate different groups, are often greater than elsewhere. There are geographical, intellectual and social demarcations. The concentration of wealth and power in Paris is in sharp contrast to the relative impoverishment of the remainder of the country, for example. The beautiful *arrondissements* at the heart of the French capital sit awkwardly with the ugly postwar concrete estates that surround them, linked by the worst in US-style highways flanked by drive-ins and neon signs. If you are with a French acquaintance in the street and someone they know stops to say hello, do not assume that you will be introduced. It is as though there is a fear to present people to one another in case they are not of the same rank or status. Fraternities, which often take liberties, remain an important watchword of the society.

The white letters 'FNAC' against a brown background identify one of France's most well known and successful high-street retail chains. It combines the sales of books, CDs, photographic equipment, videos and other cultural goods, and is staffed by well-informed employees. With such pioneering innovations as bar-code readers allowing clients to swipe any compact disc and listen to the music it contains before purchasing, it appears the very model of modernity. But how many of its customers today remember what the initials that make up its name stand for? Founded after the second world war, the Fédération Nationale des Achats pour les Cadres was a company explicitly targeted at purchases by *cadres*. It is a term that is difficult to translate into other languages, but which retains a distinctive status in France. They are management-level employees, with a well-defined place in the hierarchy, their own union, pension fund and specific legal rights.

Cadres are just one of the most visible of a number of clearly – and even rigidly – defined groups. Others include civil servants, whose administrative decisions are governed by a separate body of law, with its own statute books, courts and judges, quite distinct from criminal or civil proceedings. They have entry requirements based on competitive entrance exams: a way to test intellect, but not much help for late developers or those whose talents lie more with management skills than in understanding textbooks.

Many sectors within French society can claim their own elites. Each has its own rules, customs and codes to define its place and maintain its distinctions and privileges. All countries have equivalents, but few are so tangible or visible as those in France. While the English have their highly elitist gentlemen's clubs and old-boy networks, and the Americans their alumni associations and business circles, the French have perfected such structures far more broadly. There are discussion groups, like the reformist Saint-Simoneans, or Idées et Projets formed around Jacques Delors. There are regional and ethnic groups which stick firmly together, such as those drawn from Corsica or the Corrèze, homeland of Chirac. And there are groups formed around the *grandes écoles*, government departments, companies, trade unions and politicial parties alike. Long after their political beliefs may have changed, the Maoists and the Trotskyists of the 1960s retain the same personal clan loyalties – and mutual hatred – today. Perhaps most powerful of all, there are the civil servants who have proved extremely adept at maintaining their roles over the years through firm union action. These groups all serve as powerful networks of influence. France is a society where the idea of mutual aid (*renvoyer l'ascenseur*) and the use of connections (*pistons*) is fundamental. When you telephone an unknown person *de la part de* or on behalf of a common friend, it makes all the difference.

The clans foster very strong internal loyalties, but come at the expense of those outside – and of the general, collective interest. When just 50 per cent of French households pay income tax (against about 90 per cent in the UK), it is not surprising that many feel removed from broader civic responsibilities and prefer to make special pleadings for their own self-interested causes. Those who denounce their own tend to do so anonymously, tipping off the *Canard Enchaîné* or writing newspaper articles and reports under such pseudonyms as Favella, Socrates and Equinox. Their quasi-tribal attachments reduce the pressure for accountability on the wider community and foster a sense of impunity. In the political sphere, it was never better illustrated than the response of Georgina Dufoix, the social affairs minister at the time of the contaminated blood scandal of the mid-1980s, who argued that the government was 'responsible but not guilty'. It was a callous phrase that perfectly summarized the system of deflecting blame.

If contact between and entry into France's highly stratified elites is far from easy, exit from them is just as difficult. For the groups protect their own, recycling their members in different roles. Take Jacques Attali, for example. An *enarque* and member of the Conseil d'Etat, he was a former close adviser of François Mitterrand and bears considerable responsibility for some disastrous nominations of individuals to head newly nationalized companies at the start of the 1980s. His extravagant spending record as the first head of the European Bank for Reconstruction and Development in London cost him his job and nearly destroyed the reputation of the institution. Yet Attali has had little apparent difficulty in reinventing himself as a widely-quoted commentator and writer on the broadest range of topics, producing theatre plays and publishing books on philosophical aspects of the Internet. With the scandals of François Mitterrand's presidency fresh in his mind, Jospin may have considered it politically wise to distance himself from his former master and ministers (although he had been Mitterand's education minister). But

Jospin appointed Attali to head a commission on modifications to the education system. The conclusions, tellingly, focused more on how to encourage a few more of the top students in troubled schools to make it into the elite *grandes écoles* than on any serious reflection on ways to make such schools more attuned to the needs of its average or more poorly performing pupils.

The cult of intellectualism

When twin babies are born in Britain, the first out is considered by law to be the elder of the two. It is judged to have begun life earliest. In France, the opposite applies. The second to be born is treated as the elder because it is viewed as the first to have been conceived. No better example illustrates the difference between the British approach, focused on pragmatism, and the French philosophy, which concentrates on concepts and intellectual ideas.

Signs of the intellectual, didactic spirit of French society are not hard to come by. Travel on the metro in Paris, and you will see posters produced by the Centre pour la vulgarisation de la connaissance attempting to explain in simple terms what causes mist and how television signals are transmitted by satellite. A far higher proportion of the passengers on the trains is likely to be studying serious novels or non-fiction books rather than flicking through newspapers, chatting or studiously staring into space like their counterparts in other countries. Even the graffiti are likely to be more poetic.

It is a trait that is fostered at school, in an education system that is universal, free and highly regarded. How many other countries would attempt to teach 17-year olds philosophy as a subject in their *baccalauréat*? Or would be able to imprint a certain logical way of thinking so firmly on young minds that in later life nearly everyone reasons in threes, arguing that there are three explanations for anything? Not to mention instilling a solid knowledge of authors, whose names and quotations are frequently dropped into conversation. Go to a museum or classical concert in any part of the world, and the chances are that the French will be among the most heavily represented foreign visitors. The school system's strength is to sustain at least some hope of achieving the Republican desire for equality, laying the foundations of a system of merit based on intellectual achievement more than on family background or wealth.

No surprise that in France, intellectual property rights have long been so carefully guarded. It was the Frenchman Beaumarchais, author of the *Marriage of Figaro*, who first developed the system of *droits d'auteur* to protect authors' rights – which continues today. The country retains a tough system of *droit de suite* designed to ensure that artists' heirs continue to benefit from the rising prices of their works. France has played a leading role more recently in the fight against *photocopillage*, attempting to clamp down on multiple photocopies which undermine publishers' and authors' profits. And it has levied a tax on blank videos in a recognition that pirate taping will take place, reducing the income to those involved in producing films. French customs regulations are still among the toughest in the world, giving officials confiscating and fining powers even over those individuals who have in all innocence bought counterfeit goods into the country.

Yet intellectualism has often come at the expense of action or practical ideas. As a joke frequently told by the French against themselves puts it, the dismissive response to a foreigner's bright idea may be: 'That's all very well in practice, but does it work in theory?' The consequence has been a number of costly mistakes over the years, such as the considerable fruitless expenditure on the development of the Secam colour television standard by the French in the 1960s. The system's technological sophistication was undoubtedly greater than that of its rivals, but commercially it was a failure.

In many ways, it is desirable that the French do not measure achievement simply in crude commercial terms. It is testament to the culture that it is able to generate so many specialist books or films which only appeal to small, minority audiences. Yet there are limits to such logic. Ideas in France have sometimes come at the expense of implementation, a distaste for the nitty gritty. Academics have taken on a powerful political role, and the cult of intellectualism has at times gone to ridiculous extremes. Few senior French politicians consider their image complete today without a book of poems, a novel or a history text to their name. From Jack Lang and Pierre Joxe on the left, to François Bayrou and Nicolas Sarkozy on the right, it is not enough simply to write political texts, but worthy treatises are more desirable. Mitterrand prided himself on his *plume*. But Chirac has also indulged, and Valéry Giscard d'Estaing has even turned to romantic fiction. Not all such authors do the entire effort on their own, of course, turning instead to ghost-writers who carry out research on their behalf.

More seriously, there sometimes seems to be a belief that intellectual solutions can solve everything. A top civil servant took great pride in late 1997 in explaining how the government's newly unveiled proposals on the introduction of the 35-hour week would create additional employment. Everything had been meticulously thought through and costed, with a neat mixture of increased productivity, union wage restraint and state top-up funds all elegantly compensating for the four-hour reduction in the working week and persuading employers to hire new staff. All it lacked was common sense, as companies shed staff without replacements, the rules were tweaked to gain state aid, and unions viewed attempts to limit pay increases with suspicion.

The cult of French intellectualism is also reflected in a preference for discussion and dissection of ideas over the willingness to act. In Corsica, successive National Assembly, Senate, Ministry of Finance and Accounting Chamber reports have spelled out the problems over the years, interspersed by regular consultations, most recently starting again in late 1999. Yet action has been far more limited. Endless commissions have been convened to analyse the problems with the existing system of financing future pensions with the contributions of the fast shrinking labour force. Every scheme and scenario has been studied, and multiple projections drawn up. Few disagree that the present structure is unsustainable. But no one has had the courage to implement fundamental change.

The lure of the navel

Walk into an off-licence in London, and there are wines on sale from Australia, Chile, South Africa and many other regions around the world. Go into the equivalent in Paris, by contrast, and few bottles will be available from anywhere outside France. Britain long suffered from its paucity of home-grown food and wine. But in compensation, its openness to other cultures and a new-found interest in good living means that its supermarkets, shops and restaurants today offer an impressive variety of exotic produce. France, instead, is often tempted to concentrate only on its own.

Enter a French bookshop, and the *Guide du Routard* travel books will likely be on prominent display. Founded in the early 1970s for hippy backpackers on their way to India, the series has become one of the best-selling guides for a far broader public today. Still with an eye on budget travellers, the guides nonetheless provide a distinctive Gallic twist, with sections on "where to have a drink" in each town, and listings of the best restaurants. They cover destinations as far flung as Cambodia and Brazil. But

the best-selling guides are those covering rather less exotic loca-
tions: the regions of France. The concentration reflects the fact
that while a small elite travels to some of the most unusual places
around the globe, France as a whole remains a nation whose citizens are fiercely attached to their own territory, even when on
holiday.

With the chance to travel quickly and cheaply to somewhere
with a familiar culture and language, a country that is endowed
with good weather, magnificent and varied landscapes and
excellent food and wine, it is understandable that the majority
of the French rest at home. In just the same way that so many
other tourists come to visit from abroad, why should the French
not profit from their own heritage? But their choice is one more
example of a certain arrogance and insularity or *hexagonalité*,
based on the glories of the past. In the same way, a former *Le
Monde* journalist laments that his newspaper reports less and less
international news on its front page, concentrating instead on
domestic matters.

The introspective focus on national history runs through
many aspects of contemporary France. On a spring afternoon in
1995, for example, hundreds of spectators gathered to witness a
curious ceremony. A huge French flag had been draped over the
Panthéon, the shrine for Republican heroes in central Paris.
International invited dignitaries sat in raised podiums alongside
dozens of national decision-makers. It might have been the run-
up to the presidential elections, but the Gaullist Edouard Balladur, one of the leading candidates in the campaign, was
present, as well as Robert Hue, head of the Communist Party.
Republican Guards carried two coffins on to glass stands in
front of the monument. A procession of schoolchildren in bright
clothes bearing huge models symbolizing radium and polonium
walked towards them along a white carpet stretching back as far
as the Luxemburg Gardens. Mitterrand gave a long speech in
honour of the latest of more than 70 citizens disinterred so that

they could be laid to rest in this new setting: Marie and Pierre Curie.

It was the sort of display that France's former president adored. After his first presidential victory in 1981, Mitterrand had walked across Paris to the Panthéon clutching a red rose in his hand. But while the rhythm was reduced under his replacement, Chirac would take up the tradition when he presided over a similar ceremony in honour of André Malraux. And in 1998, on the centenary of the notorious anti-Semitic Dreyfus affair, Jospin would also select the backdrop of the Panthéon to pay homage to Zola, the author whose *J'Accuse* had helped win a reprieve for Lieutenant Dreyfus. Alain Richard, the defence minister, even saw the need to put out a public statement stressing the modern army's attachment to Republican values. France loves to indulge in such extended bouts of self-examination and historical genuflection.

France is far from closed to outside interests and trends. While the country's attitude towards Algeria may be ambivalent, *raï* music has become a mass-market product in the last few years. World music more generally – notably from francophone Africa – attracts a large, mainstream audience. The proportion of books translated from foreign languages into French is far higher than the number translated into English. Yet in many ways, France was far more open, and far less obsessed with its own history in the past, when it was busy building the Suez or Panama canals, engaging in postwar reconstruction or developing Concorde. While the country can still revel in and profit from the glories of the past, it risks failing to prepare for the future. Like the light from a distant galaxy visible on earth only millions of years after it was emitted, the *grands projets* of which the country can be rightly proud today were largely conceived and implemented in the 1960s and 1970s. Whether it is the TGV, the modernization of telecommunications or Airbus, France is now reaping the fruits of such previous initiatives. Some have continued with a momentum of their own – even beyond the end of their useful lifetime. History has shown that France is capable of shrewdly analysing a problem, catching up from behind with an ambitious solution and overtaking its neighbours. But there have been few recent, bold ideas to take the place of those devised by previous generations.

Excessive *nombrilisme* has also brought another pitfall. French decision-makers have been all too quick to label foreign trends that they were reluctant to embrace as Anglo-Saxon, ultra-liberal and by extension undesirable. Suspicion of the stockmarket, for example, and fear of foreign investment continue to haunt politicians and commentators. Yet at the turn of the century, France was a huge investor in bonds to finance the ambitious infrastructure projects of the tsarist Russian government. Its Bon Marché department store in Paris represented a pioneering step in the development of modern retailing. Even the size of the French state was only one-third of gross domestic product at the start of the 1960s, compared with 53 per cent today. The idea of France as a defensive, inward-looking country with a bloated state that stands apart with its own model of development is rather more recent than some would like to believe.

Plus c'est la même chose, ou plus ça change?

The French may have given the word 'chauvinist' to the world, but not in the way that is often assumed. If Nicolas Chauvin de Rochefort was a soldier who proved naively loyal to Napoleon, he was swiftly ridiculed by his French comrades for being so. He would have been quickly forgotten had he not been parodied first in the lithographs of the draughtsman Charlet, and then by the Cogniard brothers in a play first performed in 1831. Chauvinism is perhaps less typically French than the parody and critical spirit which immortalize the word. First appearances are often incomplete in France, and underlying the superficial impression can be a very different reality. Behind the image of an archaic country, France has been transformed enormously in recent years. Its economic strength alone – whether measured by the size of the economy, its export levels or its continued capacity to attract high volumes of inward investment – testifies to the fact that it has been able to adapt. With a gross domestic product of €1.4 trillion in 2000, it still ranked among the top five economies in the world – behind the US, Japan and Germany, but on a par with the UK and ahead of Italy. Behind each reactionary gesture, France often employs sleight of hand to construct a rather different reality.

When Chirac relaunched nuclear testing just after his election as president in 1995, it was perceived by many as a gesture of the continued legacy of de Gaulle. Yet in fact Chirac became the first political leader in France to have the courage to breach the postwar Gaullist myth, by officially raising for the first time the question of the responsibility of the French state for the atrocities committed by the Vichy regime during the second world war. He oversaw the launch of investigations into the expropriation of assets from the country's Jewish community. Under his eye, the trial finally took place of Maurice Papon, one of the civil servants who eased himself from the Vichy into the Gaullist administration, carrying a protective shield of immunity throughout his subsequent career and well into his retirement.

Chirac put an end to the brash and costly *grands projets* adored by Mitterrand, like the Bastille Opera or the Grande Arche at La Défense to the west of Paris, the façades of both of which have symbolically already begun to crack so soon after their completion. France in the late 1990s started to redefine in a more modest way its long-standing military presence in Africa, and abolished compulsory military service. Gone was the contrarian programme of nationalization that had marked the early

1980s at a time when the rest of the world was beginning to privatize its state-owned enterprises and activities. Chirac's government continued to sell off parts of the public sector, and – underneath the sometimes more ambiguous rhetoric – to embrace the liberalization of the economy.

In a television interview in late 1997, France's new prime minister rejected demands that unemployed people aged under 25 should receive additional state subsidies. He argued instead for the need to create 'a society of work and not of assistance'. It could have been Margaret Thatcher speaking, but it was in fact the Socialist Jospin. It was left-wing administrations, too, which undertook the liberalization and modernization of the country's financial sector during the 1980s. They created an electronic stockmarket more modern than its British counterpart, and a highly sophisticated derivatives exchange – albeit partly in order to help finance spiralling levels of public-sector debt by raising additional cash from the private sector. When the Jospin government unveiled its controversial legislation to introduce a 35-hour maximum working week, the measures contained many flaws. But the policy did have the effect of forcing the country's inflexible management and union representatives together to talk. And it provided an excuse to re-negotiate a wide range of other restrictive labour rules in way that was often to the benefit of employers – and could help modernize French companies.

The decision to allow France's mutuals to take over so many of the country's financial groups in the late 1990s – from Crédit Lyonnais, CIC, Natexis and Crédit Foncier de France to GAN – seemed counter-productive and insular, shielding them from competition and foreign ownership. But it also had an advantage. The payments made by the mutuals to the state to buy these groups were an elegant way to discreetly soak off much of the excess capital that they had accumulated over the years, in order to distribute it more equitably within French society. The removal of this safety-cushion of money forced the mutuals to be leaner and placed them under greater pressure to manage themselves competitively. And it was a precursor to efforts to transform the mutuals into private-sector entities, starting with the legislation to change the legal structure of the Caisse d'Epargne savings network begun in 1998.

Many of France's most eye-catching exceptions today are just that. The state is still capable of issuing decrees that seem absurdly impractical, interfering and archaic. Yet decentralization and deregulation alike have delegated enormous power away from the government in Paris, leaving the administration with considerably diminished responsibilities. State-owned enterprises may seem outdated, but most that remain are well on the way to restructuring and privatization. Cultural policy does a good job at the margins in helping foster French cinema, but its effect is small compared with the influences from abroad. Such exceptions grab the attention, but they are not representative of the underlying changes taking place in the society. Its unions are certainly capable of some extraordinary and colourful demonstrations and high levels of disruption, for example. Yet their influence is on the wane.

In many ways, France is a modern country struggling to wrest itself from a postwar corporatist straitjacket. Jospin does not have the legacy left by generations of centre-right governments in the US and over a decade of Thatcherite reform in Britain which has allowed Tony Blair to take advantage of modernization without having had to assume responsibility for the pain it caused. He inherited a country with a very different and unreformed social contract, with a political right still echoing some of the rhetoric of Gaullism and a left-wing coalition including parties that have reformed far more slowly than their counterparts in Moscow. But recent historical precedent in France suggests that by wrapping up their reforms in suitably fork-tongued ideological rhetoric, left-wing governments have in recent years been better able to implement sensitive reform than their counterparts on the right. Juppé may have been criticized when he attempted to impose controls on medical spending, for instance, but very similar measures were subsequently introduced by Martine Aubry, Jospin's social affairs minister.

While France's private sector has changed enormously in recent years, the same cannot be said of the state itself. It remains the employer of a gigantic workforce and a huge consumer of funds. Most of the job growth in France over the last few years has come through part-time and temporary work in the private sector, outside the rigidly structured employment contracts which rule over the civil service. The public sector poses an enormous political threat to those who dare try to tackle it. Juppé found that out to his cost in 1995. Jospin tried to avoid any suggestion that it should even shrink painlessly by natural wastage, simply not replacing those who retire. However, the strikes of spring 2000, which forced him to withdraw planned reforms to both the tax ministry and the education sector, showed his desire to avoid conflict. The fact that he was not willing to take a risk to his ratings two years ahead of the planned date of presidential elections highlighted the sclerosis of the political class. In the words of Claude Imbert, editor of *Le Point* magazine, "the winding back of the state will be as painful for France as decolonization was in the 1960s".

In its favour, France has enormous advantages. Its intellectualism – and its accompanying critical spirit – should be able to work in its favour to bring about reform. It has proved capable of living with – and even thriving on – its own contradictions in the past. Its civil service and business elites have proved themselves not only among the most talented in the world, but also able to smoothly adapt to changing times. The problem is that – like their counterparts in politics, the trade union movement and the media – they have often served themselves rather than the general interest of the country, leaving many of their fellow citizens behind in the process.

France is not simply coming to resemble all of its neighbours in the industrialized world. There are and will continue to be distinctions in the path that it follows, that keep it special in one way or another. While some of its exceptions have hindered its evolution, others – like the bold vision of the engineers who built the TGV – have helped or even explained it. The country's willingness to stand apart continues to be a useful stimulus to the rest of the world. But as the price of maintaining political influence and financial support, it has been increasingly forced to abandon its more isolationist tendencies and succumb to outside pressures which impose a degree of uniformity. Its policymakers have often maintained a deceit by publicly praising ideals of French exceptionalism that do not reflect what is really taking place. In doing so, they are cynically avoiding public discussion on important issues.

The real question is not whether France can adapt and modernize, but rather whether it can do so quickly and fundamentally enough. When it could have restructured the state at a time of high growth and low unemployment in the 1980s, it procrastinated and debated, pushing the burden on to policy-makers during the more difficult climate of the 1990s. Many of its recent reforms have come more thanks to the instigation of its foreign partners and neighbours than through its own internally generated willingness to change. At the start of the new millennium, its economy was picking up strongly, much as the result of low interest rates, the relatively weak value of the euro compared with the dollar and sterling, and wage restraint within the private sector. Yet again it sent out ambiguous signs with its capitulation to striking teachers and tax inspectors. There is the clear risk that it will not capitalize on its fresh prosperity to tackle structural reforms within the state.

There was a 'long hot summer' in the corporate world in 1999 which suggested a growing move away from its Franco-French reflex, best illustrated by the crossborder mergers of

Pechiney with Alcan of the US and Algroup of Switzerland; or of Rhône-Poulenc with Hoechst of Germany. But this frenetic activity was followed by a 'chilly winter'. The Pechiney deal was called off, ironically blocked by the European Commission on anti-monopoly grounds. Public-sector demonstrations forced two of Jospin's ministers out of the government. The demonstrations might not have taken place at all if Dominique Strauss-Kahn, the powerful economics, finance and industry minister, had still been in charge. But he had been forced to resign in November 1999, under judicial investigation in relation to two funding scandals. His status perfectly encapsulated the tensions and ambiguities of modern France. He spanned the political left and the right, and seemed a good modernizing force able to talk to unions and corporate bosses alike. Yet he also bridged the country's old and new political cultures. The fact that he felt obliged to resign – or would otherwise probably have had to be sacked – is at least one sign of progress towards a tougher and more independent judiciary and a fresh sensitivity to corruption. But his departure helped to trigger an important policy reversal. It also signalled the start of a slow-down in the government's pace of reform, as it began to nervously eye the risks of controversial change ahead of the presidential elections in 2002. It illustrated just how much France continues to hover between the legacy of the rigid postwar structures of the past and the challenges of the new century ahead.

References

Special thanks to David Buchan and Robert Graham, successive bureau chiefs of the Paris office of the *Financial Times*, and my colleagues John Ridding and David Owen, inspiration for many ideas. Equally, for support and friendship, Jo and Domitille. I am grateful for meticulous scrutiny of the English text to my parents Alan and Jean Jack, of the French text to Marie-Thérèse and Jacquie Sardin and Géraldine Gallagher, and for comments on particular chapters to Anne Solange Noble, Patrick Ponsolle, Philip Ogden, Arnaud de Bresson, Robert de Bruin, Julian Nundy, Marc Epstein, Nicolas Charbit and Jérôme Fournel, as well as to assorted book reviewers. To Andrew Franklin, Odile Jacob, Felicity Rubenstein, Claire Elliott, Monty Lee and Bruce Clark, without whom things would never have begun. *Mais surtout à Sandra, ma source la plus fondamentale.*

Most of the material for this book was gathered during four years' reporting on France for the *Financial Times* between 1994 and 1998. The information came through many first-hand interviews with individuals whose names are cited when they gave their permission, and others who preferred to remain anonymous. It was backed up by a wide variety of French media reports and specialist publications. On specific chapters, the following were notable.

Chapter 2   The closing of the French mind

Patrick Messerlin, 'La politique française du cinéma: l'arbre, le
    maire et la médiathèque', *Commentaire*, No. 71, Paris,
    autumn 1995
Henriette Walter, *Le français dans tous les sens*, Robert Laffont,
    Paris, 1988

Chapter 3   The pull of Paris

Michel Bauer and Benedicte Bertin-Mourot, *Vers un modèle
    européen de dirigeants?* Boyden/Abacus Edition, Paris, 1996
Institut de la décentralisation, *La décentralisation en France*, La
    Découverte, Paris, 1996
'La France a-t-elle trop de fonctionnaires?' *Le Revenu Français*,
    4 April 1998
Jean-Marc Ohnet, *Histoire de la décentralisation française*, Le Livre
    de poche, Paris, 1996
Pouvoirs Locaux, *Le spectre de la recentralisation*, Editions Privat,
    June 1997

Chapter 4   Full speed ahead

Cour des Comptes, *Le rapport public*, Paris, October 1996
Institution of Civil Engineers and Société des ingénieurs et
    scientifiques de France, *The Channel Tunnel*, Thomas Telford,
    London, 1989
Pierre Lubek, 'L'experience française du financement des
    projets de TGV', *Revue générale des chemins de fer*, Paris,
    October 1997
Babette Nieder, *TGV et ICE: les processus de décision entre la
    politique, l'administration et l'industrie (1968–1991)*. Also

summarized in *Euroscientia Forum*, No. 1, January 1998

Jérôme Spick, *Le tunnel sous la Manche*, Presses Universitaires de France, Paris, 1992

Chapter 5   Cheques and imbalances

Paul Barril, *Guerres secrètes à l'Elysée*, Albin Michel, Paris, 1996

Patrick and Philippe Chastenet, *Citizen Hersant*, Seuil, Paris, 1998

Chapter 6   The spirit of '68

Dominique Andolfatto and Dominique Labbé, *La CGT. Organisation et audience depuis 1945*, La Découverte, Paris, 1998

Edouard Balladur, *Deux ans à Matignon*, Plon, Paris, 1995

Michel Crozier, *La société bloquée*, Seuil, Paris, 1994

Hervé Hamon and Patrick Rotman, *Génération*, Vol. 1. Seuil, Paris, 1987

'Les fonctionnaires sont-ils des privilégiés?', *Capital*, July 1998

Magnum Photos, *1968: Magnum throughout the world*, Hazan, Paris, 1998

Roger Martelli, *May 68*, Messidor, Paris, 1988

Henri Weber, *Que reste-t-il de mai 68?* Seuil, Paris, 1998

Chapter 7   The inability to say 'no'

Cour des Comptes, *Crédit Lyonnais*, Paris, 1996

Jean-Yves Haberer, *Cinq ans de Crédit Lyonnais*, Ramsay, Paris, 1999

Rapport de la commission d'enquête sur le Crédit Lyonnais, Assemblée Nationale, Paris, No. 1480, 1994

Chapter 8   The extremes of power

'La chute de la maison maire', Les dossiers du *Canard Enchaîné*,
   Paris, 1997
Les immigrés en France, Insee, Paris, 1997
'L'extreme droite en France', *l'Histoire*, No. 219, March 1998
Myriam Niss, 'Ces Alsaciens d'ailleurs', *Hommes et migrations*,
   No. 1209, September 1997
Observatoire régionale de l'intégration et de la ville,
   Strasbourg, *L'immigration et les spécificités du vote Alsacien*.
   Cahier No. 17, March 1996

Chapter 9   The furthest shore

Dominique Bucchini, *De la Corse en général et de certaines vérités
   en particulier*, Plon, Paris, 1997
Gabriel Xavier Culioli, *Le Complexe Corse*, Gallimard, Paris, 1990
Nicolas Giudici, *Le Crépuscule des Corses*, Grasset, Paris, 1997
Mission d'information commune sur la Corse, Assemblée Nationale,
   Paris, No. 3511, 1997

Index